I0560676

PRAISE FOR
THE TRANSPORTATION RIGHT OF WAY

"Mr. Gilchrist has written a very thoughtful, readable, and comprehensive work. His vast length and deep knowledge of experience as a traffic engineer is evident in every chapter and in every topic he covers. This book is an important read for designers, traffic engineers, accident lawyers, and all those interested in understanding and improving traffic safety."

–Norm Keith, BA, JD, LLM, Lawyer, Investigator, Mediator, Arbitrator, Keynote Speaker, and Author

"Robert Gilchrist has five decades of experience in traffic engineering. His book examines in detail many contributing factors leading to traffic accidents such as human error, excessive speed, road design and signage, traffic signals, weather conditions, and road maintenance. A must-read for any serious student of road safety."

–Roger Barker, MA (Cambridge), MS (MIT), PEng, Retired Engineer

"A must-read for trial lawyers and forensic engineers alike. With over five decades of trial experience handling complex cases involving serious injury and death due to roadway safety failures, I found *The Transportation Right of Way* to be an exceptionally researched work in the field of transportation and traffic engineering. Robert Gilchrist brings unmatched clarity to the complex interplay between traffic engineering and the human factors and standards that govern safety. Filled with real case references and packed with authoritative sources across North America, this book is as insightful as it is accessible—a rare and invaluable resource."

–David F. Smye, King's Counsel, LLD (honoris causa, Ontario Law Society); Fellow, American College of Trial Lawyers; Firm Counsel, Mackesy Smye Lawyers

IN SUPPORT OF SYSTEM USERS
AT THE CROSSROADS OF
PUBLIC SAFETY AND PERFORMANCE

THE TRANSPORTATION RIGHT OF WAY

Robert S. Gilchrist

RIVER GROVE
BOOKS

Published by River Grove Books
Austin, TX
www.rivergrovebooks.com

Distributed by River Grove Books

Design and composition by Greenleaf Book Group and Brian Phillips
Cover design by Greenleaf Book Group and Brian Phillips
Cover photo used under license from ©Shutterstock.com/vs-arts
Car icon in Image 6.1 © Adobe Stock / Matsabe

Publisher's Cataloging-in-Publication data is available.

Print ISBN: 978-1-966629-05-4

eBook ISBN: 978-1-966629-06-1

First Edition

CONTENTS

ACKNOWLEDGMENTS

Many thanks are extended to Norm Keith, who encouraged me to embark on this endeavor. We shared our thoughts and ideas in long conversations while out running along many roads and trails. Norm, a lawyer with several publications to his name, suggested I start writing about my experiences.

However, it was Robert Munroe, a distinguished trial lawyer, who provided the tipping-point decision to carry on or trash the project while opening the way for me to see forward. I sent Robert a rough draft of the book, and he indicated he could have used the material in his work. In his review, Robert suggested that this book would be a work spanning both legal and engineering interests.

Roger Barker (PEng, ret.) and Allan Feldman also offered encouragement and insight related to engineering and related considerations, after listening to my musings about the way many travel infrastructure decisions are made that affect right of way users. Discussions with Roger and Allan were always helpful in defining the breadth and depth of the subject matter.

Finally, many thanks to my wife, Jan, for her endless patience in allowing me to closet myself away to work on this project.

PREFACE

This book is intended to be of interest to those who now are or in the future will be responsible for or must evaluate some component of the ground transportation infrastructure. It is an encouragement for those individuals to adopt multiple perspectives, but particularly that of the system user. The book is relevant to those who must rely on the documented direction, manuals, and guidance for planning, designing, operating, and maintaining infrastructure.

For those providing infrastructure, it is an encouragement for them to not only consider what they must do to satisfy the standards of the industry but also to consider how those using constructed facilities may be excluded from the protections provided. For example, intentional exclusion can come about through design or operating provisions. Inadvertent exclusion can come about by a failure to recognize human cognitive abilities and limitations. The book provides opinion and commentary relevant to those who must evaluate situations and conditions either from within the industry or while looking into the industry. Those taking on such responsibilities are encouraged to question why things are the way they are.

For those within the industry, or exogenous to the industry, who must assess the usability of the infrastructure or those using the infrastructure, this book is relevant in determining how information they acquire and rely on will affect their future course of action. More explicitly, it is encouraged for those individuals to wonder why the rules, regulations, standards, guidelines, and protocols have been written in the manner that they have. During their contemplations or evaluations, readers are encouraged to question whether there may be some bias in the rulemaking and, if so, then who benefits? Who is likely to pay the price? And who is left out?

For the most part, the ground transportation infrastructure works very well and the frequency of unintended incidents is extremely rare. The transportation industry generally recognizes the vulnerabilities of system users and attempts to accommodate many of those vulnerabilities through well-considered forethought in its guidance to those providing services. For this reason, the book should not be viewed as a critique of the industry but rather as an encouragement to further ponder the provisions of the industry in some instances and to raise questions or even challenge the industry norms from the perspective of system users.

SOME BACKGROUND

1.1 The Path to Here

My interest in transportation came into focus in 1970, when I was a first-year university student. I had a course on environmental perception and became interested in a driver's view of the road on an urban freeway. There was little in the way of human factors information on the subject at the time, and my research was thin, so the paper was not particularly well-received. However, the paper did point out to me in dramatic fashion that a good understanding of human factors is critical to the design of transportation infrastructure and the accommodation of human behavior in using it.

I then switched to a civil engineering program to learn about the design side of creating transportation facilities. I thought that those in engineering maintained a greater control of the design and implementation process. The civil program at the university had a group of enthusiastic professors who specialized in transportation, which at the time was a small but emerging niche in the broader field of civil engineering.

During my time in class and during work terms, I was exposed to a wide array of subject matter related to the transportation industry, from preliminary concept studies to design, to implementation, and finally, to some construction. However, my interest was in the softer side of engineering, and I tended to focus on the planning, design, traffic control, and operations of transportation systems.

Upon graduation, I was fortunate enough to get a job as a transportation planner and assigned the task of computer modeling transportation demands for urban growth and a proposed urban freeway ring road. After some time, I moved into the private sector while completing a master's degree, which expanded my background in traffic engineering. Traffic and transportation engineering is loaded with human factors considerations, although that information tends to be presented as facts and standards inferring expected human performance. Designers of the time accepted these human behaviors as incontrovertible truths, and there was limited concern for the system users since their needs were automatically accommodated in the applied standards. However, there seemed to be little recognition of the variation in human behavior in that material.

As a graduate student, I reflected on the standards of the time, and especially the basis of the standards. My interest grew when it became apparent some groups of drivers may not be folded into the safety net provided by the standards. Indeed, some alarming conditions described in design and control manuals seemed to be accepted by the industry, but acceptability by the public had *not* been vetted. I found this information hidden away in technical manuals with little exposure to the broader public or any persons outside of the profession. Practitioners seemed to have little interest in reflecting on the relevance of excluding a portion of the population from the standards.

Since that time in the mid-1980s, some excellent research has been done on what constitutes an acceptable standard. A working knowledge of human factors in the provision of transportation facilities has become much better understood, too. Even so, the basic design standards of the time have changed little to this day due to a multiplicity of factors. On the other hand, human factors have been more fully integrated into the control and operation of transportation systems.

In 1992, a professor from the university and I became business partners, and we established a new engineering firm that would focus on transportation safety issues. Due to the business environment of the time, the firm quickly began to focus on forensic transportation assessments and analysis of ground transportation systems. This was a natural transition encompassing a combination of facility safety considerations and their relationship to the many other aspects of facility operations. Identifying sources of failure in transportation systems requires an understanding of how people in motion may respond to situations and how much time is needed as they are confronted with decisions.

Consequently, people working in this niche require an understanding of human factors. By this time, my career, sparked by my initial interest in human factors, had come full circle. While we were better informed about the intricate relationship between human factors and infrastructure, many unknowns remained. Still, throughout the next thirty years of working in the field, the absence of specific human factors information related to systems characteristics was readily apparent.

The information in this book is compiled from my career experience as an engineer-practitioner combining the assessment of infrastructure and human activity. Based on my training and experience, on several occasions I became qualified to provide human factors information at trials related to transportation matters. These cases involved the movement of people who were harmed in some way and how the infrastructure contributed to the harm. The area of my practice encompassed all ground transportation modes of travel, including pedestrians, bicycles, and motor vehicles. While there are repeated references to human factors throughout this book, this information has been obtained through the published papers and works of human factors specialists. An excellent reference text examining the subject is *Human Factors in Traffic Safety* by Lawyers and Judges Publishing, last reviewed in its third edition.

1.2 A Basis for Considering System Users

At this point in my life, I have found that many long-accepted truths are simply opinions and subject to change with the current narratives. Many of the ideals in transportation planning and engineering are no different. Consequently, while the sciences of transportation engineering and safety can be illuminating, many facets of the industry elicit a vague or uncertain result. Oftentimes, there is little interest in further establishing the facts if they may run counter to the public narratives.

While the equations of motion stand fast with time, much within the industry of providing ground transportation comes to the forefront and then fades from view with time as industry practitioners change. To that end, I have attempted to compile revealing information that has been known to the industry for many years and can be applied routinely to benefit system users but that is often overlooked because of the inconvenience of dealing with it in critical assessments. System users include anyone using any element of transportation facilities such as sidewalks, pathways, trails, crosswalks, paved and unpaved roadways, boulevard areas, and much more. They include any means of mechanical conveyance—automobiles, e-bikes, scooters—and human-powered conveyance—walk, run, bicycle, and so on. System users may be protected, as in an automobile, or vulnerable, as pedestrians and cyclists.

This book is in part a discussion of how the transportation engineering industry operates and how this affects the system users. Those responsible for the system include all people involved in decision-making at any level. These people are the engineers and technologists engaged in the planning, design, and operations of the systems as well as the managers, supervisors, office personnel, and field staff responsible for keeping the system operating. Those responsible also include peripheral participants who are increasingly influencing the industry, including politicians, advocacy groups, legal professionals, and other stakeholders.

One theme of the book is that whether responsible for the system or simply a user, all these individuals can be characterized by a probability distribution. Both groups may be affected by self-interests, distractions, misunderstandings, poor judgment, and other influences.

As a new engineer, I believed the notion of public welfare and safety was paramount and was a hallmark for the profession. Public welfare was pitched to us first in school and then by professional organizations as the benchmark of performance. Later, I came to believe that industry protocols in some elements of transportation engineering and system management had drifted away from the notion of public safety in pursuit of other interests and varied definitions of safety, which arise in accordance with the source of the discussion. Transportation industry officials can have different opinions from others in the industry, the law, politicians, the public, or special interest groups.

To indicate that one definition of safety is more or less relevant than others is likely to reveal some dissonance among the groups. Consequently, I believe that it is relevant to question the protocols and standards of the industry. Manuals do not always include the information necessary for making informed decisions, while some design and control standards exclude a percentage of the population from the nominal safety provided therein. Where vagueness and inconsistencies exist in manuals, engineers and others should question whether the public safety protocol has been reasonably met.

Over many years of forensic transportation engineering analysis, it became clear that some travelers inadvertently fell into that portion of the population who did not perform as envisaged by the standards and manuals. In essence, the performance of these individuals was not explicitly protected by these industry safety provisions. Consequently, they could become involved in a crash and be injured through no fault of their own. Such events are precipitated by several sources, including the user, the machinery in use at the time, the infrastructure, the environment, or some combination of these.

Behavioral studies show there is substantial variation in the population. The extent of the population captured by any standard can be framed or remain an open question, particularly in the context of individual performance. For example, when out and about, we see that drivers travel at different speeds or that some drivers will choose to pass through an intersection on a yellow light while others will stop. Each of these can be viewed as a reasonable decision, and together they simply reflect a range of variation in human performance.

Forensic transportation engineering is an examination of the reasons why a system user failed to perform in a manner consistent with the attributes of a transportation facility or how the transportation system otherwise failed to provide the attributes necessary for users to safely use the facility. As many transportation facilities have been in use for decades, it is necessary through forensic transportation engineering to determine if the standard of practice at the time of design or construction remains relevant, or if actions are necessary to satisfy current technical knowledge and user expectancies.

Therefore, one task of forensic engineering is to determine if the behavior of specific system users falls within a normally expected range of behaviors as shown by the range of activity within the population and enabled by the system, not as defined by a rule of thumb, policy, standard, or a manual. Where there is a mismatch between "wished for" behaviors of the industry and actual behaviors, forensic analysis must assess whether the actions of individuals exercising typical or common behaviors were reasonably encompassed within the industry standards or simply left out. The natural consequence of such inquiry is to also assess if the standard itself is reasonable.

Whether assessing the performance of an individual or the performance of a standard, a key consideration is whether they are reasonable. The provision of safety cannot be absolute, meaning free from any and all possible harm, and any notion that it can be is a fictitious sentiment. Since absolute travel safety is not possible, it is accepted in the industry that a small portion of the population may be excluded from the protections afforded by nominal standards.

The small portion of the population excluded from a standard is referred to in this book as being in the tails of the probability distribution. Taking a speed distribution, for example, where an average speed may be 80 km/h (50 mph), some drivers travel slower and others faster. If 85 percent of drivers travel below a certain speed, only 15 percent travel faster than that speed. The 15 percent of drivers traveling faster than that speed is considered to be in the tail of the population distribution for speed.

There are several standards that encompass only 85 percent of the population. For this reason, when injuries are incurred where there is doubt about why the event occurred as it did, it is necessary to recognize potential contributions from those responsible for the system, if any.

A legitimate question, then, is: If a full range of reasonable individual performance is not accounted for in the standards of the industry, then why are the standards written in the manner that they are? More importantly, who benefits or not from the established standards? Further, in considering system users, how much safety is enough? This book examines a selection of design, control, and maintenance standards from this perspective in the context of the impacts on end users.

Still, investment in safety initiatives is subject to diminishing returns, which is to say, at some point, further investment in safety initiatives provides little or no meaningful safety benefit. While the industry inexplicably seems to have defined for itself some cusp revealing the extent of safety to be provided, people continue to be harmed because of that determination. On the other hand, not every soul can be reasonably accommodated. Therefore, unvalidated expenditures on excessive safety provisions can become a waste of funds that may be better spent elsewhere. This can occur where political and other stakeholder interventions use safety as a means to achieve other goals. Yet, in today's social media culture, those responsible for the infrastructure are likely to be poorly equipped to deal with a popular narrative.

Finally, since the standards are created out of the public view by individuals who have varied interests and backgrounds, do the standards adequately encompass the notions of public welfare and—more specifically—public safety? It would seem appropriate for the public to weigh in on these issues from time to time. One means for vetting some current or past standards is through the litigation process. New standards being proposed would likewise benefit from broadly based stakeholder input, including input from engineering institutions, professional boards, and safety advocates.

This commentary on the nature of the industry should not be considered a condemnation of industry standards. Those planning, designing, building, operating, and maintaining our transportation systems are typically well educated, skilled, and exercise ingenuity and integrity in the completion of a complex task. Due to their efforts, our road and transportation systems routinely serve the population very well.

The content of this book is intended to provide a basic understanding of the ground transportation industry to those who examine events where a person or persons came under harm. It provides to the legal profession a range of information that is available but often left unconsidered in liability matters.

For transportation engineers, this book will illustrate how standards do not always consider the ability of all to react in specific conditions. It will also illustrate how situations can simply be a trap for some system users. For example, the roadway signs or geometry of a situation may not provide sufficient time or distance for some people to assess conditions and respond in a desired manner.

Also, for the forensic transportation engineer, this book is an encouragement to consider a full range of issues, including the reasonableness of the standards.

For academics, this book is a recommendation to engender in students the notion that the industry may not perform to perfection—not unlike drivers and other right of way users. In addition, the book is an encouragement to consider not only those that will benefit from engineering actions but also those who might be harmed in some way.

This book is not intended to be an all-encompassing examination of the issues touched upon. Hopefully readers will consider the possibility that at the time an injury was incurred, more may have been in play than what appears on the surface—beyond the commentary of a few witnesses or the generalizations of those being discovered for trial. This book may be used to gain a broad view of the industry while storing the information until a section of it becomes relevant to a particular matter or case. With that in hand, it is more likely to be a reference enabling insight on some issues that will allow investigators to strip away the many veneers that can be presented in commentary and documentation during litigation in order to reveal a root cause or contributing factor of the harm.

2

FORENSICS IN TRANSPORTATION ENGINEERING

2.1 People as Evaluators

In a police evaluation of motor vehicle collisions (often referred to as a crash in the US), the principal source of causation tends to be directed toward the individuals on the scene who were involved in the incident. They were the reason that the vehicles were on the road in the first place, and they are known to have all sorts of inadequacies and poor judgment.

The list of the inadequacies assigned to drivers often appear as checkboxes on motor vehicle accident reports, which makes it easier for the police to select a fault. One collision reporting system identifies more than thirty-five driver and pedestrian actions that contributed to collision. Human error choices on the form include the assessment of driver decision-making, which is manifest in actions such as driving too fast for conditions, following too closely, or losing control, in addition to a failing driver condition such as impairment, medical condition, fatigue, or inattention. All these point to driver causation.

No doubt, many indiscretions can be placed on drivers, and by far, their actions are the most frequently cited source of causation. After all, the population can be expected to exhibit a wide range of personality traits, mental and physical capabilities, judgment ability, distress, anxiety, illness, and more. One or several of the checkboxes are likely to strike a chord with a police officer, enabling an assignment of fault.

While there are many options available in collision reporting to assign fault to drivers, there is less opportunity to recognize the influence of other contributing elements. In describing the nondriver elements, some information is collected related to environmental conditions—clear, dark, rainy, dry, icy—and the road conditions—alignment, surface type, and whether a traffic control is in place. These can be used to point to where the failure in driver performance occurred. However, there is typically only one checkbox indicating how the roadway may have contributed. The road surface condition is identified, whether dry, wet, icy, or other. There is often little opportunity in collision reporting systems to identify infrastructure failures due to geometry, traffic control, or maintenance.

This structuring of the reporting system often permits road authorities to get off scot-free even when the roadway was contributory in some way. Such an approach to assigning fault to drivers alone can be reinforced through restrictive legislation limiting road authorities' liability. Still, to the credit of some police investigators, comments on the collision report or in duty notes can provide some insights about the infrastructure.

The performance of all drivers can be assumed to fall within a normally distributed population (see Image 2.1). In view of the rarity of collisions relative to total system usage, it is readily apparent that an overwhelming majority of drivers are reasonably responsible, reasonably trained, and reasonably skilled in the execution of the driving task. For discussion, these drivers are found throughout the distribution constituting about 85 percent of the population. However, drivers who normally or occasionally fall outside of that group may require a little more time to assess and respond to a given situation. These individuals can be expected to constitute up to 15 percent of the driving population and are therefore said to be in the tail of the normal distribution.

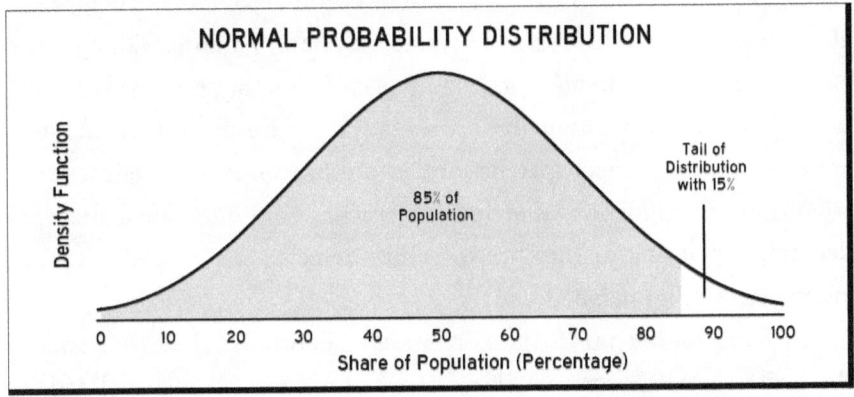

Image 2.1: Normal distribution showing portion of the population contained in the tails. (Source: Gilchrist, August 6, 2024)

While only about 15 percent of drivers fall within the tail of the distribution, those individuals may be unfairly assigned responsibility for collision through no fault of their own when things go wrong. In view of how individuals' behavior can vary from time to time, their presence in the tail of the distribution can be temporal and occur rarely, recurrently, consistently, and, importantly—inadvertently. They may be intelligent or not, lazy, poorly trained, uncaring or ambivalent, distracted, and more. The drivers may also be competent but process information slowly or incorrectly, or they may inadvertently place low priority on high-priority tasks.

All these traits, when referenced in the context of collisions, lend credibility to a narrative that places blame on the drivers while the drivers may not be the initiating source of the problem. While most drivers diligently perform within the bounds of reasonable behavior, sometimes individuals may experience a lapse in a critical situation—whether intentional or inadvertent—and their actions fall below the performance threshold necessary to avoid collision. That threshold of performance may be related to either human factors or industry standards.

With this variation in mind when considering the typical driver, it is worthwhile to recognize that those providing our infrastructure are also human, with all the same characteristics and potential failings that can be assigned to drivers. Those failings can occur at an individual level or corporately throughout the organization. In the field, these failures are more likely to affect specific locales and operational or maintenance conditions. Examples could include obstructed sight lines due to seasonal decorative planting or significant facility defects such as washouts that are missed during inspections.

Moving higher up in the corporate structure, at the other end of the professional spectrum, failings can be systemic, business-related, or related to an industry culture. These failings find their way into the policies and standards of the industry so the public feels their effects more broadly in such matters as maintenance practices and policies.

Considering the host of individuals who plan, design, manage, and maintain our travel infrastructure, the common perception is that those in charge will unwaveringly ensure that the public may travel safely. Consequently, the public assumes that those responsible for our infrastructure will always get it right and that travel can be undertaken safely. However, these professionals and their subordinates, like drivers, also fit within a normally distributed population of industry personnel and may exhibit the same range of human performance within their given responsibilities. Therefore, failures in the performance of their duties should be expected from time to time, which can lead to failing situations in the planning, design, operation, or maintenance of transportation systems. While most organizations have redundancy and fail-safe systems in place to prevent this, sometimes things just fall through the cracks. Therefore, if rarely, some industry personnels' actions will (intentionally or inadvertently) fall below the performance threshold necessary to ensure transportation systems operate well for everyone.

A case in point occurred when a supervising engineer-in-charge received a report indicating low levels of friction on a local curvilinear highway section, yet the friction levels were not found categorically deficient. The implication of the report was that more testing was required or some type of monitoring program needed to be implemented. The individual decided the friction levels were compliant with the minimum standard and shelved the report, possibly temporarily, but apparently without discussion with superiors or subordinates.[1] Inquiries were made after there occurred several crossover collisions that were well publicized in the media, which led to cries for an investigation. The result was an emergency repaving of seven kilometers of a major divided highway and a public inquiry. The inquiry alone went on for more than two years and cost more than $26M, based on the last estimate in 2024.

The context of this discussion refers to organizations responsible for maintaining travel systems and therefore presumed to be capable. They may be large organizations that have a many-layered structure from department head to field staff, including federal, state or provincial, regional, and/or municipal road authorities. However, travel authorities can also include parks and recreation departments, conservation authorities, transit operators, engineering and works departments, and private-sector systems contractors. All these organizations experience transition and change in staffing, technology, policy development protocols, and more—all while working under pressure to manage costs.

Public corporations routinely consider cutting the cost of services, often at the expense of user serviceability. In one instance of reducing maintenance costs, a decision was made to eliminate the inspection of local roadways within neighborhoods. A Yield sign subsequently went missing for an extended period and a serious crash occurred. The road authority was sued. The municipality's defense was premised on the concept that they were unaware of the missing sign. However, since the municipality had canceled its inspection program for the area, they had to pay out a substantial sum to the injured party.

In this instance, apparently it was more convenient for staff to bend under the political pressure to lower costs than to stand fast on the importance of maintaining the prescribed standard for roadway inspections. Few administrators are willing to put their job on the line to maintain or enhance existing services in the face of higher-level direction to cut costs when they are protected by a public travel authority.

The use of the term *"travel authority"* is an important one. A responsible agency is expected to maintain a comprehensive, up-to-date knowledge base and be staffed with well-trained and capable professionals. As an authority, they are also assumed to possess the tools necessary to make supportable, reasoned decisions that satisfy industry standards. Typically, but not necessarily, maintaining industry standards helps the authority to minimize exposure to liability claims. Still, situations may arise where corporate performance falls below industry benchmarks, thereby increasing liability exposure and the potential for claims.

When an alleged failure related to transportation facilities occurs, the situation is usually evaluated based on minimum threshold standards described in a given manual. Then it becomes a simple matter to determine whether the authority adhered to industry standards by satisfying the provisions in the manual. If the standards are satisfied, the authority is considered protected in the event of liability claims. Notwithstanding that, it is sometimes appropriate to evaluate whether the industry itself has performed in a reasonable manner. In such cases, public opinion, political involvement, or judicial decisions are a means to achieve resolution of the issue.

It is enticing to believe travel authorities will always place the safety of the traveling public first and foremost. Many people therefore assume that facilities—roadways, intersections, trail sidewalks, and so on—are safe for public use. For a transportation facility to be deemed safe, it must operate without the occurrence of property damage, personal injuries, or fatalities. However, our current roadways and many other elements of the transportation system have not been able to achieve this goal.

One factor is that accommodating human behavior in the use of all transportation systems cannot be all-encompassing. In considering roadways, the extent of accommodation has not been consistent across all infrastructure elements, partly due to uncertainties in the way people perform. Furthermore, the degree to which travelers are accommodated is rarely challenged. For this reason, unintended uses of technology or highway features to satisfy some personal objectives of users must be expected. Satisfying one's desire may come about by delibrate action, because of misunderstanding the technology being used, or for many other reasons. For example, adults may deliberately ride bicycles on the sidewalk rather than the roadway in some locales where riding on the sidewalk is prohibited.

Another example, this time concerning a misunderstanding of safety-enhancing technology, is that of antilock brakes. When a technology is new, some users can be expected to misuse it, whether intentionally or inadvertently. When antilock brakes were first introduced as a significant safety advancement in automotive design, those who had purchased the option placed too much reliance on the feature, resulting in a higher collision experience for those drivers. Similar results are likely when new transportation infrastructure is developed and brought into use.

Contrary to the widely held perception that those responsible should be providing safe roads, the fundamental benchmark for measuring infrastructure performance is "nominal safety" as established in policies and manuals. This simply infers that conditions satisfy the safety thresholds set by the industry standards. That should not be confused with "reasonable safety" or "acceptable safety," which is the threshold for safe operations set by others, including some individuals within the industry. The reason for this distinction is to reflect the extent of risk tolerance of the interested party who has scrutinized the safety of the facility. In this context, while nominal safety serves as the industry benchmark, it does not necessarily align with the safety expectations held by other institutions or the public.

In this sense, industry standards do not provide for safe travel but rather nominally safe travel, which is deemed to be adequate. Furthermore, spot decisions regarding safety can come from many different individuals within an authority's hierarchy of departments and personnel. It may be assumed that senior levels of an authority make a sincere effort to uphold industry standards, aiming to meet or exceed the nominal standards of the industry. But there also may be compelling influences to circumvent those intentions, including political motivation affecting design, documented or undocumented corporate policy, individual or corporate discretion, or a need to fulfill social or political expectations and narratives. While we assume travel authorities are motivated to ensure decisions reflect industry standards, many opportunities exist for the best of intentions to disappear in their execution.

In larger authorities, the best of corporate intentions is likely to prevail, using up-to-date knowledge and technology administered by well-informed, motivated professionals who recognize that a duty to the public and to safety is paramount. However, moving down through the hierarchy, the motivational context for good intentions is not necessarily pervasive. Initial intentions and vision of the end product, including travel safety, can fade with intervening opportunities and compartmentalizing responsibilities. In part, this may occur when the importance of a job well done for one group, such as design, competes with the interests of some other group, such as maintenance.

For example, if a maintenance individual views a task as an inconvenience or has a personal desire to clock out on time, corporate priorities can temporarily conflict with the best interest in public safety. This creates a risk of failing to serve the public's need. In one such case, a worker spent a quiet afternoon in the storage yard garage rather than servicing roadways during a period of ongoing snow flurries. That action resulted in a $5M payout to an individual who crashed while passing through a snow drift. While authorities may well have programs in place to avoid these types of situations, employees are a part of the population subject to the same performance influences and failings that affect drivers.

Administrative organizations may also suffer from internal degradation because of organizational structure or economic pressures. For example, departments can cut costs by reducing the qualifications of individuals who are responsible for a task. This could involve replacing engineers with technologists, or replacing technologists with technicians, or advancing foremen into management positions.

In one instance, a well-respected municipal engineer had completed a safety audit of an intersection. The ensuing report recommended several changes to the intersection, one of which was to clear the sight lines. Shortly thereafter, the engineer changed employers and was replaced with a technologist who did not follow through on the sight line recommendation. As a result, a child experienced a catastrophic injury in a serious right-angled collision due, in part, to the poor sight line. In a subsequent lawsuit, it was found that the engineering report was ignored by a technologist who made an anecdotal judgment that the intersection was safe enough. The person who replaced the engineer was not professionally qualified to counter the engineer's original report. The lesson in all this is to consider who is making important decisions and determine whether they are properly trained and ethically equipped to make decisions regarding public health and welfare.

In matters of litigation, individuals responsible for elements of the transportation systems can experience conflicting loyalties when users are injured due to a fault in the system. Departmental staff errors can affect both personal standing and corporate credibility, and a desire to preserve these can conflict with the public interest. Travel authority employees can thus experience an ethical dilemma around addressing litigation issues if they incorrectly believe that protecting the public corporation also protects the public interest. Such actions primarily protect personal interests rather than the interests of the public and especially system users.

Transportation authority staff often perceive that saving the corporation from a large settlement is desirable because it protects the public interest as represented by the public corporation. In reality, they are only protecting the financial interests of the corporation and taxpayers from paying the costs, which has little to do with public safety. Consequently, the way source material is evaluated may be influenced by the desire for a perceived favorable outcome for the corporation, which may not benefit the broader public interest.

Such an economic and face-saving approach can overlook the importance of protecting public health and safety in transportation matters, especially those who experience harm due to the system's faults. Additionally, this approach can prevent those injured by a system failure from receiving reasonable restitution. Even after a matter is resolved in favor of the system users, changes to the system may not occur due to cost or the reluctance of the corporation to admit fault.

2.2 Transportation Services and the Legal Profession

Often transportation infrastructure is examined in litigation only when substantial or catastrophic damages occur involving large lifetime care costs for an injured party. In the absence of significant economic demands related to damages, there can be a tendency to avoid the challenge and cost of evaluating infrastructure, rather than treating it as a matter of due diligence. Thus, travel authorities may not become involved in many cases where the infrastructure may have contributed to the incident.

Consequently, when the ongoing costs—assessment of damages—of a collision are well-known but there is a shortfall in funding resources, engineers may not be consulted for a forensic analysis until several years after the incident had occurred. Under these demands, forensic transportation assessments are less likely to be limited by the anticipated amount of funds to be received by the injured parties at settlement or trial.

Still, lawyers are people. More specifically, people who drive. Even young lawyers typically have a wealth of driving experience, having completed the training to acquire a license and observing the infrastructure over their years of driving many kilometers/miles. Consequently, as with most drivers, when lawyers sense something is unusual, minimal, or not fully compliant, there is typically reasonable probability they are correct. In completing their due diligence in satisfying their instincts, they will seek advice from an industry professional regarding the extent of the problem.

For lawyers, and for everyone, time is money. Both plaintiff and defense counsels seem to view transportation forensics as black-and-white issues related to whether some metric in a standard was satisfied or not. Thus, a short answer can quickly be found in a book of standards and verified by an engineer. However, transportation engineering is more than simply looking up the standards in a manual and determining if the proper metric or rules have been applied. While sometimes sufficient, such a clear-cut assessment is not always enough.

A simple comparison of site conditions to the threshold values given in a manual is not always appropriate because the construction of transportation facilities can predate the current knowledge of the industry as well as the current standards or guidelines by several editions. Furthermore, in certain instances, no standard is available. In such cases, assessments must be carried out based on the information available at the time of construction and the means by which a facility reflects the knowledge of the industry at the time of the incident. Regulatory and warning signs are one means to match older physical conditions with current user expectations. For example, Sharp Curve signs may be used where a curve may be tighter than drivers are expecting.

There is much more to transportation engineering than defined standards. Most manuals, if not all, now contain a wealth of information beyond the metric specifications. They can provide a backdrop of relevant material including the rationale for established protocols and procedures and discuss the realm of expected human performance. Other relevant information that is both directly and peripherally relevant when trying to determine how the use of a facility led to a harmful incident can be found in manuals, journals, position papers, and research put out by governments, institutions, and interested organizations.

Many general-use manuals of standards are created through multilevel committees including steering committees and working groups or consultants, usually identified in the acknowledgments and credits. Such information can be important in forensic engineering to determine the agency's level of knowledge at the time of an incident.

Other information could include human factors, such as response times, methods for providing guidance, and other considerations in their application. This information is presented in manuals to establish basic concepts. Manuals can also describe the level of safety provided, offer advice for improving safety at reasonable cost, and provide guidance on how to avoid design problems.

Beyond the industry standards, extensive information is floating around in the form of pamphlets, compendiums, and related materials. These may not have direct relevance to planning and design issues but relate well to operational and maintenance issues, as well as considerations for system users. For example, insurers produce materials on safe driving, bicycle and motorcycle associations produce materials on safe riding habits, and salt producers may explain how to use salt and salt solutions for effective road maintenance.

Some of these publications can have industry or national importance, while others may apply locally. All this information constitutes the broad knowledge of the industry and is necessary for transportation authorities to remain up-to-date. An indexed compilation of material both old and new is useful for establishing knowledge over time, which may be relevant to what an authority ought to have known at the time of an incident.

In large transportation authorities, protocols and procedures may be developed by an industrious, committed individual with extensive knowledge of a particular subject. Such material may be distributed widely or departmentalized within an organization. As staff move on, the information continuum is increasingly at danger of being disconnected, allowing gaps to form in the knowledge base. Additionally, new employees may see matters somewhat differently. Valuable organizational policies and technical information can fade from the general knowledge base of the organization. This happened in the case discussed previously of the safety review conducted by an engineer who left shortly thereafter and was replaced by a less qualified individual.

Authorities' knowledge of the broader industry can be an important and controversial issue when determining contributory factors to incidents. For example, a roadway constructed in the distant past may fail to satisfy the current standard. However, provisions to satisfy the needs of today's drivers are typically available by other means, such as traffic control devices. To properly apply appropriate solutions, road authority personnel need to understand both the design and control elements of providing adequate service. These disciplines, however, may be disconnected in some authorities, especially in larger organizations where technical expertise can become compartmentalized.

Furthermore, standards and guidelines can be written in an intentionally or inadvertently vague manner, or even contain contradictions, leaving critical decisions up to industry personnel. For example, in one manual, the need for a Bump sign is tied to the motion of unsecured objects in the vehicle when passing over the bump. As a result, the threshold of need for installing the sign is vague and inconsistent with the needs for installing other warning signs, such as curve warnings. Thus, defining the conditions for when a sign is required to warn drivers of a hazard can remain subjective despite the seemingly sage advice given by manuals.

The absence of a sign is unlikely to be a problem for those who travel a roadway frequently. A road patroller passing over a bump every day may see no concern, whereas an individual responsible for road safety could recognize a potential issue. To the unknowing driver, the bump may cause a reaction or failure to perform in a certain manner, resulting in collision. At issue is whether the driver would have responded differently if a sign had been present. In such matters, it is appropriate for the courts to determine if appropriate knowledge and care for the traveling public was applied in the decision to install a sign or not. Importantly, beyond that, it is reasonable to question whether the standard itself is appropriate given the wide variation in opinion about how the standard should be applied. This in turn provides substantial latitude for diverse judicial decisions related to similar situations.

In a discipline where knowledge is expanding continuously and individuals are increasingly placed in a career niche, obtaining an appropriate range of corporate information from an individual in the discovery period before trial can be problematic. Often, individuals presented for discovery are quite junior and simply do not have the breadth of industry knowledge or experience to handle the range of subject matter at issue. These individuals can provide only limited information, and the broader standard protocols, policies, practices, or technologies of other sections, departments, or the corporation remain unknown. Obtaining relevant information then turns to the post-discovery exchange of information—requests for the production of specific information before trial—which can be limiting and time-consuming. The information becoming available then depends on the knowledge of those making the inquiries. Thus, plaintiffs must rely on information from their own experts, who must have extensive experience in transportation engineering and organizational structure.

Licensed professionals are most likely to have broad knowledge of the range of issues through education, training, and experience. They are most likely to have variable responsibilities related to engineering and technical matters within a larger organization, even moving between departments. They are also most likely to have ethics training and be aware of their duty to public safety. Unlicensed professionals may not be required to complete the ethics training required by regulatory agencies for some practice elements.

Less senior personnel, such as technologists responsible for traffic control, may have little knowledge of the administrative protocols or design and maintenance issues. On the plaintiff side, lawyers who utilize industry personnel with limited experience may miss key information. In this context, lawyers need to know what information should be available, not just what is presented by the defendants.

3

HOW THINGS CAN GO WRONG

This chapter will frequently reference failures that occur in transportation infrastructure and systems. However, it needs to be stated clearly that our transportation systems almost invariably provide adequate and even reasonable safety for most people, which is a credit to the transportation industry as well as the host of individuals who design, build, operate, and maintain these systems. Like most drivers, those caring for our transportation infrastructure diligently perform with integrity and within the bounds of reasonable behavior according to the industry and the public trust. These individuals are well-trained, attentive, and dedicated to making operations run smoothly. However, from time to time, faults do occur in those systems because of human frailties, through wear and tear, or both. Consequently, the discussions contained herein should not be construed as a general critique of the individuals or authorities operating our transportation infrastructure. Rather, it deals with the rare and odd elements that sometimes come to light through unfortunate events.

Even in difficult driving situations or when road conditions are poor, the information provided by the signs and markings of travel authorities should give well-thought-out guidance, allowing nominal safety. Due to the dedication of industry practitioners, collisions or mishaps are typically extremely rare in our travel systems relative to the total amount of travel. Thanks to their attention to details, travel is reasonably safe for most system users. Highways that were originally designed and built in the 1950s or later generally have horizontal and vertical alignments that serve most drivers and conditions well. Facilities with alignment features predating this period are rendered reasonably safe through the provision of traffic control devices, including signals, signs, markings, and delineation.

However, invariably, not all travel authorities encompass the professionalism and technology to provide adequate safety across the transportation systems they are responsible for. Local systems and services can be established and operated by individuals who lack a background in transportation systems. For administrative reasons, the overseeing of some travel systems can be passed off to others, such as parks departments or conservation authorities. Those organizations may not have staff with the background and training to adequately develop or assess important design, operations, or maintenance activities, and may lack a predisposition to explicitly consider the necessary travel safety concepts.

In a similar vein, transportation professionals seem to be experiencing a decline in credibility, possibly due to an inability to accommodate all public views and advocacies. In a recent road safety review of a suburban roadway, the study team presented a thorough and balanced view of the need for improvements and supporting recommendations. The report recognized both the needs of system users and the desires of area residents. Meanwhile, a politician for the area presented his own recommendations based on the advocacy of a small group. This approach to evaluating transportation facilities allows the introduction of features that do not conform to proven concepts of safety and serviceability for all system users.

Consequently, adequate safety may not be provided. One example is the provision of a multiuse path that was controlled by a municipal transportation authority along one section and a conservation authority along another extended section. In the section controlled by the transportation authority, conventional bikeway signs were installed where the path crossed a roadway. In the section controlled by the conservation authority, cyclists must weave their way through a narrow offset gate on either side of a roadway in order to cross (see Image 3.1). Presumably, these gates were installed to prevent access by automobiles, not to inconvenience or endanger cyclists. Furthermore, the authority did not provide Stop signs for bike facilities where they intersect roadways, contrary to the guidance established by traffic control manuals for the area. Placing fixed objects within a bicycle facility creates a hazard, and such measures are not consistent with cyclist needs, while more appropriate means are available to prevent automobile access.

Image 3.1: Multiuse path with heavy bicycle traffic showing locked gates creating an obstacle course and hazard for cyclists. (Source: Gilchrist, August 19, 2024)

In this case, a will to provide travel amenities, such as provision of a natural setting, or to curtail an activity, such as prevention of vehicular access, overrides movement and traffic control needs to provide adequate safety for cyclists using the path. Despite being informed of these problems, the conservation authority has made no changes over many years.

In the suburban area managed by the city, vehicular access is prevented through signs and pavement markings at unencumbered entryways. Consistent with current signing practice, there are Stop signs for cyclists using the path at intersections where the path is managed by the city transportation staff.

In 1997, I met with a prominent roadway design professional and author of several standards, who mused about the decline in the decision-making skills of a premier road authority. He suggested that the decline likely commenced many years earlier with the integration of departments and the movement of nontechnical managers into key positions. While the administrative changes seemed subtle, the effects were showing over the years. At the time, the design professional was involved with other experts in a safety review of a new and yet unopened provincial freeway where the police had identified several hazardous design and control elements.

A trend toward using less costly general managers rather than technically qualified managers is a reflection of the significant pressure on engineering and public works departments to rein in the cost of providing service. As the previous chapter mentioned, one common method of cost cutting has been to reduce qualifications and experience of technical personnel for specific tasks. This has been an industry trend for many years, with engineering positions being filled with technologists and so forth. Perhaps this is one reason why there seems to be an increase of instances where observant travelers wonder, "What were they thinking?"

As one example, a median at a signalized intersection was raised to provide an elevated flower bed. It is artistically attractive but obstructs the sight lines of left-turning traffic even when no flowers are present. The situation likely came about due to political or citizen influence, desirous of an aesthetic appeal. Complaints from the public appearing in the local newspaper were ineffective in rectifying the deficient sight lines for left-turn vehicles. When one individual in charge was informed of the liability exposure of the location, they indicated that they had extended the time of a protected left-turn green light to accommodate two vehicles instead of just one in response to the complaints about deficient sight lines.

Thus, in response to public influence, the person in charge decided to modify the operations rather than deal with the real safety issue. Lowering the height of the planters would have been more costly. The visibility problems remain for the third or later vehicles in the left-turn queue. At the time of publishing (several years later), the obstructed sight line remains. Forensic engineering does not typically capture this behind-the-scenes means of fixing deficient facilities. However, the condition in the field remains and could lead to catastrophic results at some future point, which would then require the assistance of a forensic engineer.

In another example, a municipality reconstructed a three-kilometer (1.9 mile) section of a two-lane roadway that had bike lanes on both sides of the roadway. Changes were made to the previous configuration, which had incorporated some well-considered safety features for both bicycles and motor vehicles. But as a result of the reconstruction, the direction of a one-way access and egress system for a small parking lot on one side of the road was reversed. With the new arrangement, the egress driveway intersected the roadway at a very acute angle. Consequently, drivers exiting the parking area and turning right into the near lane of the roadway penetrated the far lane (for travel in the opposite direction). These drivers also found their left-side sight line along the roadway was restricted by a retaining wall and embankment extending to the limits of the driveway/bike lane (see Image 3.2). The sight line for the bike lane was almost nonexistent at a location where cyclists could easily be traveling 50 km/h (30 mph) or more on a descending grade. After several months of operation in this way, the egress driveway was relocated to provide adequate visibility. It was a situation that never should have happened with proper oversight.

Of interest, the municipality had certified safety specialists on staff. Oddly, several of the changes seem to have come about to improve the cycling experience on a roadway that had been operating well without issues for many years.

Image 3.2: Location where an exit driveway with a high skew relative to the near-side lane had a dangerous visibility restriction. The driveway was changed to a one-way entrance. The tail of the new entrance arrow is on the left side of the view, and evidence of the Stop line removed appears aligned with the wall, embankment, and brush providing the visibility obstruction. (Source: Gilchrist, August 19, 2024)

These types of problems should not occur today, given the extent of knowledge within the industry. In this author's view, there are certainly problems within the hierarchy of some road authorities. Ultimately, such organizational problems become manifest in the field when there is a lack of critical thought regarding the impacts of poor decisions, leading to insufficient consideration of the system users' needs.

Typically, drivers exercise routine care in carrying out driving tasks that they have performed many times previously, which they may perform by rote. However, on encountering less-common conditions or situations, exercising routine care can precipitate failures in driving performance, leading to crash experiences. In the above case of the exit driveway, drivers compensated in their own way by ignoring the presence of the bike lane, ignoring the visual obstruction provided, and routinely passing over the directional dividing line of the roadway in order to make a right turn.

While such glaring faults are rare in the provision of facilities, they can have catastrophic outcomes. These design or implementation failures can take years to become apparent, emerging only when the right set of seemingly unusual conditions comes together, such as in the preceding example, when an unwary cyclist and unwary driver converged at the conflict point. By that time, the individuals who originally set out the design, operations, and paper trail detailing the development process could be long gone.

Another instance occurred in an industrial area where a local industrial road was constructed with a modest descent over several hundred meters. In the middle of the descent was an appropriately designed horizontal curve satisfying the municipal and provincial standards. However, the horizontal curve included a break point on the downgrade with a 1 percent increase in slope. The change in grade was designed as a single point in the road rather than as a smooth vertical curve. Under normal operating conditions, drivers could traverse the location without issue even when the road was wet.

However, one winter during a snowfall and slippery conditions, a man's car slid off the road, striking a fixed luminaire support with the driver's door, resulting in about one meter of penetration into the vehicle. Examination of the scene and friction conditions found that given the slippery road condition, the change in attitude of the vehicle traveling over the break point was sufficient to reduce the vehicle weight on the rear wheels, allowing slippage. Thus, the loss of traction of the rear wheels caused a loss of control at the break point.

The forensic transportation analysis found that the municipal road authority had an active but draft standard at the time requiring a smooth vertical curve for a 1 percent change in grade. The design standard had been in draft form for many years but was contained in the city design standards. In the case of this particular roadway, the design was prepared by a design-build contractor and signed off by their design engineer. The design was submitted to the city and went through their approvals process, during which it was presumably examined by competent professionals, but not necessarily. As this case did not go to trial, it remains unknown how the design prepared by a consultant got past the city engineers and reviewers and whether inattention, incompetence, negligence, or even engineering judgment was the cause of the problem. Regardless, the city had to issue a large payout to the injured party.

Many manuals within the industry, as part of their foreword or introduction, refer to the need to exercise *engineering judgment* when applying the provisions of the manual. This type of recommendation is necessary to cope with the many conditions and situations that do not fit neatly into the contexts directly addressed in the manual. It allows decision-makers to deviate from the manual to accommodate unique features found in the field or new design concepts. However, engineering judgment requires the application of applied science and engineering principles, not unfounded assumptions. An example may be where terrain conditions require costly construction methods to satisfy compliance with the manual. Engineering judgment may be used to design and install a feature consistent with a speed less than the adopted design speed of the highway. These situations can be rendered nominally safe through traffic control provisions.

When this type of considered decision is made, it is necessary to document the process and to maintain a record of the protocol used for arriving at a decision in which there is noncompliance with the industry standards. Further, while the design is noncompliant, it is incumbent upon the designers to ensure that the location satisfies the industry standard of safety for public use. For example, in the case of a small radius curve, the design condition needs to be supported by traffic control provisions that warn the public of the potential hazard and inform them how to safely traverse the section. Advance curve warning signs and advisory speeds may be appropriate to ensure the location satisfies the industry standard.

I have encountered many instances in the litigation process where engineering judgment was used to justify the provision of noncompliant situations or conditions. In almost every case, there was also an absence of documentation to indicate why things were done the way they were or how the situation or condition was assessed at the time of installation. In these instances, the documentation likely never existed. Recordkeeping for this information can be nonexistent or haphazard and given little priority in longer-term record maintenance. Even so, there should not be an issue in litigation if a noncompliant location was rendered compliant and acceptably safe for public use by other means, such as appropriate traffic control.

THE IMPORTANCE OF HUMAN FACTORS

4.1 Human Factors Are Problematic

There are an astounding number of ways that drivers can become trapped, resulting in harm. Often, this occurs where conditions that drivers believe are present do not encompass the full reality of the situation or condition. While it is not the intent to deal with them all here, it may be worthwhile to briefly explore how and where system users may assume they are performing safely, when in fact they are putting themselves or others at risk. In some cases, hazards are created by system users, while in other cases they are inherent to the infrastructure.

The following is a list of system user situations or conditions where schemas may be unconsidered, incomplete, somewhat erroneous, corrupted during an activity, or just plain wrong.

- Cyclists believe that riding on the sidewalk is safe. However, drivers coming out of driveways can have visibility obstructions. Also, drivers may not expect cyclists on the sidewalk and may not look in both directions.

- On departing a driveway and proceeding to the right, drivers may not look to the right and fail to detect pedestrians and others—scooters, as an example—approaching from the right.

- In making a left turn at a traffic signal during the intergreen period—yellow plus all red—some drivers assume through traffic approaching in the other direction will stop when it might not.

- Pedestrians and drivers may believe that drivers turning left at the end of a protected left-turn phase will stop, if possible, while left-turn drivers moving ahead may attempt to complete their left turn during the red phase by penetrating the opposing through lanes before those vehicles proceed forward.

- Pedestrians can falsely believe that green lights for traffic will provide sufficient time to walk across the intersection in the same direction despite a pedestrian signal head indicating "Do Not Walk."

- Pedestrians may falsely assume push buttons for crosswalks at traffic control signals will allow them to cross on the current green phase for traffic.

- Passenger vehicle drivers, cyclists, and pedestrians can falsely believe that the mirrors on large trucks allow a good view of all areas around the vehicle, when there can be very large and critical blind spots for the truck driver.

- Many pedestrians and cyclists are unaware of the off-tracking of large vehicles when making turns and may not leave sufficient clearance.

- At two-track railway crossings, the approach of a second train may be hidden from drivers, cyclists, and pedestrians by the departure of the first. A similar visibility restriction can occur with trucks at intersections when one large left-turning truck hides from view another approaching truck moving straight through.

- In proceeding through a Stop sign, drivers may look in both directions before departing but not allow sufficient time to assess the speed or time of arrival of approaching vehicles. In such cases, the driver is known to have "looked but did not see."

- Drivers will not slow until well after the onset of snow, wrongly assuming that unless the pavement is beginning to appear white, the pavement retains most of its dry-condition friction.

- Pedestrians and cyclists may believe during low-light conditions that since they have good visibility of approaching vehicles, the driver of those vehicles will be able to see them as well.

Most of the time, these situations occur because the system user has a false assumption about their own safety. Individuals may experience these incidents, such as riding a bicycle on the sidewalk, many times and successfully complete the trip. However, in any one trip, several infrequent events can converge, causing a failure in the schema, and an injury results. Unfortunately, sometimes time and motion will allow a scenario to unfold in a way not previously experienced or envisaged.

Often, the harm comes about when individuals believe that others will act in the same manner *they* would in a given situation. For example, the driver waiting to turn left at a traffic control signal sees the light change from green to yellow, considers the traffic approaching in the opposite direction, and proceeds forward to turn left. The ensuing collision that occurs results from the left-turn driver falsely assuming that the approaching driver will stop because they (the left-turn driver) would stop in that situation.

Alternatively, the left-turn driver may fail to properly assess the speed and distance of the approaching vehicle. It may also have been that the other driver was speeding, so while the distance to collision would have typically been sufficient for the other driver to stop, they decided to proceed through the intersection using the end of the yellow and/or all red to enter the intersection.

Oftentimes, individuals simply do not anticipate the variable outcomes that are possible. Children are allowed to play in their driveways because they are in a safe space, but they can be backed over or otherwise struck by a vehicle operated by anyone not expecting children to be playing there. Adults riding their bicycles on the sidewalk because it is considered a "safe space" can be hit by a vehicle leaving a driveway. Joyriders blow through intersections for kicks, failing to consider the outcomes if they are struck by a driver on the through road. Drivers running a yellow indication fail to consider how long cross traffic will take to get into the intersection. All these cases involve a time and motion component to the crash in combination with an unconsidered evaluation or outcome.

While these examples relate to the system users, it is worth wondering if similar unconsidered outcomes can be the result of the infrastructure's design. The answer to that question is an unequivocal *yes*, possibly with more frequency than one would imagine. The following cites a few examples of problems that have happened or continue to contribute to unimagined outcomes by designers.

In the case of sidewalks, consider the designer who believes that the walk from point A to point B is most artfully accomplished by having pedestrians walk a longer route through point C, since it provides some visual interest. On the day the sidewalk is opened, a pedestrian follows the path and takes in the item of interest. However, having seen the attraction once, they forever after choose to take a straight line from point A to point B rather than the designer's anticipated route. A new path shortcut emerges (see Image 4.1). What the designer believed was relevant becomes irrelevant to pedestrians; thus the sidewalk is in the wrong place for a long time.

In the case of traffic turning right at intersections, designers in the past believed that a nice smooth and quick transition from one road to the next was important to keep traffic moving with as little disruption as possible. The turn could be done moderately quickly using a Yield sign and curving roadway with a large island, effectively installing a direct ramp. However, after many years, it was found that drivers would not turn their head sufficiently to look over their shoulder—or for sufficient time—to assess approaching traffic conditions on the through roads. Additionally, drivers may not observe nearby pedestrians. In recognizing the real and potential failures in these circumstances, many of these locations have been removed and replaced with a right-turn bay, a much smaller island, and a Stop sign that allows drivers to more conveniently look left.

Image 4.1: Example of a sidewalk leading to nowhere. The sidewalk was placed to provide the shortest connection to another sidewalk. The path leads to a signalized crossing of the highway and a nearby parking lot. (Source: Gilchrist, August 23, 2024)

In a similar vein, many designers still believe that for access from a crossroad onto a freeway, right turns from the crossroad are best handled using direct ramps so that drivers need not reduce their speed from that of the crossroad. These ramps often allow traffic to speed up as they depart the crossroad. Aside from the wasteful land consumption, this design results in pedestrians dealing with high-speed traffic, which often also exhibits substantial variability in speeds. Pedestrians can have difficulty assessing the arrival time of traffic and distance that is necessary for crossing the ramp. Often, drivers are not looking for pedestrians on these high-speed exit ramps from the crossroad and fail to notice or otherwise acknowledge pedestrians in these areas.

Oftentimes, transit stops are placed at regular intervals along a roadway so that pedestrians will have access to transit services within a reasonable walking distance. While these stops are typically at intersections, there may be little consideration given to how pedestrians are to cross the road to access or depart from the stop. Being on busy roadways, pedestrians require gaps in traffic of a certain size to allow them to safely cross the roadway at locations without traffic control signals. Yet during busy periods, the selection of an appropriate gap to use can be a daunting task, subject to error.

Granted, one may contend that pedestrians should walk to a controlled crossing (signalized crossing) if they have trouble or doubts about crossing the road at transit stop locations without some kind of control. However, pedestrians are unlikely to do so since it can be reasonably expected the transit authority would place bus stops at locations where it is safe to cross. Thus, the transit stop is a destination and an enticement to cross the roadway at that location. Suggesting pedestrians should walk to an alternative stop down the road runs contrary to the transit stop placement. It also assumes that pedestrian activity and transit usage is insensitive to excessive travel time. Such assumptions fail to consider the real characteristics of pedestrian activity.

In another example, slow-moving pedestrians may start crossing the roadway during a walk signal yet not complete the crossing before the signal indication turns to "Don't Walk." This can occur because the time allotted for the crossing movement is routinely based on an average walking speed of 1.2 m/s (4 fps) or similar for normal crossing conditions. Yet some pedestrians walk at slower speeds.

A routine walking speed is likely to be used by road authorities unless specific information is available that slow-walking pedestrians may be present. The occasional slow walker is left on their own. Where they are known to be present, provisions may be available. Some traffic control manuals enable consideration of slower speeds and recommend that longer crossing times are appropriate where there is a known regular presence of slower moving pedestrians.

Older individuals are known to walk at slower rates. Eubanks and Hill noted in one study that the fifteenth percentile walking speed for those over sixty-five years is about 1.06 m/s (3.5 fps).[1] Coffin and Morrall found the fifteenth percentile walking speed of elderly pedestrians to be 1.0 m/s (3.2 fps) and subsequently recommended that as a design walking speed for signalized intersections only near senior and nursing homes where most pedestrians are elderly.[2] Of course, slow-walking individuals can be present at any location. Obviously, some individuals walk more slowly than the fifteenth-percentile speeds. As such, the normal setting can effectively exclude an estimated 15 percent of walking seniors (and likely those with young children) who are considered to be vulnerable users of our transportation systems. Perhaps the authors of some manuals assume slower walkers could or would hurry across the road, but no foundation is presented for determining why some walkers may be left out of the signal timing protocols for normal operating conditions (1.2 m/s or 4 fps walking speed).

The question of inclusiveness in our transportation systems is a concern within the industry. Yet there seems to be an unwritten but pervasive policy that the extent of inclusiveness is about 85 percent of individual characteristics. Chapter 5 discusses additional human factors, including inferences into who is included and who is not.

4.2 The Driving Task

My informal introduction to human factors was in 1971 in a university course examining environmental perception. Information on this subject related to transportation systems seemed very thin in that program. Still, by 1975, an undergraduate urban transportation engineering course included material that provided insights to engineering considerations related to eye movement, color perception, acuity and speed-related peripheral vision, sensitivity, visual attention, glare effects and recovery, reaction time in response to stimuli, and condition of the driver.

Now, it has become well accepted that understanding human factors in transportation engineering is essential to understanding how every element of facilities and services will work, from conceptual design to ongoing maintenance. More importantly, understanding human factors enables those responsible to understand how users of the infrastructure will react to specific situations or deviate from the intended actions envisioned by the providers of the facility.

This prevents the unfortunate circumstance where, during litigation, the designer must describe their misguided hopes of user behavior after the public has routinely failed to act as desired. In this regard, travel authorities "will" people to act in a certain manner before installing infrastructure elements without effectively considering how system users may actually act.

Human factors have long been known to be important and integral to transportation and traffic engineering. Therefore, it is not sufficient to focus solely on physical standards without considering the variability in human performance and specific needs of users. In forensic engineering, simply indicating whether standards were satisfied or not is insufficient since people cannot always perform to the level required by standards. The forensic task is to determine if the situation or conditions were well-suited to human performance capabilities and whether a complete range of individual performance capabilities were universally included.

Ongoing research on driver information processing has revealed much about human performance while operating a vehicle. Over time, humans' abilities and deficiencies have become a keystone consideration in the development of roadway design and traffic control systems. However, these capabilities and limitations must be accredited to all system users, not only drivers. Children represent a special case discussed in a later section.

An early description of driver information processing appeared in the third edition of *A User's Guide to Positive Guidance*,[3] a publication of the US Department of Transportation, and is summarized below as a breakdown of driver behavior. The material reveals an understanding of basic human factors in the performance of the driving task. It also has shed light on how to use positive guidance in the design, control, and operations of transportation facilities for more than thirty years.

While most of the human senses are used in driving, up to 90 percent of all information is gathered and received visually. Drivers process information serially, one source of visual information at a time. Given the need to process multiple visual inputs simultaneously—traffic lights, approaching vehicles, crossing pedestrians, and the road ahead—drivers will compensate by juggling information through prioritizing and processing these inputs sequentially. Drivers integrate various tasks and maintain awareness of a dynamic, changing environment by sampling information using brief glances (eye fixations) and quickly shifting attention between locations (saccades). They rely on judgment, estimation, prediction, and memory to fill in gaps, share tasks, and shed lower-priority information.

Drivers collect information from multiple sources, prioritize what to focus on, process the information, make decisions, and execute control actions—all while often operating under the pressure of time constraints.

The process of prioritizing and selecting which tasks to perform first is known as *primacy*. Primacy is assigned according to the perceived consequences of *not* attending to an informational source. When two or more information sources or needs compete, the one with the highest primacy is (or should be) satisfied first. However, when juggling potential or real conflicts, opportunities for error are heightened.

In driving, control tasks assume the highest primacy. These tasks include steering, regulating speed, and maintaining headway. Secondary tasks typically include reading signs and watching for other vehicles or pedestrians.[4]

The information drivers gather and process is therefore primarily dependent on their visual search process. While the human eye has a wide range of view, not all visible information is processed. Of more than one billion bits of information reaching the retina in a second, drivers are conscious of and can act on only sixteen bits per second.[5] Consequently, drivers are able to act upon only a small portion of the information that they receive. This provides ample opportunity for something to be missed or to go wrong in the absence of some guidance such as signals and signs. Looking in the direction of an object does not mean that it is seen, and not looking directly at an object does not mean that it goes undetected.

The area where drivers focus their attention while driving is limited, making the information within that view important to what a driver will become aware of. Mourant and Rockwell found that in traveling along an open two-lane road, drivers concentrate their eye fixations on the lane in which their vehicle is traveling and to the right shoulder. Fewer than 3 percent of eye fixations were to the left of the road's center,[6] affecting whether drivers will detect a hazard in time to effectively avoid it. For example, object or pedestrian detections on the left by an approaching driver can be expected to occur later (less distance from the vehicle) than those occurring on the right.

Drivers consciously select information to process through direct observation using their central vision or by detecting a stimuli that attracts their attention in their peripheral vision. For a person to detect an object in their peripheral vision, it must contrast from the objects or background that surrounds it. Contrast may be provided by size, shape, color, brightness, and/or relative motion. In a discussion of drivers detecting pedestrians, Eubanks and Hill address the difficulty drivers can experience when the object is unexpected and intermixed with other visual stimuli:

> Pedestrians, cyclists and animals can appear in view at any time and often from a direction which is not anticipated. At night, oncoming headlights can overwhelm the visual systems and brake and turn signals can intermix. To be seen in peripheral vision stimulus must be more attention getting than all other competing

stimuli and cause the nerve fibers of the peripheral retina to fire a signal to the brain to direct central vision in another direction.[7]

Without the visual stimuli in their peripheral vision to attract a driver's attention, they may detect an object too late or miss it entirely. As objects or pedestrians move into the area of a driver's central vision, detection becomes more probable with less delay. This is why, as a motorist traveling along a through road, we occasionally see a vehicle coming to a stop on the side street at an intersection but did not observe its approach even when a clear view was available for some time. For similar reasons, pedestrians waiting at the side of the road may be undetected until a driver is very close to them—or a driver may miss them altogether even though they were in plain sight. These missed or delayed detections can occur due to a lack of contrast—no motion, indistinct color, small size—combined with the absence of any expectation of their presence. Under low-light conditions, visibility is reduced and detection becomes even more difficult.

While considerable attention has been given to the drivers of motor vehicles, the findings from research on the driving task are certainly applicable to all modes of travel. These concepts apply to a cyclist biking on the street or a trail as well as a pedestrian walking along a sidewalk. While there may be some variation in the time and space available with other means of movement, information is acquired and acted on in similar fashion, and instructions to these system users should be delivered using the same concepts applicable to drivers. For this reason, the assessment of other types of mishaps (not motor vehicle crashes) resulting in personal injury or involving off-road transportation infrastructure should be examined through the same lens that we use for drivers, with adjustments made as necessary.

Understanding driver behavior is fundamental to understanding driver performance and is also an important element in the design of acceptably safe roads and in the design and placement of traffic control devices such as warning signs. Driver behavior is also relevant to the roadside conditions and can also be affected by the maintenance of all facilities in the right of way.

Accordingly, to establish a driver-related context, the following section and Chapter 5 contain an overview of selected aspects of driver behavior gathered from over fifty years of research concerning human factors. Specific reference is made to the extremely important principle of driver expectancy. The more normally cited process of driver perception and reaction to hazards on the roadway is also presented.

4.3 Driver and Other Systems User Expectancies

There is little doubt that driver *expectancy is the key factor* when considering the behavior of drivers or other system users related to safety issues affecting the design of safe roads, the assessment of specific traffic collisions, or the evaluation of the general safety of roadway sections.[8] This important human factor can be used to explain the actions of drivers and others using our transportation systems, such as cyclists on a path or pedestrians on a sidewalk.

When approaching a green light, drivers can expect it to turn yellow. Drivers therefore have an *expectancy* related to the phase change of the signal indication. Consequently, they may prepare in advance and respond quickly when the change occurs. When approaching an intersection on a through road, drivers expect a vehicle on the crossroad to stop and wait until they pass through. If the driver on the crossroad pulls out instead of waiting, then the expectancy of the through driver is likely to be violated. The reaction times of drivers is known to be affected by these expectancies. The 1992 *Traffic Engineering Handbook* states:

> A fundamental component of this approach [to driver information processing and perception] is the concept of expectancy. Drivers operate with a set of expectancies . . . and if these expectancies are violated there is the potential for an accident.[9]

The principle of driver expectancy is also described in *A User's Guide to Positive Guidance* (second ed.), published by the US Department of Transportation.

> [Driver expectancy] relates to the readiness of the driver to respond to events, situations, or the presentation of information. It is primarily a function of the drivers' experience. If an expectancy is violated, longer response time and incorrect behavior usually result . . . control and guidance failures tend to be catastrophic.[10]

The expectancy principles developed in the 1970s and expanded on in the 1981 user's guide were effectively summarized and related to road safety by the US Federal Highway Administration. In their 1986 report entitled *Driver Expectancy in Highway Design and Traffic Operations*, the impact of expectancy violations on driver performance were succinctly stated:

> If designs are incompatible with driver attributes, or if the information displays are ambiguous or erroneous, or if expectancies are violated, drivers will commit errors, and the system will fail.[11]

That summary document also contained the following observations about driver expectancy:

> Expectancies are associated with all levels of the driving task and all phases of the driving situation.

> Drivers experience problems and commit errors when [their] expectancies are violated.

> Drivers should not be surprised.

The more predictable the design, information display, or traffic operation, the less likely will be the chance for driver error.

Drivers, in the absence of information to the contrary, assume that they will only have to react to "standard", i.e., expected situations . . .

Drivers tend to anticipate upcoming situations and events that are common to the route they are driving.[12]

The principle of driver expectancy is a powerful explanatory process. Therefore, this principle was not surprisingly also recognized and adopted by the transportation engineering community as a key element of its standard of practice. The *Geometric Design Guide for Canadian Roads*, published by the Transportation Association of Canada (TAC), has recognized the importance of driver expectancy in all aspects of the driving task and promotes the principle. The first chapter of the 1999 *Guide* lists several expectancies:

Drivers tend to anticipate upcoming situations and events that are common to the road they are travelling [sic].

The more predictable the road feature, the less likely will be the chance for errors.

Drivers experience difficulty when they are confronted with the unexpected.

Drivers, in the absence of counter evidence, assume that they will only have to react to standard situations.

The road and its environment upstream of a site create an expectation of downstream conditions; drivers are more likely to experience problems in transition areas and locations with inconsistent design or operation.

Expectancies are associated with all levels of driving performance and all aspects of the driving situation. This includes expectancies relative to speed, path, direction, the roadway, the environment, geometric design, traffic operations and traffic control devices.[13]

Consequently, it is well-known that drivers form perceptions of what lies ahead on a roadway and anticipate their occurrence based on a long history of driving experience, driving in similar settings elsewhere, as well as situations encountered on previous sections of the same roadway. In this context, the transportation and traffic engineering industry recognize that if conditions or situations that drivers encounter on the roadway meet their expectations, their driving performance tends to be error-free. If those expectations are violated, however, errors may occur and the results can be catastrophic.

Of course, these concepts are also applicable to other modes of personal transportation, as well as having some corporate relevance. Pedestrians can expect that the sidewalk is free of tripping edges, potholes, and missing cover plates (water valves). They can also have expectancies that if the signal indication is to "Walk" as they start across the street, they will have sufficient time to finish the crossing before the light changes. Cyclists can expect that designated bicycle facilities will be designed and controlled in accordance with design standards applicable to the industry. In the administration of facilities, individuals new to a job can have expectancies that their predecessors were sufficiently competent and therefore there is no requirement to reassess previous decisions. When these expectancies are unfulfilled, future problems may be anticipated.

SOME HUMAN FACTORS IN DESIGN

5.1 Perception/Reaction

The process of driver perception and reaction plays a key role in assessing driver performance.

That perception/reaction process comprises the following basic elements:

- Detection/perception: the alertness and ability of a driver to visually detect an object or situation on the roadway

- Identification: the thought process subsequently required to perceive the object and/or the nature of the situation and determine whether a hazard is present

- Decision response: the thought/decision process required to then make an appropriate selection for which action to take

- Volition: the ability to react by initiating that action (e.g., depressing the brake pedal or turning the steering wheel)

This assessment/response process applies to all driver reactions, whether responding to changes in traffic control or anticipating a pending collision. In the case of the former, the control devices must provide sufficient information and time for drivers to respond in an appropriate way. In the case of the latter, drivers may run out of time to respond, so their assessment or the vehicle maneuver may be only partly completed before the collision occurs.

Other travelers and vulnerable road users also use this same mechanism to assess many situations and conditions they encounter. For example, pedestrians and cyclists assess whether they can cross a roadway given approaching traffic and then respond by stepping into the roadway or applying pressure to a pedal to get the bicycle rolling (volition). Pedestrians assess where to move when another individual approaches on the sidewalk. Cyclists assess how to cross railway tracks angled across the road. However, since the time allocated to each step of the process can vary substantially, each condition must be assessed on its own merits.

If the maneuvers are relatively simple, the required time is relatively small. For an expected situation requiring a single, simple maneuver, such as braking a vehicle to a stop in response to a traffic signal phase change, only minimal time is needed to initiate the braking action. This would represent the lower bound for the reaction time required to initiate the braking action.

Determining the reaction time for an individual involved in a collision is fraught with problems. Most reaction time information for individuals is inferred based on a population distribution and likelihood rather than being deterministic. Determining whether an individual should have been able to respond is problematic since the situation cannot typically be replicated. When testing an individual, they have an expectancy that they will have to react. That is not the case with a pending collision. It is then necessary to speculate whether an individual can be assigned the characteristics represented by the general population or whether the individual was an outlier at that time and place. There may be inherited or legitimate reasons for being an outlier in response time.

In accident reconstruction, a common response time of 1.5 seconds is typically assigned to participants when assuming standard driver perception/reaction times for straightforward situations. Key research information regarding perception reaction times reported by Olson[1] noted that "given a reasonably clear stimulus and a straightforward situation a great deal of data suggests that most drivers (i.e., about 85 percent) should begin to respond by about 1.5 seconds after first visibility of the object or concern." Once again, there is the eighty-fifth percentile, so it can also be stated that fifteen out of one hundred drivers are unlikely to respond in this time.

For collision reconstruction, 1.5 seconds has become the benchmark reference time. The finding by Olson is consistent with the work of Summala, who found that drivers responding with a steering input to the unexpected door opening of a parked vehicle had a mean response time of 1.5 seconds and reached the halfway point of maximum displacement from the original path in about 2.5 seconds.[2] As a human factor, a similar response time may be assigned to other system users, including cyclists, pedestrians, scooterists, and more. For example, a cyclist riding near the edge of a traffic lane reacting to the sudden opening of a door of a parked vehicle is likely to react in a manner similar to that noted by Summala.

When the condition or situation is unusual or difficult to perceive, an extended response time is appropriate. Drivers should not be penalized by assuming a usual response time when reacting to traffic control devices that may be difficult to perceive, vague in their intent, or missing. The detection time for signs, signals, and markings may be substantial under such conditions. For example, drivers may become involved in a collision because the street sign they were looking for was small and/or located well away from the roadway, resulting in an extended search and longer detection time. This circumstance may be readily viewed by the police examining a collision as distracted driving, thus blaming the driver when in fact the sign size or location contributed to an extended response time.

In other cases, newly placed or temporary conditions signs that require a driver to respond may be visible for an extended distance, but the message is not delivered until the sign becomes readable based on the travel speed of the vehicle and other human factors considerations. The result can be an extended detection and identification period and very short decision period.

Many temporary, changeable message signs do not have the contrast or resolution to provide sufficient reading time, particularly where the message itself is dynamic. While many drivers may be able to handle the situation and perform without collision, the situation can entrap some individuals who process information more slowly and fall into the tails, or fifteenth percentile, of the population distribution. For example, individuals with dyslexia or who are not fluent in the language may fall into this group. Thus, where collisions occur under these circumstances, the scene conditions that were present are likely to be relevant.

The fundamental principles of driver behavior encompassing expectancy and perception/reaction time must therefore be incorporated in any analysis of driver performance when assessing travel infrastructure— roadways, bikeways, paths, sidewalks—at the scene of an incident.

Since Olson initially began his research, there has been significant interest in expected response times in reaction to a change in traffic control or a threat. The nature of the research has examined a wide range of situations involving the movement of people. This information is now finding its way into textbooks and manuals and thus is known to transportation industry professionals. However, there is more work to be done. For forensic engineers, there are now algorithms to assist investigators in determining an appropriate population response time for various situations or conditions. Of course, metadata recognizes a range of responses but does not reveal the capabilities of a surprised (or not) individual in each of the detection, identification, decision response, and volition processes involved in a specific collision. There remain significant issues in attempting to assign this information to individuals, in part because testing introduces a heightened state of awareness. That difficulty is expounded by a multiplicity of factors such as conditions at the scene, preexisting awareness, attributes of the individuals at the time of the incident, and variation in personal response time as well as considering the bounds of reasonability.

In considering this information for design purposes, 2.5 seconds has long been used as an appropriate length of time to observe a hazard and begin the avoidance maneuver, such as braking.[3] This standard is used in both the US and Canada. Over the years, this value has been reexamined many times but has remained resolute. The 2011 Green Book (formally titled *A Policy on Geometric Design of Highways and Streets*),[4] which is a national standard for design in the US, provides some insights on this standard for time. It identifies a range of response times for several conditions. For a typical driver, Green Book data indicates that for a single information source, such as a traffic signal phase change, occurring under *expected* conditions, drivers require an average of about 0.6 seconds to react, with some taking as long as 2.0 seconds. Under *unexpected* conditions with a single source of information, drivers require more time. For the eighty-fifth-percentile driver, response times are about 1.7 seconds for expected conditions and about 2.7 seconds for unexpected conditions.

After identifying this information, the Green Book reaffirms that 2.5 seconds should be used for the design of stopping distance in response to a hazard. This would apply to the situation with a vehicle coming over a hill and the driver observing the taillights of a stopped vehicle in the same lane. In selecting this value, time and distance estimates for stopping reflect an assumed taillight height, driver eye height, and travel speed. Thus, for minimal vertical curves (hills) and designs conforming to the assumed conditions, drivers are provided the nominal protection related to this simple response condition. Still, the manual recognizes some drivers may have trouble conforming to the time standard.

Realistically, coming over a hill and observing a stopped vehicle in their lane is likely to represent an unexpected condition for a driver. Indeed, many situations can cause a delayed detection or be considered unexpected circumstances. When there are two information sources, the eighty-fifth-percentile driver can take as long as 2.5 seconds to react to expected conditions, such as a signal phase change on an icy road, and 3.5 seconds for unexpected conditions.[5] In these circumstances, the manual's allocated response time excludes 15 percent of drivers or more.

The concept of applying standards that protect only 85 percent of drivers when they are performing normally is based on rationalizing the situational parameters and concluding they work for most individuals. In accepting the concept, it is assumed that facilities are built using design and control elements better than the minimums found in the standards. Where that may not be the case, it is assumed that drivers will compensate for poor or minimal elements by making appropriate adjustments to their actions, such as decelerating at a higher rate or driving more slowly. Therefore, the concept can be applied to all individuals. Most engineers seem to accept this approach as reasonable, believing that it would be too expensive to build facilities to encompass all drivers within design and control elements.

National highways and roadways generally operate well for most people with such rationalizations, and collisions suffered by those excluded from the standard are likely rare but remain an unknown. Whether one may agree with it or not, this approach to providing safe roads has been deemed reasonable by the industry. However, identifying those who may experience harm from the approach is almost impossible, and the odds of obtaining a fair resolution can be remote. With this uncertainty in combination with the propensity for the profession to exclude some system users, it seems appropriate that where there is tangible uncertainty, the system user should be given the benefit of the doubt in litigation.

This transportation industry practice has been used to define a safe response time in many situations. For example, the response time for a driver when a traffic light turns yellow may typically be set to a minimum of 1.0 second for the design of signal timing. However, some research has suggested that drivers have a mean response time of 1.2 seconds, with the eighty-fifth-percentile driver taking 1.9 seconds.[6]

Even so, the research for that information contained both analyses and rationalizations that resulted in confirming the use of the 1.0-second interval as a minimum for traffic signal timing, at least in some jurisdictions. Whether the research or the rationalizations are appropriate for public applications, the process shows the selection of design values is not straightforward and residual uncertainties can remain.

The Green Book, as well as other design manuals in the US and Canada, also refers to sight distances for critical situations, which include unusual situations drivers may encounter. The industry term for this is "decision sight distance," because the response process can be much longer than usual. These are situations that are difficult to perceive or that require complex reactions, such as speed, path, and/or direction changes. The response times for these situations can be very long, ranging from 3.0 seconds for stopping on a rural road to 14.5 seconds for a complex situation on an urban roadway.[7] References for response times for these conditions are based on studies from 1979. Consistent with the industry practice, the authors of that research did not encompass a full range of human performance in their summations regarding decision plus response times.[8] In addition, it was recommended their findings be applied to the eighty-fifth-percentile operating speed. The Green Book simply reported the findings for the determination of decision sight distance.

In a study of the decision sight distance requirement for highway exit ramps, the authors of one paper reviewed the standards presented nationally in the US and Canada. Specific attention was given to the safety the standards provided and the sustained operating performance. The study found that none of the four exit ramp terminals examined satisfied the provisions of the standards. The study therefore recommended better signing be used to overcome the deficiencies. Nevertheless, it was concluded that measured distances to objects (signs) containing the necessary information "for most but not all drivers" was sufficient to make decisions and execute maneuvers safely.[9]

Such findings are common within the transportation engineering industry, where those responsible for public safety routinely recognize and allow a portion of the driving population to be excluded from the protection provided by the standards. In the case identified, the outcome of the research was to recommend means for improvements through signing rather than meaningful changes to the standard.

Given this approach to the preparation of standards, situations or conditions satisfying standards cannot be classified as universally safe, but they can be made more or less safe,[10] since it is assumed people will adjust to the situation. In dealing with this responsibility, the industry assigns to itself the positions of judge and jury in matters of public safety. There is often no reference to benchmarks with respect to its acceptability by the public. These standards are then incorporated into public policy, often without democratic confirmation. In this context, the application of standards may be considered a discretionary decision by industry personnel.

Recognizing that industry practices are not universally safe for all users, some people may be accepting and others outraged. However, it is not the intent here to indicate what is appropriate or not, but rather to put the issue on the table. What is relevant is that the industry standards are not universally encompassing of all system users. Beyond that, it is the task of forensics to assess whether the infrastructure may have contributed to the harm of individuals involved in collisions.

Therefore, certain locations may be expected to experience unusual collision rates even when standards have been met at their nominal level. In such cases, any assessment and review of this circumstance that the providers of the facility or service undertake is often directed toward improving the safety of the site rather than evaluating the contribution of the standard. Thus, the process helps maintain the rationalizations used to develop the standards.

These types of rationalizations seem to abandon the concept of the highway providing a universally safe operating environment, shifting the onus for safe performance to some users who may not be aware of or able to handle certain conditions/situations. In this respect, a detailed examination of the collisions is required to determine if there was a systemic contribution because of the design parameters. In view of the rare but possible shortcomings of design, it is appropriate for practitioners to provide more generous designs than the nominal values of the standards, thus moving the operating conditions in the direction of greater safety. The Green Book supports this notion and points out the possibility that longer times than allocated by the nominal standards may be necessary:

> A brake reaction time of 2.5 s is considered adequate for conditions that are more complex than the simple conditions used in laboratory and road tests, but it is not adequate for the most complex conditions encountered in actual driving.[11]

To some, having this type of information included in a manual is simply an invitation for litigation. Alternatively, some believe that since the manual presents the standards of the industry, those providing facilities that satisfy accepted standards should be immune to legal claims. For this reason, some argue that there is no place for this type of commentary in a manual. A long history of vehicle operations and absence of collisions enables the industry to assume that when the nominal limits of the standard are present, safe operations exist. Consequently, omitting this type of information from the manual is justifiable.

However, the standards of the industry are not there to protect only the providers of infrastructure from claims. Their purpose is also to protect the system users from harm, and following a collision, those users have a right to know whether their actions were adequately accounted for within the standards. By doing so, a fair balance is established between the providers of infrastructure and its users, allowing for detailed assessments of cause and effect when users come to harm.

5.2 Closing on Slow-Moving or Stationary Objects

Sometimes situations or conditions occur where people are injured and evaluators believe the drivers involved could have clearly seen something was about to happen, had lots of time to react, but incredibly, made little effort to do so. Two situations are presented: The first involves a pedestrian fatality involving a clearly visible train. The second involves a passenger vehicle running into the back of a truck.

In response to the situation involving a daylight pedestrian fatality at a railway crossing in an area flanked by urban development, the site was visited to observe the circumstances of the person struck by the train. The railway line was straight in the direction the train was coming from, passing through a wide, shallow depression. The crossing had active signals and gates for traffic. The visibility condition allowed the approaching train to be seen for more than two kilometers (1.2 miles). The train's intense headlight could be viewed at a very great distance during the day and at night. When viewed from the waiting point at the crossing, the train seemed to take a very long time to arrive. For much of the wait, the shape of the train was obscured to some extent by the glare from the headlight. The view of the train suggested it was approaching head-on in slow motion.

When the train reached a certain closeness, the warning system became activated and a set of gates closed the road in the usual fashion. However, no gates extended across the sidewalks, and the path across the tracks remained open for use. As the train approached, the size and shape of the front of the engine eventually became definable despite the glare from the headlight. As it passed, it seemed to do so at a very high rate of speed—much faster than was anticipated from watching its approach. In this situation, the detection period was very long. However, as the engine neared the crossing, the identification period was short.

This situation relates to the assessment problems present when a vehicle is heading straight toward a stationary observer and only the vehicle outline is visible. Though warned, the pedestrian, in the time available to them, could not work out the problem involving the walking clearance time for the tracks and the arrival time of the engine. Mortimer, in the *Accident Reconstruction Journal*, indicated that for oblique views of an approaching train, individuals must rely on the changing size of the approaching train to estimate its distance[12] but provides no inference about the success rates of such observations. As the observation angle increases, speed and distance estimations improve.

The situation where a moving object is heading straight toward an observer is known as "looming." In this case, the pedestrian was part of a group of individuals who experienced a failure to assess the looming danger, even though the train was plainly visible. This human factor response suggests that design provisions for railway crossing gates where there are sidewalks need to also include gate provisions for pedestrian (and cyclist) facilities. However, the looming problem plays a role in other situations involving other types of system users.

Looming can also be a problem for drivers, especially at night when the only visible signs of a hazard are a vehicle's lights. In examining the looming problem for drivers, Olson and Farber[13] identify the distance at which a driver overtaking a stationary or slower-moving vehicle will first realize how rapidly the space is closing and that some imminent response is required. Prior to this distance, a driver may have perceived that they are closing on a lead vehicle that is stopped or slow moving, but they are unlikely to have full knowledge of the closing circumstances. The time to collision is not identified until the approaching vehicle is very close.

Of course, the hazardous nature of the closing situation can be exacerbated by the contrast afforded by the object. In the case of closing on a slow-moving vehicle, all that may be visible are the taillights or possibly some other information that is difficult to interpret. In the case of only two taillights being visible at a distance, the problem is two-dimensional rather than three-dimensional, exacerbating the problem of identification (step two in the perception/reaction process).

Accumulated research has determined that when the angular velocity of an approaching object—indicated by its growing size—exceeds an average of 0.0035 radians per second (rad/s), drivers are able to assess the relative velocity between vehicles.[14] As usual, this may not include everyone. Recognizing the range in performance, Tijerina found the angular velocity threshold enabling assessment of closing speed to be about 0.002 and 0.004 rad/s.[15] To assess individual ability, it is necessary to assume most system users can assess closing speed for angular velocities of less than 0.004 rad/s. Thus, an application of the industry practice has again allowed for the exclusion of some system users.

These findings may be used to identify the distance at which the time to impact will occur for any given closing speed. For example, consider a situation in which a driver becomes able to assess closing speed on an object at an angular velocity of 0.003 rad/s. If a driver approaches the rear of a 2.45 m (8 ft.) wide bus at a closing speed of 70 km/h (43.5 mph), assessing the speed differential commences about 128 m (420 ft.) from the bus. The driver of the approaching vehicle has that distance to come to a stop if the bus is not moving or a somewhat greater distance if the bus is moving in the same direction. On wet pavements, a driver is provided with a perception-reaction time of 2.5 seconds, where a design stopping distance from 70 km/h (43.5 mph) is 110 m (361 ft.).[16] Consequently, a driver who commences assessing the closing speed at that threshold of angular velocity may be able to bring their vehicle to a stop under this design condition.

For a driver traveling at 100 km/h (62 mph) closing on a stopped truck, identification of the time to collision for half of drivers likely occurs when the driver is 150 m (492 ft.) or 5.4 seconds from collision.[17] The design stopping distance is 185 m (606 ft.) with a drag factor of about 0.3. Allowing the design driver 2.5 seconds of reaction time, they would require 125 m (410 ft.) to stop based on a drag factor of 0.7. Still, an analysis of looming shows that collision was more probable for the fiftieth-percentile driver making the identification at this distance. Obviously, some drivers require more distance and time based on their individual circumstances. Including an eighty-fifth-percentile driver would shorten the stated time and distance to impact. The same method can be used for the assessment of approach to slow-moving vehicles.

Once again, this type of assessment assumes that all drivers would react in a certain manner, while the data indicates substantial variability. Under difficult viewing conditions, the distance at which identification occurs can be substantially shorter. Some drivers could easily be at risk of being assigned an inappropriate response rate they simply do not possess, given the situation. Again, determining the response capability of an individual is likely to be situation and condition dependent. Hence, determining a reliable fixed response rate for an individual post-collision is also highly unlikely. On the other hand, calculations can determine if a driver responded in an appropriate amount of time. In other words, it may be possible to determine if a driver responded well but not if they responded poorly.

In more difficult or confusing circumstances that may prolong assessment and thereby delay reaction, collision may be substantially more likely. For example, consider the situation where the driver of a vehicle approaching another vehicle or object checks his rearview mirror for nearby traffic when preparing to change lanes. This is a task that may take as little as one second or possibly much more. If the assessment of closing speed is delayed by just one second, collision would occur. Therefore, it is readily apparent that drivers do not have much time to complete the assessment of closing speed and to initiate an appropriate response on approach to a slow-moving or stopped vehicle ahead of them.

This circumstance can be especially critical in the event of lane blockages on high-speed roadways. It may arise with left-turning drivers assessing oncoming traffic, as a result of a collision blocking a lane, or during queuing for a highway exit. In such scenarios, drivers approaching the end of a queue need to vacate the queue lane or come to a stop. Either action is subject to human factor restrictions that limit the likely success of either maneuver.

The circumstances associated with looming can be present in other daylight situations as well. Many drivers have experienced the situation where, when passing through an intersection with a Stop or Yield sign, they quickly look both ways and then proceed forward. Upon checking a second time while in motion, the driver detects an approaching vehicle. The search methods and timing in coming to a stop have been reported to be in the range of 1.1 to 2.6 seconds.[18] The data is again characterized by a probability function. Given the issues with respect to time of arrival as established in looming situations, these times may be too short to avoid collision in some instances.

For instance, when undertaking a right turn at an intersection, many drivers have been taught to look left, look right, then look left once more before initiating a turn. But if a driver fails to take sufficient time for any one of these observations, a collision can result. They may well see a vehicle approaching but fail to assess its speed and time of arrival due to the looming problem. The situation may be a case where the driver "looked but did not see" the moving vehicle due to the lack of movement contrast in looming, or more specifically, a lack of dwell time in the search direction.

In the case of the slow-moving or stopped vehicle, the onus is on drivers to recognize the situation and perform successfully. In the case of the railway crossing, recurrent lane blockages, and similar situations, the travel authority bears some responsibility for the safety of the situation since there are methods available to deal with the situation through infrastructure elements. Either way, this discussion shows that even reasonably skilled, reasonably attentive individuals can become entrapped by the dynamics of an emerging condition that is unfamiliar or difficult to perceive.

5.3 Selection of Speed

The industry holds that drivers will travel at a speed at which they are comfortable. Pignataro wrote about this in 1973:

> A driver's desires govern most driver actions. Drivers and pedestrians often do not react to controls and regulations unless they appear reasonable. This must be considered when regulations and

controls are established; however, some regulations that might appear to be unreasonable to the road user, but are necessary, must be backed by proper enforcement.[19]

This basic human factor of drivers can readily be observed on most roadways where almost all drivers exceed the legal speed limit by a moderate amount. To illustrate this point, the speed profile of one collector street is summarized in the following:

The roadway is situated within an urban area and can be classified as a two-lane suburban collector road of about 1 km (0.6 mi.) in length that is relatively straight with some small hills and stop control at both ends. There is roadside residential development on large lots with residences set well back from the roadway. There are no pedestrian generators along the roadway, but it does have an asphaltic concrete shoulder sidewalk on one side. There are forested sections with trees and shrubs located close to the pavement. Lane widths are 3.5 m (11.5 ft.). The posted speed is 50 km/h (30 mph). Traffic counts and a speed study were completed in 2011, finding there were about 2,500 vehicles per day on the road.

In the area of the speed survey, this roadway has the appearance of a rural road. The mean speed of traffic was about 60 km/h (37 mph), or about 10 km/h (6 mph) over the maximum legal speed limit. The fiftieth-percentile speed was about the same as the mean speed, while the eighty-fifth-percentile speed was 69 km/h (43 mph) or 19 km/h (12 mph) over the speed limit. In 2022, the speed limit on this roadway was dropped to 40 km/h (25 mph). This may well have been done as part of a general reduction of speed limits on urban streets or in response to a couple of new residents on the roadway wishing to have it repurposed. With the imposition of the new maximum legal speed limit, personal observations suggest there is little to no change in the speed profile.

Speed surveys in locations such as this confirm that drivers rely on the situation, conditions, weather, personal needs, and risk tolerance to determine a suitable driving speed as much or more than solely relying on maximum speed limit signs. In this situation, there are no cues in the appearance of the roadway to indicate to drivers that speeds slower than the previous speed limit are warranted. As the speed limit is dropped from a higher speed in an adjacent section on entering an urban area, the lower speed limit signs are posted in one direction only. The speed limit signs that are now posted may be viewed as unreasonable, so drivers continue to use the roadway in a manner that they have traditionally felt appropriate.

A study undertaken by Transport Canada examining the attitudes of Canadian drivers shows the characteristics of drivers found on local roadways like the one described previously are widespread. The results are of interest not only to the development and implementation of roadway safety features but also transportation forensics. Results of the study are summarized in the following extract:

> Overall, we find that the definition of speeding is elastic, that Canadians perceive themselves to speed much less than other drivers, and that their assessment and descriptions of their personal instances of speeding are often relatively benign. Seven in 10 drivers admit to exceeding the speed limit at least occasionally, particularly on highways (81 percent). The average speeding amount is 12 kilometres over the limit on highways, 10 kilometres on two lane highways/ country roads and 7 kilometres on residential streets. From a definitional standpoint, many people believe that while they might be "technically speeding," they are not driving in a way that endangers either themselves or others. Moreover, one in two drivers (52 percent) agrees that people should keep up with the flow of traffic regardless of the speed limit. It is also interesting to note that most people believe it is just as dangerous to drive 20 kilometres *under* the speed limit, as it is to drive 20 kilometres *over*.[20]

These observations obtained through study groups have important implications in determining the design and operation of roadways. In effect, the observations show that other transportation systems elements are adapted in various ways for personal benefit. The situation is similar to when pedestrians find their own path, thus adapting for their benefit a situation not considered reasonable, as in a sidewalk location. This study shows that drivers perform in a similar manner for their perceived benefit while considering their safety concerns.

In the same vein, it is reasonable to expect that pedestrians walking beside a roadway will want traffic to move more slowly, as it is perceived to be more safe. Consequently, pedestrians can also be expected to cite that speeding is a significant problem and reduced speeds are necessary as they adapt conditions for their own use. A conflict thus arises between the preferences of different system users. However, as shown previously, simply lowering the speed limit is unlikely to provide a desirable result for either pedestrians or drivers. Even so, as the information of the Canadian study was obtained through self-reporting by surveyed individuals, the study is expected to underreport the incidence of speeding. There is some evidence of underreporting from other data sources. While the incidence of speeding the study reported for residential streets was 7 km/h (4.3 mph), the average speed on the residential street described previously was 10 km/h (6 mph) over the limit.

Traffic engineering practice has long stated that speed differentials are an important means for managing safety. Confining the speed differential to a smaller range where all vehicles are traveling at similar speeds is anticipated to reduce the frequency and severity of collisions.

The Institute of Transportation Engineers recognized the importance of accommodating the actions of a larger share of drivers and noted from an engineering approach that the speed limit may be set to the eighty-fifth-percentile speed of drivers.[21] This approach to speed signing is not universal[22] but is commonly cited by the industry, so the industry's practice to exclude a portion of driving performance is evident once again. It is unclear if 15 percent of drivers are inattentive to their speed, have simply drifted outside the bounds of reasonableness, or are speeding irresponsibly. The basis for selecting this value for inclusion is not readily apparent within the industry, nor is its applicability to specific settings. However, it is likely to be an untenable position in the context of human adaptation if a speed limit is raised to accommodate this range of drivers. The research shows that in raising the speed limit, the average speed of traffic on the roadway is likely to increase, while lowering it is likely to have a marginal effect unless accompanied by other changes.

This understanding of the human adaptation of vehicles and highways for travel and transport must be considered in the context of collision experience. It indicates that the legal or posted speed limit may be unsuitable as a benchmark to define speeding. Even so, the posted speed limit likely contributes to a driver's choice of travel speed while considering the risks of being ticketed if exceeding the speed limit. Most drivers believe that traveling in excess of the speed limit is reasonable. Therefore, defining excessive speed can be somewhat elusive and subjective. Is it 10 or 15 km/h (5 or 10 mph) over the limit—or something else? Can it be different for different types of roadways or different types of situations? Is it reasonable to lower the speed limit and still use the same criteria to define speeding?

Each situation is likely to be different and possibly require a different definition. As a benchmark, one might use the threshold set by the transportation industry and use the eighty-fifth-percentile speed or some range around that percentile. While this would not resolve the issue, it does point out what most drivers using a roadway believe is a reasonable speed given the setting, the traffic control, and design features.

This human response presents a dilemma to those designing roadways. Further, it can be argued that the tendency for drivers to travel at speeds greater than the limit is a reflection of the historic approach to the design of roadways. Conventional design theory is intent on allowing drivers to feel comfortable at the posted speed of the roadway. Beyond that, it is necessary to account for various roadway conditions as well as drivers who may inadvertently—or intentionally—test the limits of those conditions.

In applying these requisites, there is also a desire to have vehicles stay on the roadway when navigating curves at the posted speed when the pavement condition is less than ideal, including times when pavement friction may be low due to ongoing wear and tear or accumulation of contaminants such as oils, snow, and ice. To accommodate these types of issues, design manuals rely on the provision of a design speed that is higher than the legal maximum speed limit posted on roadside signs.

In the US and Canada, the concept of design speed has been adopted at the national level and set out in successive manuals since at least 1960. Agencies that issue national standards include the manuals of the Transportation Association of Canada (TAC)[23] and the American Association of State Highway and Transportation Officials (AASHTO).[24] Geometric design standards are also issued at the state and provincial levels. For the most part, there is reasonably consistent correspondence between manuals. However, some manuals provide more detail for their standards, illustrate alternative treatments, or present a slightly different view of the issues.

The Ontario Ministry of Transportation has set standards for design for a very long time. The manner in which their manual determines a speed appropriate for design is relevant in considering vehicle operations for most collisions.[25] The description of design speed may vary somewhat in other manuals. However, the basic concept as set out in the Ontario Ministry of Transportation's manual appears in the following:

> A speed is selected for the purpose of design and correlation of the geometric features of a road and is a measure of the quality of design offered by the road. It is the highest continuous speed at which individual vehicles can travel with safety on a road when weather conditions are favorable and traffic density is so low that the safe speed is determined by the geometric features of the road.[26]

Design speed is used as a control for all the design elements of roadways, including horizontal and vertical alignment, roadway cross-section, visibility requirements of drivers, the roadside environment, and traffic control. Traffic control standards may be set according to design or posted speeds or operating conditions. In the case of the latter, there may be provision for the design speed of the roadway. Typically, the maximum speed appearing on regulatory speed limit signs is lower than the design speed of the road. The practice of the industry is to have the regulatory speed limit of a roadway be 10 to 20 km/h (6 to 12 mph) less than the design speed.[27] The higher differential is applicable in rural areas as well as key facilities in urban areas. This consideration reduces the likelihood of collision for those drivers who inadvertently or willfully exceed the regulatory speed limit by a moderate amount.

As a consequence of this approach to design, road authorities commonly use design speeds of 100 km/h (60 mph) for assessing existing rural roadways with a regulatory speed limit of 80 km/h (50 mph). Freeways with a 100 km/h (60 mph) speed limit may have a design speed as high as 130 km/h (80 mph). Some urban roadways have a design speed that is the same as the posted speed limit. Presumably, this may be rationalized on the basis that, at lower speeds, crashes may be less severe regardless of the contributing causes. Whether that type of assumption pans out depends on the type of collisions that occur.

As all elements of roadways are typically designed for speeds much greater than the posted limit, it should not be surprising that operating speeds (the speed of most vehicles) may be well above the posted speed limit. As stated previously, it is understandable that a driver's speed selection seems to inherently, if unknowingly, gravitate to the design speed rather than the maximum legal speed limit as posted.

5.4 More on Response Time and Variation

When approaching a hazard, a driver's selection of speed and path may be considered a three-part process. As with the perception/response sequence, the process involves recognizing the hazard, identifying the options, and selecting an appropriate course of action. The options include speeding up or slowing down, steering right or left, or some combination of these. However, the success or failure of the decision process depends upon the complexity of the hazard, number of choices, and magnitude of each action that may be determined under time constraints.

Factors that degrade the ability to make appropriate decisions include:

- Vagueness in defining the hazard location or magnitude
- Insufficient time to choose between alternatives
- Inability to identify appropriate alternatives
- Insufficient information to make the right choice
- Misleading cues that may seem relevant but are not

When there is a failure in speed or path selection arising from any one of the above factors, the results can appear in the form of collisions.

An example of how response times can vary is demonstrated through analyzing a lane change. As with any driving maneuver, lane changes are not spontaneous events—they require time and distance. The physical task of drivers executing a lane change to the left requires steering movements in the following sequence:

1. Steering to the left to initiate the turn.
2. Steering to the right to terminate the turn, allowing the vehicle to move across the lane division line.
3. Steering to the right to align the vehicle path with the new lane once it has been entered.
4. Finally, steering to the left to terminate the turning action once the path alignment with the lane has been found.

Research has shown that passenger vehicles moving at approximately 90 km/h (56 mph) will take an average of approximately 5.1 to 5.3 seconds to complete a lane change. However, drivers are not consistent in the amount of time they take for a lane change.[28] Lane changes may take as little as 3.1 seconds or as long as 13 seconds. Much of the research relates to the proximity of a leading vehicle and the time to collision. An instance in which the time to collision with a vehicle directly in front (obstruction) is not a factor may be when lane changes take longer. Lane changes on a busy road may also take longer. Further, most research materials on this issue relate to the observed lane change time for the drivers of passenger vehicles.

Based on this information, a driver who is aware of a lane blockage ahead would require at least 5 seconds and possibly as long as 13 seconds to complete a lane change on a high-speed facility. However, individual drivers may well take longer, particularly if there is other traffic in the vicinity that may delay or impede the maneuver. Consequently, a minimum decision sight distance for a freeway may be assumed to be the distance traveled in approximately 13 seconds at 100 km/h (62 mph), about 360 m (1,180 ft.).

Such information is important in the determination of merge and exit lane lengths in allowing vehicles to move into or out of traffic while traveling at highway speeds. Lane changes to the right may be more difficult due to the problems associated with vehicle detection in blind spots. These features of the highway also have assumptions related to the speed and density of vehicles on the highway. The problem is exacerbated when vehicles are moving across lane division lines from both sides of a lane. These locations are referred to as weaving sections. Where drivers are required to check for vehicles two lanes over in their potential maneuver space, the maneuvers are more complicated and can take longer. Careful attention is required in the assessment of design conditions or the forensic investigation of collisions within weaving areas.

Many other situations exist in which assumptions are made about the time required to initiate a maneuver. A commonly examined time is that of stopping distances due to a simple hazard, discussed previously as no less than 1.5 seconds. To encompass an adequate range of drivers, highway design for the purpose of stopping has used a value of 2.5 seconds for more than fifty years. Yet in 1992, the Institute of Transportation

Engineers pointed out this reflects stopping due to a simple hazard and that 15 percent of drivers may be excluded from the protection of this standard. It is not within the scope of this work to specify all the human factors contributing to perception and response times. However, for those interested, *Human Factors in Traffic Safety* (third edition) has an excellent and extensive discussion of perception reaction time variations for many circumstances. One researcher concludes that it may not be possible to assign a time to the detection period and that if individuals take 2.5 to 3.0 seconds for the balance of the response process, that time may be reasonable.[29]

In evaluating the suitability of roadway information obtained from signs, many standards govern their size, color, shape, reflectivity, message content, and location. These characteristics affect drivers' detection and identification time of signs. Where situations are assumed to be familiar to drivers, traffic engineering practice may apply very short perception reaction times. In the case of traffic signals, the time may be as short as 1.0 second.

Yet contrary to this value, research suggests the average response time is 1.3 seconds,[30] which has led to some controversy in the industry. Studies have shown that, at the eighty-fifth-percentile level, driver response times to the onset of a yellow indication range between 1.5 and 2.1 seconds.[31] Some argue that this variability is related to the distance a driver is from the signal when the phase change occurs. Drivers farther away may be more casual in responding to the change.

If drivers tend to be casual about reacting in most situations, they may be more indecisive when they are closer to the signal since their expectancies come into play. This is especially relevant in the case of long intergreen times (yellow plus all red). In either case, uncertainty persists regarding how effectively signal timing accommodates those who take longer than most to respond to a change in the signal phase.

As a final note, the detection period can be significantly longer when signs or signals are partly obscured or faded. In some instances, there may be no standards affecting these situations. In the case of faded signs, while the sign may be clearly visible during the day, detection at night is delayed. Signs located too far from the roadway may not be detected at all. Fortunately, there are standards that specify requirements for these situations.

Detection of approaching vehicles on a side road may be delayed by the presence of vegetation that obscures the view when the ability to detect a vehicle is important. Roadside obstacles, barriers, retaining walls, accumulated snow windrows, and more can partially obscure sight lines, resulting in delayed detection or cues missed entirely. As previously stated, replicating the suddenness a driver must respond to a situation can be very difficult due to the awareness of the participants involved in any replication. In such cases, the detection time available to involved parties can be a matter of opinion and not much else.

One example involves the visibility of approaching traffic from a side road. In one instance, a steel beam barrier provided a partial obstruction of approaching traffic on the left from a stop location on the side road. Due to the geometry of the location, a clear view of the upper portion of passenger vehicles was available during daylight conditions. However, after dark, the barrier obstructed the headlights of approaching traffic over a length of about 150 m (490 ft.) before emerging into view close to the intersection. No Stop line was present. The intersection operated without any issue for many years. However, one night, a vehicle was struck even though the driver of the struck vehicle had come to a full stop and checked for traffic. The driver's visual search failed due to the intermittent obstruction of approaching headlights. While there was a diversity of opinion about the visibility conditions, there would have been little issue if a Stop line had been present.

As a final note, there can be many instances when the detection interval of the response sequence may be extended through no fault of the driver and an application of the typical response times can entrap system users. Assigning system users qualities they do not have or could not exercise in a situation may extend the harm caused by infrastructure.

6

GUIDING THE SYSTEM USER

6.1 Positive Guidance

The concept of positive guidance was developed in the 1980s and has since found its way into transportation engineering texts and manuals, including geometric design and traffic control manuals, while having relevance to roadway maintenance. In brief, the concept provides drivers the information they need to avoid hazards, when and where they need it, and in a form that will best allow them to perform safely.

Driver expectancies are aligned with the roadway features and operations by means of positive guidance. While the concept has been part of the engineering industry for many years now, it may be overlooked or set aside during design and control exercises. This chapter highlights the critical role of positive guidance, using examples to illustrate its importance when assessing travel conditions during forensic investigations.

The principles of positive guidance are particularly relevant when drivers encounter uncommon conditions that may constitute a surprise or be inconsistent with their expectancies. Through observing the application of design and control practice over many years, drivers have come to expect they will be informed of potential hazards present. They can also expect instruction in how to proceed by the application of traffic control devices, including signs and pavement markings. While the principles of positive guidance are typically incorporated into straightforward design and traffic control processes, their effectiveness can be undermined by intervening opportunities.

In one instance, a safety analysis was conducted to identify the needs of drivers and cyclists at a level railway crossing. The location included a cycle path adjacent to a railway that crossed a collector roadway at an acute angle. The initial layout was determined by recognizing the needs of each system user, safe practices, and positive guidance. However, in the next stage in development of the crossing, the system's designers incorporated changes redirecting cyclists away from a desired path to another one they would likely ignore. This illustrates how an initial plan can be modified to conform to other objectives during second- or third-generation revisions of the design. Notwithstanding that, signing should be used to manage expectancies in a manner that allows safe performance in all situations.

Traffic control devices are used to assist the driver in selecting an appropriate speed and path. Information is conveyed to the driver through several principles of sign placement and easily recognized attributes involving contrast recognition. In describing positive guidance, the 1992 *Traffic Engineering Handbook* of the Institute of Transportation Engineers indicates that information given to drivers should be dictated by four essential principles.[1]

Those principles include the following:

- Primacy: Information is to be presented in order of importance with the most important information presented first.

- Spreading: Information transmitted to drivers is to be spread out over distances that will maintain manageable information processing loads for drivers and allow them to react.

- Coding: Information is to be consistent and organized according to shape, size, color, and more.

- Redundancy: Information is to be repeated and may use differing traffic control devices.

An example of redundancy in signing is the messages provided for terminating lanes (lane closures) on higher-speed roadways. The first warning sign is set well in advance of the location where the lane ends. However, if drivers do not need to act on information within a reasonable period, they can inadvertently shed it from their memory, even if the information is important and they will soon need to act on it. To enhance safety through redundancy, the sign indicating the lane termination is introduced a second time. The first advance sign is therefore supplemented with a second warning sign located where the pavement begins to taper, closing the lane (a hazard location).

Redundant signs on the left should not be considered a replacement for primary signs on the right but rather an enhancement that may improve detection and visibility of the primary sign. Operations and maintenance personnel who are not properly trained can circumvent the important function of redundancy. One example is where a sign was placed on each side of the road to warn drivers they were approaching a roadway hazard (speed bump). The primary sign was allowed to be overgrown by vegetation. A cyclist struck the hazard, fell, and experienced serious injury. Even while traveling at lower speeds than an automobile, he had not detected the redundant sign. Had the primary sign been visible, it is highly probable that the fall would not have occurred.

When the road authority was informed of the vegetation blocking the sign, the subsequent brush trimming operation along the roadway did not attend to the vegetation obstructing the subject sign. In this instance, the maintenance people seemed to believe that one sign was sufficient, even though it was on the wrong side of the roadway and out of central vision.

As an example of how initial well-thought-out intent can change upon consecutive reworking, the *Ontario Traffic Manual* provides some insight. The multivolume manual provides some excellent information related to providing for driver needs in the section discussing positive guidance. However, in some instances, there is a disconnect in the manual between what those needs are and the provision of traffic control. For those interested, the section discussing positive guidance captures the preceding four principles in a somewhat haphazard way. Why that has occurred is unknown, but the effects are apparent in other sections.

For example, the section in the *Ontario Traffic Manual* discussing Stop signs indicates that Stop lines on the pavement *may* be provided, which runs contrary to positive guidance. This feature not only provides redundancy but also indicates where vehicles are to stop at the intersection. The section in the manual discussing pavement markings indicates Stop lines *must* be provided. Because they are directly in front of the driver, rather than at the side of the road, they are in line with a driver's most active sight line, enabling effective detection.

However, many authorities interpret the manual to mean that Stop lines are optional and do not install them, thus defeating the principle of redundancy and degrading the positive guidance intended by the manual. Installing Stop lines can be a significant expense for road authorities, as it tends to be labor intensive. For road users, the absence of such lines can place more onus on drivers to detect Stop signs and make decisions about where to stop, thus moving away from the intended safety provided by the traffic control devices.

Managing positive guidance can be challenging where there is a need to modify traffic control on a scheduled or regular basis, or where the signs are at risk of being displaced. There can also be a disconnect between an original concept in traffic management (or design) and the application of traffic control devices in the field. It is also sometimes the case that a temporary condition is inconsistent with signing due to construction progression or because physical conditions change during construction without a thorough vetting and updating of the traffic control provided. Devices can also go missing, be poorly placed, get vandalized, become hidden from view, or deteriorate with time and use, making them ineffective in providing positive guidance.

The *Ontario Traffic Manual* has also recognized the problem with mishandled positive guidance:

> Traffic control devices not only serve to structure expectancies, they tend to violate expectancies if misapplied, inconsistently applied, are absent when needed, present when unneeded and/ or ambiguous.[2]

This traffic control manual therefore recognizes that where road conditions may vary from driver expectations, signs and pavement markings are required to alter drivers' expectancies and enable them to deal with the hazards present. Drivers must be warned with appropriate information far enough in advance to respond in a reasonable manner. When positive guidance is absent and driver expectancies are violated, many (or even most) drivers may still be able to cope. However, there is a much greater risk that some drivers will not be able to respond as the road authority "wills" them to in the absence of specific instruction. Forensic investigations should be able to identify mismatches between how designers expect individuals to perform and how they may reasonably perform.

One instance of an ongoing deficiency in positive guidance is in the design and placement of street and guide signs. These signs use lettering too small to read at the posted speed limits and are often poorly placed, making their detection difficult.

6.2 A Failure in Positive Guidance at Work

Positive guidance recognizes that time and distance is necessary for drivers to assess a hazardous condition and undertake the necessary action to avoid the hazard. For construction zones, this process is managed using information handling zones. The areas relevant to establish positive guidance are set in accordance with two key driving requirements discussed previously.

First, *stopping sight distance* is the distance required to bring a vehicle to a stop, considering the time to detect, identify, and understand the nature of the hazard (perception) and react to it (move foot to brake), and then bringing the vehicle to a stop through braking with a moderately intense effort.

Second, *decision sight distance* is the distance required to detect a difficult-to-perceive information source or hazard in a roadway environment, recognize the potential threat of the hazard, select an appropriate action, and complete the maneuver safely. Both sight distances are relevant in this example related to a recurrent standing queue in the right lane of a multilane highway. In this situation, the highway was a facility some travelers used regularly and others occasionally or rarely. Therefore, not all drivers were familiar with the roadway or the recurrent queue.

The situation involved a collision between a stopped vehicle in a live freeway lane and a vehicle approaching from the rear at a high rate of speed. The stopped vehicle was at the end of a long recurrent queue in a rural area. The road authority was well aware of the situation and had time to put in place an action plan allowing drivers to deal with the conditions in a safe manner. The primary information drivers needed was sufficient warning of time and distance to observe the queue of vehicles ahead so they could avoid collision by either changing lanes or stopping. The queue of stopped vehicles varied substantially in length by time of day, day of week, and season. Consequently, the queue's end was constantly shortening or lengthening. The queue typically blocked the right lane of a freeway facility while the left lane continued to serve advancing traffic at highway speeds.

The object was therefore to inform drivers that the lane ahead was blocked and give some indication of the distance to the end of the queue. Drivers could expect they would have a reasonable opportunity to perform in an unhurried manner. A reasonable distance that had been found to work and one familiar to drivers is the lane closure protocols associated with construction zones on freeway facilities.

In this situation, vehicles in one lane or more are required to change lanes in advance of the lane blockage. This requires 360 to 470 m (1,180 to 1,540 ft.) (decision sight distance). Beyond that, drivers need sufficient distance to bring their vehicle to a stop, as a lane change may not always be possible. For design purposes, this requires 245 m (800 ft.), while allowing 2.5 seconds of reaction time and slowing at a moderate g force of deceleration of 0.35 g (stopping sight distance).

Because the queue's length would vary substantially, the location of the lane blockage was not static. From studies of the queue, the road authority had developed and installed an automatic queue warning system. These systems typically include detectors embedded in the road designed to notify an operations center of stopped vehicles. The system was installed, but within a short time its failings were evident. The new warning system could not service longer queues because the sensing capability of the system did not extend a sufficient distance along the highway.

The road authority responded by establishing a series of protocols for managing the queues on sections of the highway not served by the automatic system. They set up a mobile warning system that could move with the queue. In this sense, the queue was similar to a mobile construction zone, thus requiring mobile protections.

The authority's traffic operations manual clearly described the sign requirements for construction zones. The protocols were based on the concept of positive guidance in providing appropriate information at the appropriate time. There are several information handling zones on the roadway leading up to a construction hazard.

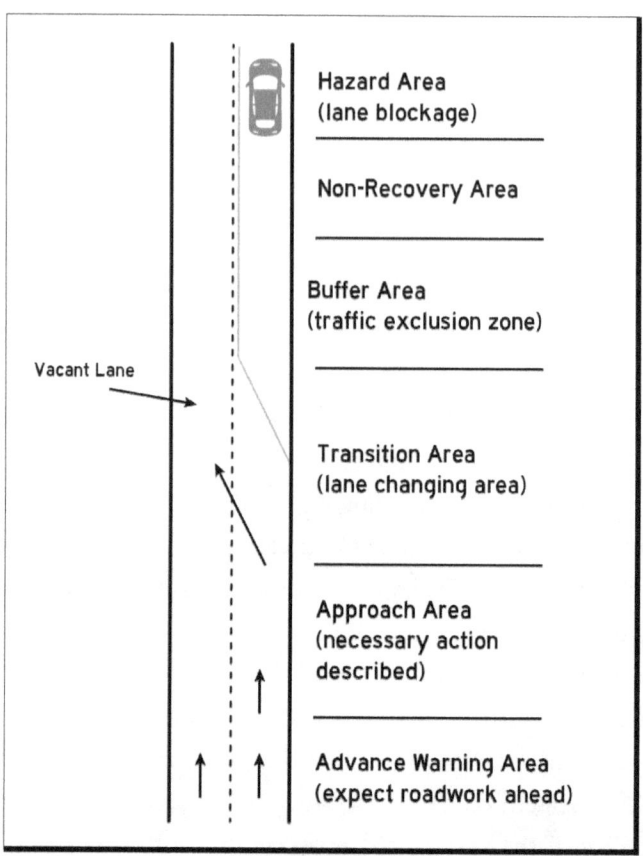

Image 6.1: Layout showing temporary conditions for a lane blockage. (Source: Gilchrist, August 2, 2024, adapted from *Ontario Traffic Manual*[3])

The areas are identified by signs and flexible drums (black-and-orange barrels) in the following manner:

- The *advance warning area* is upstream of the hazard and beyond the distance required to make the necessary decisions to safely avoid a hazard (decision sight distance). At best, the hazard may be visible at the downstream end of this area. The area is used to display low-priority and supplemental information while starting to shape drivers' expectancies. No action by the driver may be required in this area.

- The *approach area* is upstream of the hazard beginning at the start of the decision sight distance and ending at the start of the stopping sight distance. Optimum hazard visibility should occur near the end of the advance zone or at the beginning of the approach area. When the hazard is not visible, additional warning information should be located there. Drivers use this area to complete necessary maneuvers, such as a normal-speed lane change to safely bypass the hazard. An adequate decision sight distance is required. As noted, this includes the *transition area* marked in Image 6.1.

- The *non-recovery area* is an area upstream of the beginning of the hazard. The area begins at the start of the stopping sight distance and ends at the hazard. The hazard's visibility is important in this area, so speed and path information are displayed here. Drivers entering this area at a high rate of speed are at risk of having insufficient stopping sight distance available for collision avoidance. This includes the *buffer area* marked in Image 6.1.

- The *hazard area* commences with the hazard. Information at the beginning of this area is provided to enhance drivers' awareness of the hazard. In the example of the recurrent standing queue, this area would commence at the rear of the last vehicle in the queue and extend the length of the queue. Hence, this was the hazard area of the subject collision.

Rather than using the construction zone protocols for guidance, the road authority was using two trucks to try to manage the lane blockage at the time of the collision. The end of the queue was identified by a single crash truck with a high-level flashing yellow light stopped on the shoulder near the queue's end. The truck had no text message informing drivers of the queue. As the queue varied in length, the truck was located just in advance of the end of the queue, and drivers were provided with no information about the purpose of the truck. Because the truck was located on the shoulder, drivers could easily believe roadside work was occurring in that location since no directions were provided. Consequently, there could be substantial uncertainty about the purpose of the truck. Also, its flashing lights could reasonably draw a driver's attention away from the end of the queue. Further, a longer queue could extend beyond the stopped truck. Backing the truck along the shoulder would be noncompliant with the highway traffic regulations.

The road authority was aware of a potential for drivers to be exposed to an unmarked end of queue without warning when it extended beyond the parked truck. To mitigate some of this risk, the authority subsequently placed another crash truck farther away from the limit of the queue. The second truck was the same in appearance as the first, thus providing no information about the condition ahead.

As the queue lengthened, the distance to the leading crash truck was reduced, and when the queue grew so long as to stretch rearward past the lead crash truck, it would loop around between two interchanges and pull up to stop some distance behind the second truck. During this move, it would leave a single crash truck (the second truck) parked on the shoulder some distance from the end of the queue. Contrary to the well-considered provisions for lane blockages in construction zones, this dynamic lane blockage was intermittently marked by a single truck stopped on the shoulder with only a flashing bar activated.

While the authority had adopted important concepts for managing safety, neither the principles of positive guidance nor the explicit provisions of the manual related to lane blockages were applied in handling this situation. Inevitably, an individual rear-ended a stopped truck in a live lane under daylight conditions. At the time, one of the warning trucks had left its stopped location to reposition itself beyond the end of the queue.

A protocol similar to the warning system for lane closures in construction zones would have served the requirement to provide positive guidance to drivers. Also, a comprehensive and well-thought-out sign plan would have enabled explicit thought to be devoted to the concepts of positive guidance while recognizing the needs of system users. Documentation accompanying the plan would have set out the necessary principles for managing traffic in accordance with the road authority's own standards for lane closures on high-speed roadways. However, no such documentation was forthcoming. The road authority had a completed and documented plan to warn drivers of lane closures using positive guidance at construction sites. This is the type of warning system that drivers could reasonably expect.

However, the queue of this situation was not at a construction site. While the operations were managed by an experienced road authority, the personnel involved did not appear to have a background in construction or the handling of lane blockages. They did have experience with highway maintenance. The reason for the significant disconnect between the principles for handling a situation and the actions of the road authority have not been determined. However, the people in charge were either not well-acquainted with the manual and/or were reluctant to expend the effort or cost of assigning appropriate resources to the problem as required by the manual.

In this situation, both the road authority departments and contracted services failed in adequately managing expectancies for both the authority and system users. Those with administrative responsibility in the authority expected others having some responsibility to get the queue management protocols right, when in reality, no one implemented the appropriate protocols of the authority for lane closures. People of differing backgrounds relied on the experience and training of others who were ill-equipped to properly assess the situation and to establish the provisions of positive guidance that would have allowed travelers to operate safely. Had the principles of positive guidance been used to guide the actions of the road authority, the subject collision would likely not have occurred.

SAFETY IN A SEEMINGLY SAFE PLACE— THE HUMBLE SIDEWALK

From human factors research, it would seem that we are not well suited to moving at speeds more than a moderate running pace of about 10 km/h (6 mph) or about twice the speed of a walk. This basic limitation has spurred humans to improve efficiency by traveling faster, first by domesticating animals and then by mechanical means.

The aforementioned moderate running pace provides a closing speed of about 20 km/h (12 mph) for two runners approaching each other from opposite directions. Walking speeds in hallways or pathways typically provide sufficient response time to avoid collisions with other pedestrians even when there is limited sight distance. A pedestrian encountering an e-bike or powered skateboard with much higher closing speeds on a sidewalk is more likely to experience problems.

Historical literature is replete with examples of terrible collisions and fatalities on urban streets ever since horses were trained and used for travel. The world's first self-propelled motor vehicle was built by William Felton in 1803. By 1861, there was sufficient conflict in the UK to introduce speed limits of 16 km/h (10 mph) for powered motor vehicles. By 1865, that speed limit was viewed as too high and was reduced to 6 km/h (4 mph) in the country and 3 km/h (2 mph) in town, about that of a typical pedestrian.[1] The justification for these measures was related to wear and tear of the roadways caused by heavy machines and included the interests of public safety. While not the first instance showing how flexible public opinion and policy can be, it shows these considerations have long influenced the nature of our transportation systems.

The risk of a collision and possible injury exists wherever the paths of individuals, vehicles, or other mobility devices interact, which, in engineering terms, are referred to as conflict points. These conflict points occur where paths meet head-on, cross, merge, and in some cases, diverge. Conflict points can be present for all modes of travel (vehicles, bicycles, pedestrians) or across modes of travel (motorized vehicles vs. bicycles). A sharp turn on a highway may also be considered a point of conflict. All of these are situations or conditions where system users must make decisions. Those decisions may run afoul of the decisions of others or the decisions of those providing the facilities.

This chapter examines conflicts and hazards on sidewalks because they are seen by many to be a safe place compared to other facilities. Likewise, walking is perceived as a safe travel mode relative to other modes of transportation. There is much less motorized activity on sidewalks, operating speeds are lower, and the energy associated with crashes is less likely to have long-term harmful consequences. So, should they be considered a safe transportation facility?

All of us have experienced the situation of approaching another individual walking on the sidewalk and becoming uncertain about which way to pass by them, leading to a feint to the right as they feint to left, resulting in a looming conflict as both are on a possible collision course.

One or both parties stop or change course to establish a clear path around the other, avoiding collision. In this context, walking may be thought to be a safe activity, meaning without injury. Even if there is contact in the form of a bump, the individuals are unlikely to experience an injury. Of course, walking on a sidewalk and tripping can result in severe injuries when it happens so quickly that an individual is not able to move their hands and arms quickly enough to break the fall.[2] These types of experiences suggest that sidewalks may not be safe—particularly when higher speeds are involved.

7.1 Sidewalks Are Not Safe

In view of the preceding discussion, walking cannot be certified as a safe activity nor the sidewalk certified as a safe element of public infrastructure. Pedestrians may encounter a wide variety of hazards, with injuries arising from a failure to safely negotiate them. Some of the hazards have been built into the design of facilities, while others have emerged over time, and still others are temporal in nature.

Walking can be considered hazardous when the walking surface contributes to a trip and fall because of an uneven surface where users are expecting a level surface with adequate friction. One example of where this can happen is at the raised edge of a sidewalk that has been lifted due to frost heaves or settlement. When this occurs, the issue is whether the walking surface was sufficiently level or smooth to be deemed nominally safe as determined by the industry standards or reasonably safe as determined through public or judicial review. In the case of the former, engineers set the standard. In the latter, the standard is set by public scrutiny.

As with drivers encountering a hazard, for pedestrians and other sidewalk users to perform safely, they must detect the hazard, identify it as a hazard, determine a course of action, and initiate a response with successful avoidance. In the case of two people approaching each other on a sidewalk with a closing speed of about 10 km/h (6 mph), typically visibility is sufficient for one or both individuals to complete each step of this process before bumping into each other. However, when there is not sufficient visibility (low light and/or low contrast objects) such as on a crowded sidewalk, or where an obstruction exists, or where a mobility device (bicycle, scooter, hoverboard, power wheelchair) is used to increase travel speed, collision between pedestrians or other users can inadvertently occur. One example is at the intersection of two sidewalks where a person's view of the intersecting sidewalk is obstructed.

There are many opportunities for the collision avoidance process to be corrupted. The threat imposed by hazards does not have to come from the infrastructure elements but can come from the way the sidewalk is utilized by pedestrians and others or the environmental conditions. Some unusual situations can exist that extend the identification time because the hazard is not readily identified or the actions of other parties are unusual and not readily interpreted. For example, an early morning runner on a dark multiuse path beside an arterial roadway experienced severe injuries when struck by a fast-moving e-bike lacking a headlight. Gaze direction, inattention, or obstructions may delay detection by individuals using the sidewalk. There may be insufficient time and distance to assess a hazard or to choose from multiple possible responses, resulting in a longer period prior to volition. In the case of the runner, one or several of these, including environmental conditions, may have been at play.

Finally, the selected maneuver may not be completed in time. Still, at walking speeds, there is typically sufficient time for approaching pedestrians to complete the process, allowing each to go their own way without incident. Thus, if a sidewalk is properly designed to manage the pedestrian volumes with pedestrian closing at speeds of 10 km/h (plus or minus), is appropriately separated from vehicle incursions, is maintained to provide an even surface with good friction, and is used appropriately, then it may be considered reasonably safe.

A related term that is sometimes used in the industry is that of *substantive safety*, which is somewhat different from nominal or reasonable safety. Substantive safety refers to a condition in which there may be collisions, but the frequency and/or severity of those collisions is consistent with other facilities that do not have an unusual collision experience. This is evaluated through numerically identifying the experience of many other facilities and concluding that the subject location is not an outlier. Consequently, a facility believed to have substantive safety can be a condition not satisfying the nominal safety of the standards. Still, such locations may have an exposed liability where rare, even once-in-a-lifetime events come together, resulting in collision.

Hazards on the sidewalk can take many forms. Some hazards are related to elements of sidewalk design and are easily correctable. A design-related obstacle can be present wherever an individual must lift their foot by an unusual amount to step over something. We have all misjudged the height of a stair from time to time and stumbled forward. A similar effort is required in stepping over a curb onto the sidewalk from the road or parking lot or stepping over a tire bumper in a parking lot. The successful transition of hazards in these locations requires assessment time by the traversing parties. A standard barrier curb is 10 cm (4 in.) high, which seems to be a relatively simple feature for most of us to traverse, given they are reasonably visible and a common feature that many of us have stepped over successfully in a lifetime of experience. Nevertheless, this feature can present a significant hazard to ambulatory and nonambulatory individuals alike. Every once in a while, our toes may catch on them, resulting in a stumble or fall.

Pedestrians use the same perception/reaction process as drivers when encountering hazardous situations requiring a response. The task of stepping onto the curb starts with the *detection* of the curb, which may be missed due to inattention or because it is difficult to see, such as when one steps down off the curb and the height is not clearly known, especially in poor lighting conditions. Next, *identification* is necessary to recognize the potential hazard and potential for injury if the curb is not successfully traversed and a fall occurs. Also, the pedestrian must effectively *decide* how high to lift their feet to clear the curb while remaining in forward motion. To conclude the process, the *volition* phase requires the pedestrian to lift their feet to clear the curb. The forward motion places a time constraint on the activity in that if it is not done quickly enough, a fall may occur. The time available to accomplish these tasks may depend upon the visibility conditions, forward speed of the pedestrian, and more. The whole process is completed in the blink of an eye. However, many situations require much more time.

Any fault or interruption in the process can result in a trip, fall, and potential injuries. Even though the location is detected and identified as a stepping hazard, faults in the assessment can occur if the height is not accurately determined. The pedestrian's time available to assess can be curtailed by factors such as the desire to avoid other people, traffic conditions, traffic control signals, personal awareness, and a host of other distractions. These days, a common reason for missed detections arises from looking at a mobile device. Also, a failure in the assessment can occur if the pedestrian does not take sufficient time to assess the height of the curb. Therefore, a sidewalk cannot be considered safe, as a fall can result in an injury.

Hence, there is a need to consider whether the transition from the street to the sidewalk is acceptably safe or reasonably safe. Accessing a raised curb from the street is recognized as a hazard, and even more so for people with mobility issues, limited sight, mobility devices, and more. Most design standards now contain drawings indicating how the transition should be constructed to accommodate a variety of users. The design usually takes the form of a ramp with no ledge that may tip a wheelchair user. These design considerations can render access provisions to the sidewalk to be nominally safe or reasonably safe. However, features of the design may still cause problems for some people.

Sidewalk injuries can occur from non-design-related issues as well. Over winter, sidewalk slabs can be lifted by frost heaves and not settle back into their original position. Sidewalk slabs may settle or tilt when improperly supported next to a slope. When one slab is more than 1 cm (0.4 in.) higher than the next, it can present problems to pedestrians and other users, such as people with mobility aids. For example, a friend of mine running on a sidewalk tripped over a 10 cm (4 in.) water valve opening that was missing the cap. Her broken elbow required extensive surgery and several permanent metal fittings.

For many pedestrians, especially older pedestrians, heaved sidewalks can present a hazard threat. Some pedestrians bring the toe of their foot forward with only a small clearance from ground level. The low height of the sidewalk discontinuity in this range has low visibility and poor contrast, making it less detectable. This situation is compounded by an assumption that a sidewalk is a safe place to walk and so pedestrians do not look for tripping hazards, and expectancies can be violated. Hence, falls can occur because of missed detections or identifications.

Hence, the passive, nonthreatening, humble sidewalk cannot be considered safe because it can be proximate to the cause of injuries. Design and maintenance can overcome or mitigate some of the problems. Still, some hazards are related to the design. For example, people bumping into each other on the sidewalk is typically considered human error. They approached at low speed and therefore should have been able to avoid collision. However, if the sidewalk was too narrow to accommodate pedestrian traffic, it can be contributory to injuries if a bump causes a fall. In this context, the bump may be related to poor design since the sidewalk was not wide enough to accommodate pedestrian flows.

7.2 Overcrowding

It is known through sidewalk capacity assessment methods that every pedestrian requires a certain space for travel and maneuvering. The 1985 *Highway Capacity Manual* of Washington, DC, identified capacity limitations for pedestrian and cycling facilities. The manual presents how pedestrians interact on sidewalks and establishes levels of service based on demand and width for both straight sections and intersections, just as it did for roadways.[3] While this information may seem of little relevance to some designers, it can be critical in considering the transition of streetscapes to multiuse activity areas incorporating signs, outdoor restaurant tables, transit stops, benches, and so on.

In one case, I was required to provide an opinion in a matter where a pedestrian had stepped off a crowded sidewalk and was struck by a passing vehicle. The circumstances of the collision focused on the driver and the pedestrian, eventually blaming the pedestrian. However, a site inspection of the sidewalk revealed that it was located near a busy tourist area. Local restaurants had convinced the municipality to partition the sidewalk to allow on-street dining, which had been granted under license. Tables were set up on the sidewalk and fenced in. In addition, numerous obstructions on the sidewalk included poles, newspaper vending machines, sandwich board signs, and mailboxes.

At the time of the collision, during the peak of pedestrian activity in the evening, the residual width of sidewalk was insufficient to serve pedestrian flows, and the pedestrian had stepped onto the road to conveniently avoid other pedestrians. Thus, in serving the desires of the adjacent business interests, the sidewalk became less safe and failed to satisfy the function it was originally designed to do. As such, there was an engineering failure in the assessment of realistic operating conditions. Study and observation was required before the intrusion into the sidewalk space by streetscaping was allowed. If the potential for overcrowding had been identified and determined to be acceptable prior to narrowing the usable sidewalk space, there would have been an issue of design negligence.

In this example, attempting to accommodate business interests through design alone was unlikely to provide a safe sidewalk. However, engineering design, operations, and maintenance actions together could have made the sidewalk safer for public use to avoid injuries. For example, the sidewalk could have been made wider through the elimination of parking to accommodate more pedestrians. Fencing could have been installed to reduce the likelihood of pedestrians stepping onto the road, although the capacity of the sidewalk would remain an issue.

In other settings, engineering and design treatments can overcome or mitigate hazards. For example, the grade and subgrade of the sidewalk can be designed to limit the likelihood of lifting sidewalks. Also, the provision of accessible ramps can remove the tripping hazard at the transition from a crosswalk to a sidewalk. Sidewalks that have experienced frost lifting can be marked to temporarily increase the conspicuity of the ledge before grinding is used to remove the hazard. The marking of a vertical discontinuity in the sidewalk would enhance the contrast of the hazard, making it more easily detected and providing more time for users to respond to the hazard.

7.3 Winter Maintenance

Pedestrian traffic on a snow-covered sidewalk compacts the snow, typically over a narrow path of trampled snow where repeated use has leveled the snow to some extent. With sunshine and time, the surface will turn into an uneven icy crust that makes walking difficult. Observations indicate that pedestrians may shift their travel path to the roadway when this occurs.

Of course, ice is always a problem for pedestrians, whether an effort was undertaken to clear the snow from the sidewalk or not. Residual ice after snow clearing or icy surfaces from refrozen meltwater is also a hazard for sidewalk users. Haphazard winter maintenance of sidewalks makes them unusable for those requiring assistive devices. Hence, sidewalks can be particularly hazardous during the frost-prone months.

Many transportation departments within urban municipalities do not provide winter maintenance for their sidewalks within the roadway's right of way. Rather, they often shift responsibility from the municipality to property owners through municipal bylaws requiring residents and business owners to clear their sidewalks within a certain period after a storm. This type of bylaw provides the municipality with a significant expenditure saving. Of course, for business owners, a snow- or ice-covered sidewalk on their property can be a significant liability. Also, they do not have a means to shift responsibility to others. Snow clearing is required by business owners to make their property accessible to patrons but not so much for residents. Consequently, the snow clearing of sidewalks in many urban areas can be haphazardly done—if at all.

Further, the requirements for clearing sidewalks can vary substantially within the same municipality. Amalgamated municipalities illustrate this point. In at least one case, one of the former municipalities continued to fund sidewalk clearing through its municipal taxes while the others did not. The amalgamation did not unify this situation. Where snow clearing is not included in taxes, the condition of the sidewalks at any time can be highly variable. Some residents are contentious about clearing the whole sidewalk. Some do a minimal amount by clearing a narrow path, while others make no effort. In some locations, the city may instruct a resident to clear the snow if there is a complaint. In the locations where taxes support the clearing of sidewalks, they typically become usable within twenty-four hours of a snowfall event.

Of interest, the province of Ontario has established winter maintenance standards for sidewalks that municipalities are to follow as a provincial regulation. The winter sidewalk maintenance regulation was introduced in 2018, sixteen years after the winter maintenance regulation for roadways was enacted. In the case of sidewalks, the regulation allows forty-eight hours to begin clearing snowfall but allows 8 cm (3 in.) of snow to remain on the sidewalk surface indefinitely. The municipality is only required to commence clearing ice from the sidewalk forty-eight hours after it has become aware of the ice.

Of course, trampled snow turns into compression ice, even on sidewalks. Given these conditions, there is no obligation under the regulation for a municipality to provide reasonably safe sidewalks within a reasonable time period. While many municipalities have generally adopted the regulation for its application in the case of roadways, some continue to rely on bylaws that are typically enforced only on demand (in response to complaints) for winter sidewalk maintenance.

There is no accommodation in the regulation for those requiring assistive devices. Pedestrians may not be able to stay off the sidewalk for forty-eight hours. They may have travel needs for work, medical appointments, personal business, and so on. However, due to the provisions of the bylaw and the regulation for winter maintenance, there is no incentive for a municipality to provide reasonably safe travel conditions for those using sidewalks. One is left to wonder what the purpose is of the regulation. Was it established for the users or the municipalities? In this context, there may be an opportunity here for the public to impose a workable standard required of municipalities in regards to winter sidewalk maintenance.

This regulation appears to be established as protection for municipalities, allowing slow or nonperformance rather than a call to action to prepare sidewalks for public use. On the surface, it seems intended to protect municipalities from liability claims for a period of forty-eight hours (and possibly much longer) after the event or the emergence of awareness. If there is no complaint or explicit inspection for ice, no action need be taken. If action is taken, the regulation allows only localized servicing, permitting other icy areas to remain. At the very least, there seems to be a significant conflict in the regulation between the need for public safety and other municipal interests, such as staffing demands and public resources.

7.4 Technological Adaptation

Beyond the initial concept of providing a walking space for pedestrians, the use of sidewalks has been adapted for other uses serving old and new technologies alike. With increasing incentives and public demand for active transportation, significantly more cyclists are using sidewalks than in the past. Cyclists as well as the users of emerging technologies and new forms of electric vehicles (EVs) have adopted the sidewalk as their preferred operating space. New technologies include motorized skateboards, e-bikes, e-scooters, and more. At the same time, sidewalks are increasingly used to park and store mobility devices.

While the provision of bike lanes and bikeways has grown dramatically in the past ten years, these facilities are not necessarily considered reasonably safe by some users. I have frequently observed adult cyclists on sidewalks adjacent to bike lanes. In one instance, I was chastised by a cyclist on a sidewalk immediately adjacent to a bike lane because they claimed I was in their path. There are now many more modes of personal mobility devices than even ten years ago, and the number of modes is growing. These devices include bicycles that can travel at speeds much higher than 10 km/h (6 mph). I have observed competitive cyclists undertaking speed and endurance training on multiuse paths. Many of these motorized and nonmotorized vehicles can reach speeds of 30 km/h (19 mph) or more, much higher than acceptably safe travel speeds of walking conditions.

Riding a bicycle or motorized vehicle on the sidewalk can be quite dangerous in its own right. Sight distances are easily obstructed, and drivers crossing the sidewalk at driveways and intersections are not looking for such rapidly moving vehicles. Right-turning drivers may not look to their right along a sidewalk before entering a roadway. In one instance, a sidewalk cyclist died after being struck by a vehicle as it was exiting a parking lot. The cyclist was thrown into the path of street traffic. The driver likely crossed over the sidewalk before coming to a stop for the roadway, if they stopped at all.

With the intensified use of sidewalks by personal vehicles capable of speeds much faster than 10 km/h (6 mph), the risks to pedestrians are likely to increase. The severity of injuries arising from such collisions are affected by speed, mass, rigidity, projecting surfaces, and more. Higher speeds are associated with more severe injuries. Whether or not these devices are acceptable vehicles for use on sidewalks has not been determined or enforced by many road authorities. Some law enforcement protocols likely place less priority on enforcing compliance with bylaws due to the frequency of more serious crimes and in considering critical public reaction to this enforcement. Still, without enforcement, people are likely to experience harm due to the continued use and misuse of infrastructure in this way.

Added to these operating conditions is disagreement among the users who harbor variable perspectives related to the intended or appropriate use of sidewalks. Implementing enforcement can be problematic, particularly where there are advocacy groups or a general tolerance by the public for allowing use of sidewalks by these various vehicles. Legislation and regulations are often lagging in managing the vehicles we now have access to. Given this situation, disagreement between the public, legislators, and industry professionals about how to resolve issues must be expected.

The complexity of some issues is further increased by the lack of enforcement. In one large city, adults and adolescents ride bicycles (a legal road vehicle) on sidewalks even when a bicycle lane is directly adjacent to the sidewalk. Acceptance of unconventional—and even hazardous—uses of sidewalks can be reinforced by the frequency that cyclists use sidewalks without facing consequences. In addition, police are reluctant to enforce bylaws where the infraction is considered a misdemeanor.

The likelihood of an injury to a cyclist colliding with a pedestrian is reversed relative to being in a collision with a motor vehicle. One can appreciate that when an adult or child is struck by an adult cyclist, who is often wearing protective gear while riding on the sidewalk, the pedestrian is more likely to sustain greater injuries than the cyclist. Contact by the rigid components of bicycles provide significant opportunities for fractures, punctures, and abrasions. Hence, cyclists' preference to travel on a sidewalk may be related to the expected consequences arising from a potential collision with pedestrians being perceived as much less severe than if they were to be struck by a vehicle on a road. At the same time, it is quite common to see scooters for the ambulatory challenged to be using the roadway. The scooter user likely experiences a significantly better ride quality using the road rather than bumping over sidewalk joints every few meters, heaved or not.

Adding to this mix of transportation modes that have repurposed sidewalks are problems associated with mass balance and closing speed. In the context of emerging travel modes that move more rapidly on the sidewalk, engineering and design issues have become increasingly complex. This complexity is exacerbated by poorly formulated or lagging legislation and regulations as well as a slack approach to enforcement. The absence of enforcement is an enticement for noncompliant use.

The technological adaptation of devices for personal use is a fundamental element of human nature, extending beyond cyclists on sidewalks or scooters on roadways. We can see it everywhere and in all human activity.

The importance of this was first driven home to me in the mid-1980s, when it was reported that drivers with the loudly acclaimed safety enhancement of antilock braking systems (ABS) were shown to have more collisions than those without. Drivers did not understand the capability of the new braking system or placed too much reliance on its capabilities. Now, with most vehicles equipped with ABS, the distinction may have disappeared.

However, the rapid emergence and adaptation of new technologies to improve our lives challenges infrastructure service providers with both increasing and more complex demands. The growing popularity of personal mobility devices may ultimately lead to a repurposing of the sidewalk.

7.5 Planning Versus Design

The design and implementation of transportation facilities must be considered from the perspective of a diverse user group with variable capabilities. A short time ago, I became aware of reconstruction plans for a major two-lane arterial roadway functioning as an extension to a freeway. A bikeway and sidewalk were to be constructed on the north side of the roadway only. The road section was about 1 km (0.6 mi.) in length. Examination of the plan showed that if constructed on the south side, the back of the curb would encroach on the corner of one property. Constructing a sidewalk on the south side would have necessitated acquiring a parcel of land measuring about 10 sq m (108 sq ft.).

Discussion with a city engineer indicated that the city was generally reluctant to acquire lands for these purposes. A safe crossing location would be provided about midway along the length. The road authority did not consider that pedestrians and cyclists would be required to walk along the south side of the roadway to reach the crossing location, possibly trespassing on the private property or entering onto the roadway to get past the pinch point.

In reality, it is likely that pedestrians would attempt to cross the roadway anywhere along its length to get to the safety of the sidewalk since defined crossing locations were so far apart. In managing the safety problem, the road authority completely ignored the needs of some pedestrians (and cyclists) due to the effort required in securing the necessary parcel of land. As this roadway is a busy arterial roadway providing access to a large community, the incomplete design necessary to satisfy pedestrians is significant. As such, it can be considered a human factor failure in design. The built-in hazards of the sidewalk placement will be present for a very long time (or until a pedestrian is struck). Still, the road authority is likely to be free of liability because pedestrian-vehicle collisions can be blamed on the users whether or not there are too few gaps in traffic for pedestrians to safely cross the road during many hours of the day.

7.6 Summary

Thus, even a seemingly simple sidewalk, a passive element of the transportation infrastructure, cannot be certified as safe. The safety that it can provide is a function of its life cycle of activity from concept through construction, operations, maintenance, and use to the present day. Its safety is determined by the experiences of its users—those who are successful in avoiding injury or who sustain injuries—each expounding a different view of reasonable or acceptable safety. However, independent of those views, the fact that people do come to harm while using a sidewalk means they cannot unequivocally be certified as a safe haven for pedestrians or anyone else who uses them.

8

THE NATURE OF TRANSPORTATION ENGINEERING

Transportation facilities, by their nature, are a product of applied science. Due to the complexity of transportation systems, the engineering interest does not end with the completion of design. Engineering concepts and principles are used in all aspects of managing transportation facilities throughout their life cycle. Yet the wide-ranging mandates of the public transportation authority in providing these facilities are continually challenged by the need for adequate funding.

While failures leading to system problems and hazards to the public are generally rare, their sources can occur at all levels of the transportation authority. Though we like to believe that everyone involved in a task is dedicated and carries out their responsibilities to the best of their ability, they are just people and, like drivers, are subject to occasional indiscretions. Failures may occur because of the manager who gives too little attention to a recent report or field staff who just want to get home early. While often innocuous, some indiscretions can result in harms incurred by the public. When this happens, authorities move to protect themselves by a variety of means.

When individuals experience harm, there are many paths to resolution, only some of which involve assessments to determine contributory elements. The assessment process may stop with the police investigator who fills in some checkboxes noting the driver's contribution or the condition of the roadway at the time of the incident. In some cases, the investigation may be extended to the police providing commentary related to the infrastructure or maintenance of a facility. However, police investigations of the transportation facility are typically superficial and do not represent an expert opinion such as that of a licensed engineer. In the case of significant damages and legal action, a thorough forensic investigation of the transportation facilities may be undertaken. However, these seem to generally be avoided, possibly because of the time and expense involved.

To complete an assessment of the transportation facility, an analyst requires general engineering-based knowledge recognizing the life cycle considerations of the facility and the ability to render an expert opinion. On the other hand, the analyst must be equipped to delve into the details to identify the appropriate methods for analysis and drawing conclusions. For example, while the curve design and sign control may be relatively available, the evaluation of human factors elements or pavement condition ride quality, such as bumpiness, may only be available through specialized companies with task-specific equipment. These types of companies are often reluctant to take on plaintiff work for fear of damaging client relationships since they work almost exclusively for transportation authorities.

Investigations of transportation facilities can be expensive because of the substantial resources available to the authorities for their defense. Engineers representing the plaintiffs can expect their assessments to be reviewed by multiple firms offering specialty services. It was not uncommon in the work of the author to be simultaneously confronted by four or five firms or individuals retained by defendant authorities.

In one case involving a freeway management failure, the plaintiff engineer was dealing with seven different engineering firms retained by the defendants.[1] Assessments of transportation facilities must not only establish a detailed description of how and why the collision occurred but also identify whether the planning, design, traffic control, system operation, and maintenance of the facility satisfied appropriate standards of care.

Cases involving a major loss can be settled with little or no two-way dialogue between the lawyer and the transportation engineer aside from a report addressing the liability issues. Often, the engineer is not even informed of a settlement. Therefore, an engineer assigned to examine a collision involving a major loss may not be fully aware of the importance of the engineering analysis. For this reason, the following discusses elements of transportation engineering that may occasionally be expected to play a significant role in resolving cases in a settlement or at trial.

8.1 Engineering as Applied Science or Unsupported Opinion

In forensic engineering, I have often requested documentation regarding important design decisions when a transportation facility is under scrutiny. Unlike the example from the preceding chapter of the design decision to place a sidewalk on only one side of a major arterial roadway, it may be reasonably assumed that the design provisions for motor vehicles on a roadway fulfill all industry standards and specifications to ensure the curves are matched to vehicle speeds, thus limiting the extent to which vehicles will slide off the road in poor weather. We presume transportation engineering to be the result of well-educated industry practitioners diligently applying well-established protocols and standards based on the physical sciences. The roadway, sidewalk, and bikeway specifications are all set to the standards of the industry, and the engineering firm responsible for the design will put their license into play and sign off on the design, producing an engineered product satisfying acceptable safety.

But is this how things really work? In the event of an incident, it may well be necessary to verify the design elements of the roadway to recognize their potential contribution. In the example involving the sidewalk provision, the design omitted the sidewalk on one side of the road. One can scour design manuals for the country, state, and municipalities to search for a standard requiring sidewalks on both sides of arterial streets in urban settings. Some may even have such a standard. However, these provisions are not likely to be found or could be found with vague guidance indicating a sidewalk "may" be installed on both sides of the road, or that sidewalks may be absent in some sections.

The reality in the example is that, in this current age of healthy living, pedestrians are out walking, and in the absence of sidewalks, there is a potential for harm, especially at night, when visibility may be poor. In any event, sidewalks represent a significant expenditure, particularly if land for the sidewalk must be acquired (as in the case described in section 7.5). Hence, if designers decide that a sidewalk is not required, substantial benefits are likely to be accrued by the facility's owner, not the user. The owner now has an engineered facility while having paid for only one sidewalk.

At issue is whether the decision to eliminate the sidewalk on one side is a well-founded decision based in science (or standards) or simply a decision of convenience, making it a discretionary decision. In the long-term operation of this facility, the lack of a sidewalk may never become an issue if no harm ever comes. In the fullness of time, the designer's and owner's actions may never be scrutinized. Thus, one may argue that the daily use of the facility shows that it is safe and that the decision to eliminate one sidewalk was a good one. At the same time, the engineer or designer was able to save the owner an expenditure.

However, and more to the point, the incident of a pedestrian attempting to cross the roadway to get to the sidewalk and being struck by a vehicle may not occur for decades after the facility becomes operational. Still, the potential for harm remains a real possibility throughout the life cycle of the condition. This is precisely what happened in one case in which the author was asked to provide an assessment of the circumstances of a pedestrian injury at a bus stop in an industrial park.

If someone is struck crossing the road to access the sidewalk, an initial assessment would likely be that the pedestrian must have been inattentive or careless, and if the hunt for contributions stops there, the owner may never be confronted with a claim. Such a view of the pedestrian activity offers convenient support for the owner. On the other hand, when a vehicle-pedestrian collision occurs, the incident may be examined in the context of conditions the pedestrian confronted, making the design and operation of the facility relevant to resolving the matter. In this way, decisions of discretion made during the design can be scrutinized at any time throughout the life cycle of the facility.

For the elimination of the sidewalk on one side to be technically supported, at least two key matters must be considered. The first examines the life cycle operational issues. As the roadway is an existing facility, substantive information about its operation and the potential for conflicts between pedestrians (and cyclists) crossing the road and motorized vehicles will be available. If it is not, this information can be acquired through field study. Relevant information includes the design documents and field studies. Information about the temporal variation in traffic and the number of pedestrians may not be known but can also be obtained through field studies at any time and compared to the documents produced in planning the facility.

This information is then used to determine if there were sufficient gaps in the traffic stream to allow a pedestrian to cross the road at points of access along its length at the time of its design or at the time of an incident. The distance between crossing locations can assist in determining whether pedestrians are likely to cross midblock or not. Human factors considerations will assist in determining whether pedestrians are likely to walk to the nearest assisted crossing location. That type of consideration provides insight to whether (and where) pedestrians will cross the road and whether the elimination of a sidewalk is reasonable over time. The result can be compared to the safety of pedestrians walking along the side of the road without a sidewalk to access the assisted crossing locations.

The outcome of this type of assessment can vary widely depending on the width of the shoulder, likely access onto private lands, snow and ice conditions in the winter, and more.

Based on this information, engineers can determine that the absence of a sidewalk on one side of the road is acceptably safe. More explicitly, this could infer that pedestrians can safely cross or walk along the roadway and thus the incident was deemed the pedestrian's fault. Such decisions are entrusted to the engineers and designers because it is assumed they consider public safety as paramount. However, "acceptably safe" implies that collisions remain possible. In choosing to believe the situation as established by the road authority is acceptably safe, one is left to wonder if public safety is paramount to the sidewalk decision. Or do such factors like land acquisition and construction costs play a prominent role?

Further, in the absence of specific standards and/or detailed studies of the matter, is the decision to exclude the sidewalk an engineering opinion or a decision of convenience? Is it a decision that should be left in the hands of the engineers or one that requires the full scrutiny and approval of the public? Does the decision have a suitable focus on the safety of the traveling public? Is the decision supported by meaningful analyses and documentation when there is no applicable standard? Are there situations that are not encompassed within the safety of a standard, such as walking along the road at night to access a crossing location? Finally, and perhaps most importantly, do such decisions represent public policy, or are they discretionary decisions by the engineers or designers?

These questions may not be easily answered, considering the range of possible opinions, biases, or vested interests within the industry personnel and those influencing industry decisions (advocacies, politicians, and so on). Consequently, such questions may be resolved only through litigation. Still, the outcome of the litigation process is more likely to simply allocate responsibility for the collision. The process is not likely to determine whether there was a failure in a broader context encompassing the manner in which the industry treats its system users through its standards and protocols.

If studies were conducted by the owner, including walking speed for crossing the roadway and stream gaps size measured in seconds (frequency and duration of stream gaps) to determine the extent of difficulty for crossing the road, this would be an engineering calculation, and the decision could be categorized as an engineering decision. Otherwise, it may be deemed there was no engineering element in the decision. But it may still be argued to be an engineering matter, and the liability exposure of the engineers could become an issue. However, if no calculations were undertaken or the calculations were performed by contracted services, there was likely a failure to perform due diligence or a significant lack of oversight. In the absence of documentation, justification for decisions fade with time. Evaluations can then focus solely on conditions at the time of the event.

8.2 Transportation Facilities as an Engineered System

Whether we're examining a logging road used by a few vehicles weekly or a superhighway serving hundreds of thousands of vehicles per day, the principles of design of transportation facilities are dependent on applied science.

For example, the determination of acceptable sight distances is dependent on the time and motion of vehicles and independent of roadway classification. Curve radii are determined from travel speed and road-tire friction to ensure that vehicles do not slide off the road when passing through curves, independent of traffic volumes. For nominal or acceptable safety in operations, the same science is applied to pedestrian facilities, bikeways, multiuse paths, parking lots, and more.

Similarly, applied science is used to determine winter maintenance requirements considering the properties of snow, ice, chemical freezing point depressants, chemical reaction time, and more. The application of science is used in almost every aspect of the design, operation, and maintenance of transportation facilities throughout their life cycle to provide acceptable safety for public use where a duty to the public is paramount. The provision of these facilities, therefore, falls within the discipline of engineering.

8.3 The Nature of Engineering Activity

Engineering is the process of converting pure science into usable products. Hence, it is an applied science. Due to size, cost, or complexity of the products, engineering services may extend to the care, operation, and maintenance of those products. Individuals, along with their associated corporations, assuming responsibility for the products and services are identified as professional engineers—persons with specialized and professed knowledge. The outcome of engineering is products or services that may be used by others to safely perform a task to their benefit. Transportation engineers provide infrastructure such as roadways and the controls for their operation.

Those using the product are likely to have knowledge only of how to use the product. Frequently, the client and user will remain uninformed about aspects of the science and technology of the product development, operation, and maintenance and simply choose to use the product in their preferred manner. The engineer is then in the privileged position of determining how the needs of their client are best served, including a responsibility to determine the extent of acceptable safety for the public.

Associations of professional engineers recognize the nature of engineering as a process with several distinctive characteristics arising from the reliance of the public on engineered products.

As cited by one association, the engineering process is a distinctive process for the following reasons:

- It satisfies an indispensable and beneficial social need.
- Its work requires the exercise of trust, discretion, and judgment, and is not subject to standardization.

- It is activity conducted upon a high intellectual plane, requiring a body of distinctive knowledge (science) and skill (art).

- Engineering knowledge and skills are not commonly held by the general public. They are the result of tested research and experience acquired through a special discipline of education and practice.

- It has a well-developed group consciousness for the promotion of knowledge and professional ideals, and for rendering a service to society.

- It has legal status and well-formulated standards of admission.

- It has an ethical code that ensures an appropriate level of conduct.

- Finally, it should be noted how engineering is the only profession where the primary responsibility is to a third party, the "public" in the true sense.[2]

Still, the client—including the public—has a place in determining the thresholds of acceptability. In the context of today's social environment, the public is endeavoring to achieve greater usability and safety at less cost in the provision of engineered products and services. This is a natural process usually associated with competition in the private sector, where usability, safety, and cost are often traded off. However, this competition also flourishes in public-sector engineering, where there is very broad and intense competition for the expenditures of tax dollars in arts, social services, health-care services, and policing, as well as within engineering or public works departments.

Morrison and Hughes describe the engineer–client relationship dynamic.[3] The goal to satisfy competing objectives in cost and utility often moves the design or operations of products closer to the practical limit of its functionality (or safety).[4] As a result, there is greater uncertainty about how well the product will perform in the hands of its users. The need to satisfy multiple objectives with greater uncertainty creates conflict between the client and those providing engineered products and services. It is also a process in which the client (and the public) would like to assume greater control in decision-making. Thus, participants are engaged in continuous effort to limit the autonomy of those providing the engineered product or service. In such an environment, it is perhaps understandable that those providing the engineered product or service may be less than willing to fully accept the responsibilities placed on them by their client. Consequently, those providing the engineered products and services and those acquiring them are in a constant state of tension.

8.4 Transportation Engineering as a Reflection of the Day

Like many professions, transportation engineering can be substantially influenced by externalities. Changes in how engineers may perform their task arise from advances or trends in engineering, social/industry trends, or public demand. Litigation is certainly one of the most compelling influences. This is perhaps rightly so, as the results of litigation may be viewed as statements of acceptability by the public regarding specific actions of the engineering profession. The results of litigation allow engineers to reflect on the job done and provide insight to the demands of the public. The effects extend to defining areas of intensified research; determining funding levels for design, operations and maintenance, and enhanced training programs; and assessing procedures and protocols. Fortunately—or unfortunately—confidentiality agreements associated with out-of-court settlements can limit the circulation of information. While this may protect the reputation and limit liability for individuals or corporations, it can also restrict the dissemination of information that could benefit the industry and the safety of the public. One's view on this issue is simply a matter of perspective. For these reasons, case law and legal opinion should be of interest to engineers.

On the other hand, transportation engineering is open to scrutiny by those outside of the discipline who are willing to pursue an issue.

Manuals, standards, and technical documents are readily available and now often downloadable from agency websites. Transportation engineers are required to present plans and projects to the public for assessment before various hearing boards and panels. Transportation engineers also like to exchange their ideas and experiences through professional associations, conferences, and casual exchanges of information.

However, perhaps most importantly, the public has a vast and long-term experience with using transportation facilities (roads, bikeways, sidewalks). Therefore, when the public identifies unusual conditions or potential hazards, there may in fact be a safety issue or hazard present, and subsequent evaluation requires open and considered thought. During my career, I was regularly contacted by lawyers and other individuals who suspected design or operations issues were present in specific locations yet could not identify what exactly was the problem. This type of query should be considered seriously because with all the experience systems users have with available travel systems, such as roadways, for them to raise questions shows they have experienced a violation of expectancy. System users, just like professionals, can know when something is out of sync.

When questions are raised, professional examination of the matter confirms whether a problem is present and provides the details. Unfortunately, an injury often must occur before the public, the transportation industry, or members of the legal profession pay attention. Further detailed investigations of the field conditions can then specify the problem and identify the contributory elements. This relationship means that transportation engineers must expect interactions with a well-informed public.

This discussion brings to light the time-sensitive nature of decisions arising from engineering endeavors. One example relates to the one-way street systems popularized in the late 1960s. The original thinking in the provision of numerous one-way streets was to improve efficiency in travel and significantly enhance safety through a reduction in the number of the potential conflicts that street users (drivers and others) were exposed to at any time. The safety improvements were available to both motor and nonmotor travel means. For example, a pedestrian crossing the street or the driver of a vehicle entering the street had only to look in one direction for approaching traffic, thus simplifying the decision process.

However, over time, the safety benefits were not managed well. A groundswell of anti-auto sentiment by advocacy groups, corporate media, and social media pointed to the one-way system as the proximate cause of harm due to the efficiency in moving traffic. Slowing vehicles down in a two-way system was proposed and widely accepted as the appropriate solution. This narrative was deemed to provide a safer pedestrian environment, though there is evidence to the contrary.[5] It remained a matter in which motor vehicle drivers could not gain a voice. It seems industry personnel deemed challenging the projected narrative through empirical evidence to not be worthwhile, given the potential backlash. If the public narrative demanded a two-way street system, the transportation industry could provide that infrastructure. This is but one example in which infrastructure changes were implemented in response to the public narrative.

The information available to manage transportation issues has dramatically increased since the 1960s. Over the last twenty years, an increasing number of manuals have been written to address missing or vague information in previous versions. Now, specific elements of design or operation often appear in separate manuals, each of which may be updated independently as necessary. Design manuals issued by recognized agencies may be reissued every five to ten years. For some agencies, the issuing of manuals may well have become a revenue stream. As a result, industry personnel must always be informed of newly released information. This can lead to differences in the way information is presented, depending on the composition of the review process in any forensic analysis. Consequently, inconsistencies in manuals and protocols, while rare, may arise. Where inconsistencies exist, the appropriate manual must be selected and used.

To highlight this issue, consider a manual of traffic control devices that was parsed to update sections regularly without reissuing the whole manual. The section detailing regulatory devices indicated that Stop lines *may* be used at intersections, while the section on pavement markings indicated that Stop lines *must* be used at intersections. To avoid installing Stop lines, a road authority could refer to the first wording, from the section on regulatory devices, as the standard of practice, despite that manual referring the reader to the section on pavement markings for more information. Still, the two conflicting recommendations are *the* standard for pavement markings at Stop signs.

While pavement markings are a simple traffic control device that provides redundancy for the Stop sign, the provision of Stop lines costs money. Where there are thousands of intersections, the costs can be substantial. Further, whether as a matter of convenience or engineering judgment, not all industry professionals agree with the nondiscretionary use of the Stop line.

The vague and conflicting terminology of the manual allows readers to apply their own interpretation and discretion. Road authorities often interpret the terminology to mean Stop lines are not required. Therefore, Stop lines are not installed or may be allowed to fade at some important intersection locations.

In the presence of litigation, one can appreciate the desire of road authorities to refer to the commentary of the regulatory manual rather than the standard specifically setting out provisions for Stop lines. Further, one can appreciate road authorities' desire to modify the manual so Stop lines are optional as a means of reducing expenditures. While such a decision is likely to move away from safety-conscious operations, it could make life easier for the road authorities.

Consistency in applying standards depends on who controls the production process of the manual, and the results are likely to vary according to the opinion and bias of the controlling group. Of course, the authors of the manual face a dilemma in changing these wordings. In a move toward convenience and less cost, the term "may" could be used in both sections. However, this could reasonably be interpreted as self-serving. In a move toward safety, the term "must" could be used in both sections, but that would require better management and more costs. Perhaps leaving it as is is the most convenient solution so the inconsistency in terminology can be dealt with piecemeal during litigation. This is just one example of how manuals may come to be modified or not to serve a particular perspective.

The competition for funds between government departments also imposes strain on the internal relationship between those providing engineered products and services. In this way, the client can be any transportation authority, whether a state, provincial, or municipal corporation. In limiting budgetary increases, departments must decide how much of any service is needed or whether some services are needed at all. In this respect, the employer-engineer relationship of the public and private sectors is similar.

Furthermore, as the supplier of engineered products and services, the engineering responsibility of the corporation is clear, as outlined by many professional regulatory bodies that state public welfare, including or implying safety, is paramount. However, as previously cited, the public is not limited to those constituents funding the travel authority but rather all users of the facilities. Thus, the industry has a dual responsibility, which opens the door for discretion in balancing the interests of taxpayers—who may be incorrectly viewed as the public—with the broader needs of all system users—the actual public.

8.5 Transportation Engineering Activities Defined by Professional Engineers

One professional engineering licensing agency has defined the extent of services regarding the professional practice of traffic and transportation engineering.[6] Encompassed within the practice is a wide range of activities, including the management, planning, design, operations, and maintenance of transportation facilities. Within the general discipline of traffic and transportation engineering is a list of fourteen different types of studies contributing to the provision of transportation infrastructure. Among others, the list includes studies of bicycle facilities, traffic safety studies, neighborhood impact studies, traffic operations studies, and transportation social planning studies.

In outlining these studies, the agency has set the scope of engineering activity and defined the range of responsibilities in the provision of transportation services. The scope of services defined by this licensing agency for professional engineers is typical of the scope of services required by many licensing agencies, standards-issuing agencies, and transportation associations. In all of these, the safety and security of the system users is a recurring theme.

These studies illustrate the responsibilities of practitioners in serving the public need and in giving due consideration to safety issues in their work. Others looking into the responsibilities of professionals can reference this information to determine if the professional responsibilities have been met.

In undertaking bicycle studies, for instance, four essential areas of endeavor are identified. Beyond the engineering aspects, these also include education, enforcement, and encouragement. Therefore, the engineering activity does not end with design but continues on several fronts applicable to the facility's life cycle. Within these activities is the concept of monitoring and maintenance, both necessary elements to gauge the ongoing health of the facility and safety of the public. Of course, these principles also apply to other modes of transportation as well.

The licensing agency clarifies that neighborhood impact studies do not need to be initiated solely in response to proposed changes due to new development. These studies can be initiated at any time. In this context, it is recognized that a travel environment is not static over time, and ongoing inspection, monitoring, and review are required. Municipal agencies undertake studies to address the operational concerns raised by local ratepayers, business associations, school groups, interested individuals, and, importantly, system users. All these groups should be of legitimate interest to engineering management. Thus, all user groups should be explicitly considered in the design, operation, and maintenance of facilities. Identifying existing deficiencies is a precursor to the development of effective solutions, particularly where safety and/or the duty of the engineer to the public may be a concern.

In defining traffic safety studies, the licensing agency indicates:

> The onus is on road jurisdictions to take reasonable steps to identify and correct road safety problems. Initiatives should address problem prevention and/or reduction. A road jurisdiction should demonstrate that it is expending a reasonable amount of its resources to monitor and resolve the problems. These initiatives serve two major objectives: to provide both a safe road environment for road users and an improved position for the road jurisdiction to respond to liability claims.[7]

Importantly, the statement refers to road users in general and is not limited to motorists. Those who prepared the statement in 1994 recognized that transportation systems are multimodal systems serving more than car or truck drivers. Encompassed within these initiatives is the notion that some road users such as cyclists and pedestrians are more vulnerable to harm because of collisions than those who are enclosed within motor vehicles. Interestingly, some geometric design standards offer less or even no guidance in how to adequately accommodate these vulnerable road users. For this reason, the interests of cyclists and pedestrians may only be pursued when advocacy draws attention to them. To overcome this situation, it is necessary for there to be consultation with special interest groups as well as a review and examination of materials, policies, and manuals from external agencies. External resources include guidelines and manuals published by respected transportation organizations that may not be considered a standard of the industry but nevertheless represent common sense or reasonable practice.

Regarding the investigation of safety, the licensing agency raises the important concept of collision prevention. A travel authority may recognize a hazard before or after collisions occur. Both are necessary after the design and construction of facilities. Proactive methods seek out hazards that may not have generated a collision experience to date but continue to pose a threat to system users. Reactive methods respond to the collision experiences that have occurred. Together, these methods enable a balanced safety monitoring program.

The licensing agency specifies that the transportation social planning study must consider both social benefits and impacts. Socioeconomic characteristics include psychological makeup, income level, stage in life, and physical condition of the users, as these attributes determine an individual's ability to use the facility. The safety analysis encompassed within these studies includes effects on the facility's users and nonusers. The transportation social planning study emphasizes the potentially broad impacts as well as the need for engineers to consider users' performance across a range of age, gender, ethnicity, and socioeconomic status.

Consequently, human factors are an essential foundation for decision-making in the provision of engineered transportation products and services. To address broader needs, engineered products and services cannot focus solely on a single group of system users. Doing so would allow potentially serious consequences to impact other, possibly much larger, user groups. For example, as stated previously, it is essential to consider how pedestrians can safely cross the street, especially when enticements such as bus stops are present. If a sidewalk is provided on only one side of a bridge structure, pedestrians must have an acceptably safe way to access the sidewalk or otherwise cross the road upon departing the sidewalk.

Given the description of engineering activities identified by the licensing agency, the practice of engineering in the context of transportation facilities encompasses a wide scope of activities, including consideration of public safety, human factors, and travel activity.

8.6 A Potential for Harm

Users of a product often possess only enough knowledge to operate it routinely, enough to perform the intended function. Drivers or others using transportation facilities cannot be expected to intuitively know how or where specific threatening conditions or circumstances exist or how to safely navigate an unexpected hazard. Also, system users cannot be assumed to have spontaneous insight for coping with hazards they encounter. These issues are often addressed in forensic assessments but can be overlooked when evaluations rely only on facility specifications found within standards. This oversight can result in assigning capabilities to system users that some individuals may not possess, even if such capabilities are assumed at an aggregate level.

System users decide to travel based upon their history of trip making and a reliance on having at hand the necessary information for completing successful trips. Even so, there may remain unknowns, and unexpected situations may be encountered. In this respect, transportation facilities are not engineered to uniquely match the abilities of individual travelers.

The public purchases engineered products (any commercial product such as lawn mowers, clothes washing machines, vehicles) without specific knowledge in how to use them. Therefore, the potential is always present for a user to be inadvertently harmed by a product in some manner. This is also the case for those using travel facilities.

Users require appropriate instruction in how to use a product. Many consumer products come with an instruction manual. While the user may not read the manual, the supplier of the product fulfills their responsibility in providing it. It is up to the user to determine the extent of their compliance. This is also the case for travel facilities.

In the same way, the infrastructure (roadways, sidewalks, trails, bikeways) and its support facilities (the roadside) are products of engineering and, therefore, users require instruction on how to safely use them. Driver training programs provide initial instruction. Yet, formal training in how to use some facilities for some system users can be absent. Pedestrians are not instructed in how to use a sidewalk or how to cross the street at an intersection with traffic control signals. Often, these facilities are simply there to be used.

Due to the variability in travel facilities, not all information can be provided to the user before they undertake a trip. Still, the user's required documentation—for example, a driver's license—informs authorities that they have been trained. Further, users are provided with instructions via signs, signals, and markings along the way.

This is not always the case for pedestrians and cyclists, who may not have much experience or specific training in using transportation infrastructure. These travelers receive instructions visually through observation of the road or path ahead, possibly in combination with signs and markings providing specific instructions. For example, cyclists on multiuse paths require speed signs to safely share the path with pedestrians who may have small children or dogs with them. Providing signs is one means for transportation authorities to fulfill their responsibilities in providing instructions to system users.

A system user may fail to complete their trip because of inadvertent or intentional actions such as inattention, looking in the wrong direction, and more. The characteristics of a facility may limit the ability of users to use it successfully due to issues with how the facility was planned, designed, operated, or maintained. Industry professionals may experience failures in conceptualizing problems, dealing with engineering compromises, failing to consider a reasonable range of human performance, or not adequately predicting how the engineered products and services will be used.

In a simple example, worn dirt pathways across a lawn between two sidewalks illustrate the desired line users establish for themselves, whereas the sidewalks indicate the desired line set out by designers. The pathway illustrates a failure by the designer to properly assess user needs. When these types of failures occur, it is often the case that the product or service was simply not used as willed by the designer. Failures to use a facility properly can also occur when the user was not provided with sufficient instruction, such as through the application of control devices like signs, or as a result of misdirected design or implementation.

A history of engineering experience shows most products undergo evolutionary development as technology improves and more is learned about how a product is used. The product evolves and adapts to the changing needs of users, as well as to advances in science and engineering. In the above example, a sidewalk could be installed where the worn footpath indicates pedestrians' preferred route. Similarly, attitudes toward what defines an acceptable product or the use of a product or facility are subject to change. Also, statutes, regulations, and standards may fail to align with public needs. Therefore, it is inappropriate for those providing engineering services to be complacent with the design, operations, and maintenance of engineered products and services. Ongoing monitoring and maintenance related to the use of the products and services is required, which applies to transportation facilities as an engineered product.

Associations of professional engineers have self-imposed (or have had public-imposed) regulatory rules and codes intended to maintain a high standard of integrity and avoid user injuries. The legislated requirement for engineers to create and apply a code of ethics for the practice of engineering provides a legal commitment to the public to ensure that engineers "shall regard their duty to public welfare as paramount."[8] To support these ideals means engineers must be vigilant and must maintain a continuous effort in the management of engineered systems to assure the public they are provided with reasonable safety. To do this on an ongoing basis, engineering associations assist in this endeavor by producing guidelines for the development, operations, and maintenance of transportation facilities.[9]

The need to consider public welfare as paramount can become confused with the need to serve constituent national, state, provincial, or municipal interests, which may well be corporate interests. That is, the corporation may be deemed to represent the public. However, this is an inappropriate perspective for engineers because the municipal corporation is not controlled by engineers and maintains a wide range of objectives. The municipal corporation makes choices between competing interests, including the extent of public safety to be provided.

The engineer's mandate is not flexible, as their duty to the public—not to the public corporation—is paramount. For example, an economic benefit accrued to the corporation (reduced expenditure) may benefit only those represented by the municipal corporation—the taxpayer. Such measures undertaken at the expense of the traveling public's safety may compromise the engineer's duty. Individuals (including nonresidents or other general system users) can be excluded from the accrual of benefits when there is a crash-related consequence (increased crash rate).

Therefore, when economic objectives regarding the design, operation, and maintenance of facilities are prioritized, the owner may benefit but not the public. On the other hand, it is within the prerogative of elected governments to determine who may be protected or excluded from legislation. Tolerated exposure levels for hazards, drinking water, and food are examples of how governments mitigate risk. In this context, the concentrations of harmful elements within the food chain are regulated. Permitted concentrations are typically based on statistical inference rather than deterministic analyses. These levels of risk tolerance become public policy and have the force of legislation. While these levels of concentration are considered safe for public use or at least use by most people, the percentage of the population that can come to harm may not be discretely known, even if it is considered to be very low. In this way, some individuals may not be protected by these government policies.

In the case of structural engineering, a common design approach is to identify the maximum loading and then add additional loading to serve as a safety factor. Therefore, structural failures remain unlikely even after some deterioration. This is one means by which a duty to the public is inherently paramount. In transportation and traffic engineering, a common approach is to include 85 percent of drivers within the design requirement, thereby allowing 15 percent of drivers or vehicles to fall outside the range of design or operations. The share of users falling within this range is obtained from sampling studies, so it also inherently contains some uncertainty.

The genesis of this approach is unknown. It may well have predated current regulatory requirements. Even so, the approach directly conflicts with the engineer's duties, which are to regard their service to the public as paramount. Whether this concept of inclusion encompasses "public safety as paramount" is subject to interpretation. The absence of a reference to safety can be viewed as a workaround to the safety issue—not unlike some standards used by the industry. To avoid this dilemma, some engineers' regulations specifically identify safety to be part of that duty.

Excluding such a large percentage of the public from the safety encompassed within design protocols would seem indefensible in the context of engineering mandates. Therefore, it is clear that other considerations are influencing this common engineering practice. In my years of practice, I never came across a situation where the eighty-fifth-percentile threshold had been directly accepted as public policy. Indeed, while manuals provide a standard or guidance in the design or operation of facilities, the percentage of the drivers, vehicle population, or system users excluded may remain unidentified in many situations or conditions.

For perspective, the yellow interval for traffic control signals is relevant, as previously discussed with human factors (chapter 4). One manual sets the interval based on the posted speed limit, allowing a response time for drivers of just 1.0 second in some instances.[10] Research has shown the observed mean response time by drivers was 1.3 seconds, and the median was 1.1 seconds. The derived eighty-fifth-percentile perception and brake reaction time, excluding drivers' response lag time, was 1.2 seconds.[11] Therefore, some drivers are disadvantaged by the chosen response time for reacting to the onset of a yellow signal at intersections with traffic control signals.

The standards of the industry citing a 1.0-second response time to a yellow change interval may not include a source reference or any discussion related to the percentage of the public who may not be able to respond in this amount of time. This short response time would seem to assume that drivers are able to detect the change from green to yellow the instant it occurs. It would further assume that if drivers belatedly detect the change or have a slower response time, they will adapt by braking more intensely over a shorter distance. However, the response time does not include the hapless driver who may be looking at poorly displayed street name signs or potential threats already at or near the intersection, such as vehicles waiting to turn left. In this way, the developers of the standard have hidden information that may well be relevant to collision events.

Some forensic investigators use research to arrive at definitive conclusions when there can be substantive uncertainty. In one case, a power company was replacing a hydro pole 300 m (984 ft.) from an intersection with traffic signal control. It was after dark in a rural area when the company cut the power to the illumination and traffic signal for a four-way intersection. The police and the road authority were not on scene. Both roads went dark for more than a kilometer (0.6 miles) in every direction. Shortly thereafter, a right-angled collision occurred. In their assessment of the collision, forensic engineers indicated that a Signals Ahead sign located some distance from the intersection, the pavement markings, the Stop line, and street signs should have made the drivers aware of the intersection and the potential for other vehicles to approach the intersection. The two vehicles came into view at right angles, 1.2 to 1.7 seconds pre-collision. This was deemed to be sufficient time for either or both drivers to avoid collision. Yet neither driver was able to perform as determined by the forensic engineers.

In this case, the forensic engineers assigned the following information to the unsuspecting drivers:

- Previous knowledge of the intersection and its location
- Assumed driving speeds for both vehicles (without post-collision analyses)

- Assumed the drivers could respond appropriately to the unexpected other vehicle (within 1.5 seconds)

- Assumed neither driver had altered their driving speed on approach to collision

- Assumed the cues would be visible to the drivers at a reasonable distance

- Assumed the drivers could detect and identify the emerging cues to arrive at a conclusion (traffic signals not working) within the shortest possible time

In fact, the analysts could not replicate the conditions and thus had no independent knowledge of the situational conditions the drivers encountered or their performance capabilities. The above conditions attributes were therefore *assigned* to the drivers by the forensic engineers. Further, the analysis ignored the drivers' expectancies and failed to recognize the human factors that transportation and forensic engineers need to be acquainted with.

There was no evidence in the report that the analysts had ever acquainted themselves with the parameters associated with decision sight distance. Yet those parameters indicate that drivers require much longer times to perceive and respond to unexpected, vague, and difficult-to-interpret conditions. The forensic analysis was clearly biased in the direction of the public utility while adding to the harm incurred by the involved individuals. The analysis was enabled by relying heavily on hindsight bias and a limited interpretation of human factors to promote a case for the power company rather than acknowledging the range of variability in human performance.

Of course, this begs the question: What percentage of the population of facility users should be included in the planning, design, operations, and maintenance elements of facilities or in the forensic assessment of incidents? The concept of using an eighty-fifth-percentile threshold as a means to limit the economic burden of infrastructure development has been in use and accepted by the industry since the beginning of transportation engineering and, by extension, forensic engineering, if not the public. Those who plan the transportation systems are likely to indicate that the concept works well since users can adjust to the circumstances in some way. Those falling into the bottom fifteenth percentile, who are excluded from consideration and harmed in some way, are likely to indicate that it does not work. However, there is little incentive to identify these system users when harm does occur.

As a forensic transportation engineer, it is the author's view that whether an engineer or transportation authority decides to adhere to a standard or corporate policy or not is a discretionary decision. It is then the purpose of forensic assessment to determine whether that decision contributed to the harm an unincluded individual experienced. This raises the question of whether standards are public policy or not. If they are not public policy, their application is therefore discretionary and possibly subject to litigation. It would seem this is an issue to be resolved in many jurisdictions.

I have often considered that road authorities are able to choose between adhering to the standards or not. When they do not, the consequences can be in the form of litigation or a payout arising from it. Sometimes the cost of the consequences far outweighs the cost of adhering to the standards. As such, the cost of noncompliance through payouts to claimants is considered part of the cost of doing business. In this way, products (roadways) and services (maintenance) provided by transportation authorities (municipal corporations) is no different from the manufacturing of any product offered for general consumption, such as automobiles.

Whether or not the planning, design, operations, and maintenance process should include 85 percent of users or 100 percent of users is a discretionary decision, and the transportation authority can expect payouts to those in the 15 percent of the population who are excluded and then harmed. Such payouts could be considered in contingencies when preparing budgets. However, the likelihood of a legal challenge to engineering standards is very low, in part because of the complexity and expense of such a challenge and in part because of the difficulty in identifying the contribution to the harm. On this issue, I have not encountered lawyers willing to take on this challenge. Still, I believe that it is a matter open to public scrutiny, particularly in instances where the standards are unduly weighted toward limiting liability rather than ensuring the public can travel safely.

STANDARDS OF THE INDUSTRY

9.1 A Predisposition to Blame the Road User

Collisions can occur when there is a failure in one of the three components that enable safe travel: the vehicle, the driver, or the road. In investigating the cause of collisions, almost 90 percent are attributed to human failure (human error of the traveler). There should be little wonder in this regard. One collision reporting form identifies thirty-four actions and conditions that point to the road user as contributory in some way. In comparison, there are only three actions under the traffic control condition that indicate the road as a contributory factor. All three of the conditions may be considered temporary, such as icing. There is no consideration in the report that specifically deals with a design condition. By this means, the collision report inherently points to "human error by one of the involved parties" as the principal cause of collision.

The collision reporting system gives credence to the contention expressed in the *Transportation and Traffic Engineering Handbook* of 1982 indicating that drivers are expected to comprehend design and control inadequacies and compensate for them in the driving task.[1] The propensity to focus on drivers in collisions produces the potential to overlook contributing sources of probable cause. This approach to collision assessment is not conducive to the provision of road safety, as it can effectively hide root causes related to the engineering interests.

Yet it would be unfair to shift focus entirely from the system user to the providers of the service. Without a doubt, there are many irresponsible, careless, inattentive, and ill individuals who drive when everyone would be better off if they refrained. However, it is important for those examining collisions or hazards to avoid focusing on just one possible contributing factor, whether drivers, vehicles, or the roadway. Advocacy may become more apparent when there is a valid or unexplained element of an event that has not been evaluated.

In one case, a motorcyclist passed through 90 percent of a 90-degree curve without incident and then crashed on exit. A helmet video record showed no change in speed. In this case, there was a kink at the end of a right curve and no transition section to make the road align with a second left curve. On many occasions I have visited a location anticipating I would not be able to find an infrastructure contribution, only to realize that a contribution to the harm is highly likely. This was one such case. In these matters, the site may operate without incident for years—possibly decades—without the defects being identified. However, that can all change when a rare series of events come together in time and space in a coincidental way.

It could be said that human error is the principal cause of all collisions because roads and vehicles are designed, constructed, operated, and maintained by human effort. Thus, in combination with driver actions, there is a human context to all collisions. With this view of collision events, human error may not relate to one of the involved parties but rather any aspect of the transportation system as well. If all the sources of human factors contributions are to be tested, evaluation of the roadway and setting is warranted.

It is well-known that there can be a clear relationship between the proximate cause of collision and deficiencies in the design, control, operations, and maintenance elements of road systems. However, only within the last decade have these relationships begun to be quantified and published in geometric design standards and guidelines. If all potential sources of human error are to be evaluated, an examination of the travel environment is warranted.

9.2 The Development of Transportation Standards

The development of standards is not a straightforward activity because the extent of knowledge is not absolute. While physics and deterministic calculation support some standards, uncertainty and knowledge gaps exist with respect to many elements of our transportation systems. Determining appropriate values to include in manuals is complicated by the extent of variation in system users' behaviors.

As discussed previously, how much of that variation to include affects the number of people who may not be protected by the nominal limits set forth in most standards documents. There may be no definitive thresholds for some elements of transportation systems. For example, lane widths, which can differ, are often set according to traffic speed and intensity of use but also with consideration for how traffic may wander around within a lane. Lanes that are too narrow experience more frequent excursions, while lanes that are too wide encourage lane splitting (side-by-side vehicle operation). In such cases, standards reflect a consensus of opinion by those assembling a standard.

The design, traffic control, operations, and maintenance of transportation facilities are carried out within a framework shaped by legislation, regulation, engineering judgment, research, calculation, and artistic license. Industry standards of practice may be entrenched within regulations, defining manuals, guidelines, long-term practice, best practices, and even so-called rules of thumb. Just about any organization or institution may issue manuals offering standards or guidance, although those having state/provincial or national recognition generally represent the overarching standards of the industry. Travel authorities may also develop in-house standards to serve local needs while recognizing the requirements of other levels of government.

Since the turn of this century, a defining trend in manuals for the design, control, and maintenance of facilities has been to label standards as guidelines. One reason for doing so is that using the word "standards" created concerns about litigation when not applied verbatim. Also, a manual described as a standard allowed confusion as to whether the standards were inherently regulations. Some view the label as a first line of defense against litigation. In practice, regardless of the label, these manuals represent the minimum limits of described elements and present the lower bounds of sound practice but are not specifically mandatory.

A manual that uses the word "guide" or "guidelines" allows individuals to apply its recommendations based on oversight parameters, experience and judgment, training and assessment, and case-specific considerations. More recent manuals have been written in a manner allowing greater latitude in applying the standards to achieve other design-related goals while not compromising the safety inherent to the minimum limits. Users of the manuals are encouraged to apply rules in a manner that exceeds the minimum limits stated to move the product in the direction of enhanced safety. For this reason, guidelines cannot be simply treated casually, despite the label.

Whether labeled as a standard or a guideline, these manuals represent the lower thresholds of sound practice within the industry. When minimum limit standards are not satisfied, those with a duty to the public can expect less support from the engineering industry should collisions occur, as well as greater liability exposure. On the other hand, there can be reasonable cause for why the standards cannot be applied as recommended. Getting all the parts of the puzzle to fit as best possible can leave some shortcomings within the finished product. In these situations, it is necessary to document the situation, determine the variance from the standard, and implement ways and means that the safety of the condition has been maintained.

Standards are often developed under contract to third parties, with committees of practitioners representing stakeholders approving them. Depending on the complexity of the issues, there may be an oversight committee and a technical committee populated by practitioners, experts in the field, or persons who are recognized by a host organization as the most qualified to handle the matter. The host organization could be any government-supported travel authority or agency. Committee members can also be individuals that a contributing transportation authority wants to have on a committee independent of their qualifications.

Draft standards are determined for the committee, which then meets with the stakeholder organizations to review and comment on them. The stakeholder may recommend changes, which the committee further discusses and reviews. Changes to the draft standards may be determined at any step in the process. The standards may be circulated to experts, practitioners, or others with considerable experience and interest in the subject matter. The provisions are then modified to meet the stakeholder's needs and finally adopted by the committee. The foreword of most standards identifies the individuals and their associated stakeholder organizations who contributed to the approval or adoption of the standards contained therein. In forensic investigations, the list of participating individuals is useful in identifying the extent of knowledge that may be held by various parties at the time the standards were developed.

As these committees are composed of select persons engaged in the industry, the resulting provision of standards represent their values as well as the goals and objectives of the organizations they represent. For this reason, the makeup of the committee reflects the quality of the end product and the nominal safety experienced by the public. Committees dealing with matters of national scope are typically composed of individuals having a national presence and drawn from a cross section of the industry, including academics, researchers, state/provincial governments, and industry practitioners. A broad composition enables the development of broadly based goals while recognizing their duty to the public (and safety) as paramount.

Alternatively, committees drawn from too small a cross section could allow more discrete corporate or advocacy interests to become entrenched in the standards. A narrow committee composition can harbor a restrictive perspective and give preference to a narrowed range of goals while devaluing the need to maintain a paramount duty to the public. Standards are intended to balance multiple issues, including safety, economics, and environmental and societal challenges. Each influencing factor can have a predominant or subservient role in the development of standards.

The provisions of standards represent the risk tolerance that the committee is willing to assign to the public, based on their defined threshold of acceptable safety. Public evaluation of the decisions represented in the standards is rarely seen as a judicial issue. In other words, the values of those individuals assembling the standards are taken as absolute, presumably considering their duty to the public as paramount. Variability in opinion and risk tolerance represented by the select individuals approving standards is rarely questioned. The public does not have an opportunity to weigh in on the standard of risk tolerance. As response times for traffic control signals demonstrates, this approach to design can leave a portion of the population unprotected by manuals written for industry practitioners.

Furthermore, it is almost impossible to test a committee's presumptions through the litigation process. Litigators tend to focus on whether the standards were appropriately applied. There is little interest in whether the standard itself was reasonable. The reasons for this are likely varied. Challenging the standard can be seen as divergent from the principal issues at hand (harm causation). In addition, challenging a standard can be an expensive, time-consuming activity involving the review of extensive source materials, committee documentation, correspondence, and more.

In geometric design, design manuals generally agree on issues related to horizontal and vertical alignment, roadway cross sections, intersections, interchanges, and more. These basic standards have been in place for a very long time and are used pretty much universally by road authorities. They are subject to review and reassessment from time to time, which sometimes results in minor changes. Still, a comparison of standards across jurisdictions will reveal their provisions are premised on differing assumptions, leading to differing standards for the same condition.

Forensic investigations therefore must examine the standards that were in force at the time of site construction. In one case that came across my desk around 2016, a property owner of a strip mall was sued for not having a barrier curb and bollards that may have prevented an errant vehicle from jumping the curb in a parking lot. The vehicle had entered a parking space fronting onto a sidewalk and then proceeded onto the sidewalk, resulting in catastrophically injuring a small boy. It was found that when the mall was constructed, the guidance offered to practitioners was to use only low-level curbs without bollards. An important standard of the day advised that the low-level curbs were less of a tripping hazard and therefore encouraged.

Today, barrier curbs may be considered more appropriate in stopping a vehicle, as they provide a bump for vehicles that advance too far into a parking space, thus restricting vehicle penetration of pedestrian areas. However, they are unlikely to prevent vehicular access to a sidewalk even at relatively low speed. Perhaps as a sign of the times, some locations now have supplementary fixed-in-place bollards for heightened security of people and property. However, they were not a standard of practice at the time of the mall construction or at the time of the incident.

The basic alignment standards have been found by the industry to function reasonably well over time, even if some drivers are excluded by the provisions of the manual, such as in the case of minimum driver eye height, or they do not consider a full range of hazards on the road, as in how object heights on vertical curves exclude the provision of small objects. Other standards may not be so comprehensive, whether by committee decision or missed consideration. Some standards can be unreasonably vague and subject to interpretation, providing greater latitude in the way users of the manual interpret the information.

For example, one winter maintenance regulation addresses the presence of ice and the depth of snow but provides no guidance on managing slippery conditions. This source can be used in forensic investigations to present differing opinions between plaintiffs and defendants in the interpretation of a need for winter maintenance. Even though less snow has fallen than some minimum limit requiring servicing, slippery conditions can prevail through compaction of small quantities of snow on the road. This compacted snow is a form of ice but is not recognized by the standard. It can take the form of what some refer to as "black ice,"[2] which is simply ice that is difficult for drivers to detect. The standard should have a reference to "slippery conditions," as that is when vehicles start sliding off the road. The absence of "slippery conditions" from the standard has likely spared the road authorities significant expense over time.

Consequently, a standard, guideline, or policy cannot be viewed as an unbiased presentation of information that considers a duty to the public (and safety) as paramount. However, examining these manuals in this context can be time-consuming and expensive. To fully assess the nature of the standard and determine who is appropriately served or not, it may well be necessary to examine the source documents. These documents would include:

- studies and research
- calculations
- meeting notes of committees
- related correspondence

The required depth of such information may not be available where the service is contracted and the contractor is not a party to the matter.

Geometric design standards offer only nominal safety in the construction of roadways and other infrastructure elements, such as bikeways. Since the standards are often not all-encompassing, additional resources may be necessary—in the form of manuals, guidelines, and regulations—to identify acceptable safety in transportation facilities. Also, external resources can impact facility development and operations and influence engineering judgment. Managing these facilities involves a balance of risk between the individual who may experience a major loss, acceptable safety, and the return on investment of the public or private corporation. Decisions related to how transportation facilities are constructed can often determine who assumes the risk of some collisions and who pays the costs under specific circumstances. While individuals may be excluded from the standards by their specific human factors, including response time and eye height, determining whether they were victimized by the standard can be difficult to impossible to resolve analytically.

No doubt our transportation facilities are serving the vast majority of the public's safety needs fairly well. However, some individuals may fall through the cracks due to design, operations, and maintenance at any point during the life cycle of a facility. Therefore, it is appropriate for those outside of the decision-making processes to have an opportunity to weigh in on whether standards for transportation systems provide acceptable safety for the public use, and, more specifically, those who may have been harmed. Litigation is one way to achieve this, while possibly having significant influence on engineering practice. This process is one of several that enable transportation systems providers to reconcile their concepts of acceptable safety with those of the larger public.

9.3 Engineered Services Under Municipal Control

The public sector provides a wide range of engineered products and services, including the design of transportation systems, water distribution systems, wastewater collection, structures, and more. Due to the technology and complexity of some of these services, their control, operation, and maintenance can fall within the framework of engineering services. These services relate primarily to the surface transportation system but may include the management and operation of transit services and solid waste collection. Engineered transportation facilities allow for the movement of goods and people via primary travel modes, including human-powered systems, motorized systems, and, more recently, a combination of both. Yet there is indeed a growing number of means by which people get around that all require accommodation. Guidance in how to handle these situations may be missing, resulting in fractured, ad hoc implementation between jurisdictions.

Yet there are growing demands for service in the rapidly changing and competing modes of motorized and active transportation services. For example, should a fast-moving electric scooter be used on the sidewalk, roadway, or in a bike lane? What design, operations (speed limits), and maintenance provisions are required to accommodate their use? There is great uncertainty about how to best serve the varied demand. In the absence of specific legislation, regulation, or standards of practice, the owners of transportation systems are left to their own opinions on how to provide for system users in a reasonably safe manner.

Consequently, both users and the owners of facilities continuously adapt when broad guidance is absent. For example, e-bikes, hoverboards, and scooters are capable of speeds of 40 km/h (25 mph). Owners see these vehicles as active transportation suitable for use on sidewalks and pathways, while using the roadway is viewed as hazardous. The perceived vulnerability of those using these transportation modes on the street therefore moves some motorized vehicles onto the sidewalk regardless of their suitability. Pedestrians become vulnerable. On the other hand, paths and sidewalks are determined to be too uncomfortable or unsuitable for slow-moving vehicles, such as motorized wheelchairs, and the roadway is preferred, despite their vulnerability in that location.

In dealing with these situations, system providers often lag in policy development and enforcement, which tends to reinforce the entitlements of the system users while allowing advocates to control much of the narrative about how system operators should manage their facilities to ensure public safety. These are difficult problems for road authorities because there is a logic to arguments pulling both ways. It is likely convenient to do nothing and to let the answers be provided on a case-by-case basis related to specific events. Whether or not judicial decisions apply on a system-wide basis can be a matter of the language and interpretation of the decision.

9.4 A Potential for Confounding Performance

In the field of engineering, responsibilities should not differ depending on whether the end product or service originates from the private or public sector. Both produce engineered or engineering-managed products, and the users of those products are susceptible to harm if they prove defective. However, there is a perception that the private sector is more prone to compromising on cost while the public sector is not. This notion is wrong. Experience has shown that even recently constructed facilities can have built-in design deficiencies arising from cost consciousness.

A case in point was the new Highway 407, providing service across north Toronto. This was Ontario's first toll road, providing a glimpse into the future of travel. Before the highway was opened in 1997, police noted several built-in hazards in a guided preview inspection. Some of the hazards were not encompassed by design standards. Also, several locations on the highway did not satisfy the design standards of the time.[3] On review by a panel of engineering practitioners and academics, the highway's opening was delayed while significant safety-related modifications were installed, including both physical and traffic control improvements.

A more recent example from 2022 is that of the pavement marking on a newly resurfaced roadway with a bicycle lane/cycle track. The bicycle facility is protected in advance of the right turn with a 30 cm (12 in.)

concrete barrier, which terminates quite close to an intersection with a left curve but continues on the far side. The pavement marking for the centerline followed the bicycle lane and pavement widening. As a result, the curve design radius was corrupted because the centerline now directs vehicles toward the barrier on the far side of the intersection. Autonomous vehicles following the painted curve require a significant steering input midway through the curve to avoid contact with the cycle track barrier. When a driver is manually steering a vehicle that is not under autonomous control, most drivers prefer to cross over the centerline on the near side of the intersection to properly follow the design curve, thus avoiding additional steering adjustments within the curve. While additional steering inputs may be fine on a dry pavement to avoid the barrier, there is a definite crash potential when the pavement is slippery.

Experience has shown that while good intentions may be present during a facilities' design phase, the constructed facility and its long-term operations and maintenance may not remain true to those intentions. In one example, the safety analysis of a recently completed redesign and roadway reconstruction program was circumvented when a hydro company subsequently placed its utility poles near the bottom of the substantial roadside ditch. The utility poles presented a hazard to drivers, as the area was intended to be clear of objects for errant vehicles departing the road. The ditch configuration would direct these vehicles toward the poles, as the slopes were nonrecoverable.

While the road authority was concerned about the presence of such hazards in the ditch area, the utility company was an independent corporation not under control of the road authority. The safe design and location of utility poles has been a component of roadside safety manuals for a very long time. However, this information does not always find its way into the design libraries of utility companies or the thought processes of those directing the installation of these roadside objects. In the event of a collision, extensive back-and-forth efforts can occur between the road authority and the utility company to assign blame.

In another example involving street lighting in an urban area at a freeway interchange with an arterial road, there were three levels of jurisdiction at play, including a private freeway operating authority and upper-tier and lower-tier municipal road authorities. Several streetlights were nonoperational at an interchange that included a direct on-ramp with a sidewalk crossing the ramp. A middle-aged pedestrian was killed one dark and drizzly night. The lower-tier road authority was outraged they were involved in the matter because they had no roadway in the area and therefore did not carry out regular inspections there. However, they were responsible under contract for replacing streetlights that were no longer working along the arterial road. A lack of administrative oversight in both municipal road authorities likely contributed to the absence of inspections. Of course, the pedestrian was blamed for stepping onto the roadway with a vehicle approaching. The pedestrian may well have stayed on the side of the road had they known the approaching vehicle would accelerate rapidly because the direct ramp onto the highway could be taken at 80 to 90 km/h (50 to 55 mph). The case was settled without going to trial.

In considering these issues, it is conceivable that everyone involved in these situations believes everyone else is competent at their job and further believes that everyone is doing their part to produce a product that is safe for public use. But all of those involved also appear to see a limit to their own responsibility and feel that someone else is responsible for making the connection between the design and its suitability for ongoing use by the public. It is possible that the utility company did not consider the roadway as their problem when they installed the poles or that the inspectors of the arterial roadway did not see the replacement of the lights as an upper-tier roadway responsibility. Both cases represent cracks in the fabric of road safety where people can end up harmed when oversight is lacking.

It is the author's view that these issues should be of significant concern to the transportation industry. As technical knowledge has expanded over the last twenty years, there seems to be a trend in which professionals are increasingly slotted into niche responsibilities. This trend can limit the experience of those advancing into senior positions where they may not have an appropriately broad perspective or the necessary knowledge to manage public safety. At the same time, the trend of promoting individuals based on nonmeritorious advancement may already be influencing some infrastructure, operations, and maintenance, thus impacting public safety.

9.5 Safety Inherent to Design and Operating Standards

There is a general conception, even among transportation engineers, that geometric design standards provide safe roads. To evaluate this concept, consider just three of the many elements of accepted design standards. First, the minimum height of a vehicle to assess visibility for the design of intersections near a hill is 1.3 m (4.3 ft.). Yet, several models of vehicles have a roofline below that height; a Mazda Miata, for instance, has a height of 1.24 m (4.07 ft.). With these vehicles, a driver eye height that satisfies the minimum may not be assured. The same is true for vehicle visibility requirements at intersections and driveways in hilly terrain that requires a vehicle height of 1.3 m (4.3 ft.). Similarly, the vertical curve standard does not consider the effect of headlight height, which may well not be visible over a hill after dark. Second, on crest vertical curves, drivers are provided with sufficient visibility distance to bring their vehicle to a stop in advance of an object 0.38 m (1.25 ft.) in height, the minimum height of a taillight.[4] In the US, an object height of 0.6 m (2 ft.) is used. The selection of this height is rationalized in the following manner.

> The selection of a 0.60-m object height was based on research indicating that objects with heights less than 0.60 m are seldom involved in crashes. Therefore, it is considered that an object 0.60 m in height is representative of the smallest object that

involves risk to drivers. An object height of 0.60 m is representative of the height of automobile headlights and taillights. Using object heights of less than 0.60 m for stopping sight distance calculations would result in longer crest vertical curves without a documented decrease in the frequency or severity of crashes. Object height of less than 0.60 m could substantially increase construction costs because additional excavation would be needed to provide the longer crest vertical curves. It is also doubtful that the driver's ability to perceive situations involving risk of collisions would be increased because recommended stopping sight distances for high-speed design are beyond most drivers' capabilities to detect objects less than 0.60 m in height.[5]

This rationalization has interesting terminology, which illustrates the extent to which system users may be incorporated into the standard. There is contention that objects of less height are seldom involved in crashes, that smaller objects do not impose a risk to motorists, and that accounting for smaller objects would substantively increase the cost of construction. It is also stated to be doubtful that drivers could perceive situations involving risk of colliding with smaller objects since the perception of risk at higher speeds is beyond most drivers' capabilities. While these attributes may be assigned to most drivers, it is clearly evident by the vagueness and uncertainty of the terminology that some drivers who could avoid collision with a lower object height are excluded from this standard.

Unfortunately, due to the nature of litigation, the standard would likely not play a role in the assessment of events where individuals experienced harm arising from the standard itself. Such would be the case where a driver swerved off the road to avoid an animal or slid off the road because of a snowdrift. Even the lower standard of 0.38 m (1.25 ft.) for vertical curves does not recognize the presence of lower hazards, such as small animals or ice, on a road surface. Yet other conditions within this same manual do require the pavement surface to be visible. Finally, approach sight distance to an intersection for a Stop condition is premised on an assumed approach speed to the Stop sign of 30 km/h (19 mph). On the other hand, if a sign is missing or visually obstructed, a speed reduction from the posted maximum speed limit is unlikely.

Therefore, these basic parameters of the design standards can exclude portions of the driving population (and their passengers). In the case of drivers purchasing low vehicles, the drivers will likely remain uninformed of their noncompliance with design standards. Even the very few who do become knowledgeable are unlikely to change their mind about purchasing such vehicles. After all, these vehicles are all approved for use on US and Canadian roadways, so there is no indiscretion in their purchase. Thus, designers are advised to provide more generous designs than the minimum limit values of the standards.

Flatter vertical curves are more costly to build. Securing sight lines may require additional lands and ongoing maintenance. Due to diminishing marginal returns on investment from including more of the population in design elements, there may be an economic benefit to the transportation authority to accept specific design elements and then hope for no collisions rather than to further invest in infrastructure safety. Yet the basic standards have been in use for many years, and road systems are generally deemed to provide acceptable safety, while transportation engineers allow for the potential for collisions to occur.

Manuals can therefore leave a portion of the user population exposed to some specific types of hazards. In doing so, the standards effectively prioritize an undefined cost point on the safety continuum over the engineer's paramount consideration of public welfare in road safety. This raises questions about the extent to which professional engineers' concept of welfare was meant to include trade-offs between individual safety and narrower interpretations of public welfare, which may include economic considerations. Therefore, it is reasonable to question design manuals and whether the associated infrastructure is consistent with generally held professional ethics where public welfare is considered paramount.

Such considerations involving the level of protection set by standards or manuals are typically not exposed in a public forum. The relationship between a collision and design or traffic control may not be readily apparent and is often overlooked, often because of the collision reporting systems. For example, an accident report will show a collision occurred because the driver lost control due to the road condition rather than because the driver could not see the low-level snowdrift or patch of ice in time to respond because the minimum standard was used for the crest curve. The relationship between safety and public welfare may easily remain undisclosed.

An example of problems that can be present in the standards relating to this circumstance is the manner by which manuals assess the condition of bumps. Warning signs are frequently used to inform drivers of potential hazards. Drivers are informed of potentially hazardous conditions ahead by traffic control devices including signs, signals, pavement markings, and delineators. As of 1982, the *Manual of Uniform Traffic Control Devices for Canada* (*MUTCDC*) indicated the following requirements for the installation of a Bump sign.[6] In 1988, the US Federal Highway Administration (FHWA) requirements for a Bump sign also stated these requirements:

The purpose of the BUMP AHEAD and BUMP signs is to give warning of a sharp change in the profile of the roadway that is sufficiently abrupt:

- to create a hazardous discomfort to passengers:
- to cause a shifting of cargo: or
- to deflect a vehicle from its intended course when the bump is crossed at speeds 25 percent higher than the normal driving speed . . .

As of March 2001, the *Ontario Traffic Manual, Book 6, Warning Signs* (*OTM*) continued to provide guidance to road authorities based on the provisions of the *MUTCDC* from twenty years earlier. However, there were some salient changes as set out in the following, which remained in place as of 2020:

- to deflect a vehicle from its intended course when the bump is crossed at the posted speed
- Drivers typically need to slow down to negotiate the bump in a safe and comfortable manner.[7]

The first change reduced the speed at which the bump would be able to deflect a vehicle from its intended path. Thus, the requirements were changed so that no sign would need to be provided for dangerous bumps for vehicles traveling at lower speeds. What this meant for drivers is that dangerous conditions could be present in areas with lower posted speeds, yet road authorities would not have to put up signs identifying their location. In considering the safety of the change, it must be acknowledged that it was a definitive move away from safety. In considering the effect on road authorities, it could be expected to reduce their liability exposure as well as their vigilance in detecting or repairing bumps. In this way, the committee approving the change reduced the safety previously inherent to traffic control, in the opinion of the author.

The second additional phrase in the standard is both interesting and confusing. It is unclear whether this is a message delivered to drivers or the road authority. For the road authority, it seems to frame a condition in which bumps are conditions on the road where a driver needs to slow down. However, the context is that drivers need to slow only when there is a likelihood that the bump will deflect a vehicle from its intended path. If there is no shift in cargo, discomfort to passengers, or deflection of a vehicle from its path, no sign is required.

This approach to sign placement contradicts the manual's underlying premise, which emphasizes positive guidance as a key element in addressing potential hazards rather than permitting the existence of actual hazards. Certainly, under slippery road conditions, this characteristic would present a significant danger to drivers who poorly adjust their driving to match the condition at the time of contact with the bump. As previously stated, as of 2001, the *OTM* also recognizes the problem with mishandled positive guidance as indicated in the following:

> Traffic control devices not only serve to structure expectancies, they tend to violate expectancies if misapplied, inconsistently applied, are absent when needed, present when unneeded and/ or ambiguous.[8]

Surely, allowing conditions on the highway that could cause a shift in cargo, discomfort to passengers, or a deflection in the vehicle's intended path for travel speeds near to the posted limit could be considered potentially hazardous at any time. In addition, the standard for bumps seems to remove any safety cushion since a great majority of drivers travel at speeds higher than the posted speed limit. Roadways are designed to accommodate that condition. The standard also fails to recognize the potential for snow or ice on the roadway. Thus, drivers are exposed to a hazard but not informed of it.

These same conditions can be present on roadway curves that are well signed with both advance warnings and degree of hazard—sharpness of curve indicated. By comparison, the Bump sign provisions run counter to the roadway safety provisions determined for curve warnings and the premise of positive guidance—and, arguably, common sense.

By 1995, global concerns for collision experiences were becoming more focused on the means to improve roadway safety, and by 2000, the FHWA had changed its approach to the provisions of Bump signs, moving to install such signs in the interest of road safety. The concept of positive guidance was well-known at the time, and the need to warn drivers of potentially hazardous conditions and provide adequate information sufficiently far in advance to allow successful performance had become mainstream knowledge. It is noted the FHWA provisions for a Bump sign were to remove the onerous restrictions indicating the following:

Section 2C.21 BUMP and DIP Signs (W8-1, W8-2)

Guidance: BUMP (W8-1) and DIP (W8-2) signs should be used to give warning of a sharp rise or depression in the profile of the road.

Option: These signs may be supplemented with an Advisory Speed plaque (see Section 2C.42).[9]

However, traffic control provisions for Bump signs in Ontario did not follow those in the US. On rural arterial roadways with a good ride quality, road users do not expect sudden changes in vehicle attitude. This expectancy is shaped through past experience in using these roads and their current experience of traveling the road they are currently on. If the ride quality is good and free from surface defects on a preceding section of the road, a driver expects to have a similar ride quality on other sections of the same road, unless warned of a change.

A discernible bump on the road can therefore constitute a surprise condition, and drivers may incorrectly react to the condition with too much or too little steering, braking, or acceleration—particularly under low-friction conditions. Upon being warned, drivers can exercise caution and alter their driving technique to match the expected road condition.

In review of the guidance provided to manual users, the use of the Bump sign is extremely restrictive, indicating that users must experience a hazardous discomfort—presumedly for a person of normal health. The Bump sign is different from other warning signs, such as those marking hazards on the roadside. Application of the Bump sign inherently requires drivers to respond by altering their normal routine by proceeding cautiously, possibly at a lower speed and/or getting a grip on the steering wheel.

Yet the broader premise of such manuals is to warn drivers of potential hazards. In this context, these manuals recognize that a hazard is any condition that may produce a collision when drivers do not respond successfully[10] and any location where extra caution may need to be applied.[11] Successful performance is dependent on the ability of drivers to identify a hazard, recognize its threat, and decide how to proceed,[12] all of which may be accomplished through signs.

Upon seeing some warning signs, such as hazard markers, a driver may not need to take any action. For others, drivers are provided with advance warning to prepare for the hazard and follow the instructions, for example, by gently turning the steering wheel for a Curve Warning sign. However, for a Bump sign, there must be a physical displacement of cargo or a feature that will deflect the course of a vehicle before the sign is required. Warning drivers so they may apply sufficient grip on the steering wheel to maintain a steady course through the bump would be consistent with other warning signs. On this basis, the provisions of the manual for a Bump sign are inconsistent with those of typical warning signs. One can only imagine the impact on collision experience if curve warning signs were posted only where cargo was required to shift at the posted speed. Still, a vehicle deflection in passing over a bump can occur under low-friction conditions when differential drag on the wheels of a vehicle may create wheel slip.

The preceding discussion illustrates how individual elements of some manuals can corrupt overall intentions or otherwise distort a common theme to provide signs that serve the needs of drivers rather than the road authority. In two separate cases involving a bump on rural roads, drivers lost control of their vehicles; one resulted in a fatality and the other in serious injury. In neither case was there a sign indicating that a bump was present.

In the first case, a confirmed errant driver was intentionally exceeding the speed limit while holding a can of pop. On hitting an unsigned bump—which was the result of subbase settlement creating a dip in the road surface—his vehicle slid off the road into a poorly designed ditch, resulting in severe injuries to his passenger. It was uncertain if the driver was moderately or excessively irresponsible. Regardless, had a sign been present, the driver would have had an opportunity to modify his behavior and proceed with caution to avoid collision. If the driver did not exercise caution upon seeing a sign, the matter would likely not have proceeded to trial.

In the other case, a railway had been abandoned on an upper-tier busy rural highway. On abandoning the line, the track and channels were left in place, but warning signals, pavement marking, and other information devices providing notice to drivers had been removed. This was done so that school buses would not have to stop at the dysfunctional crossing as a matter of law. However, over time, the elements left in the road deteriorated, creating a bump that had been repaired a couple of times before the collision. Testing of the highway for roughness prior to the collision showed that the location was the only one in need of repair over a 17 km (10 mi.) section length at the time of the collision. After dark one evening, during an intense snowfall, snow covered the area, obscuring the surface of the crossing and the bump that had formed.

Traffic on the roadway was moving well under the posted speed limit. Still, a small vehicle struck the hidden bump at the crossing and lost traction in its rear wheels, causing the vehicle to slide across the roadway and into the path of an oncoming heavy vehicle. In this case, the bump was hidden from view and the road conditions were less than ideal. Had the bump been repaired or drivers warned appropriately of its presence, the driver would have had an opportunity to adjust his driving accordingly, even though the bump may not have shifted cargo at the speed and time of the collision.

9.6 The Standards Held by Standards Committees

Current geometric design standards have been undergoing development for well over sixty years. Throughout that period, classical physics, preliminary studies, assumptions, analyses, and opinion were instrumental in allowing committees of design experts to provide design standards that would allow engineers to provide what they believed would be acceptable safety for roadways. Although information was sometimes inexact and further study was needed, the need for some benchmark level of performance could not wait. Public agencies adopted the standards, and the public generally seemed to accept they had been provided with acceptable safety. Over the years, the standards have been reviewed, reassessed, and expanded. While much has changed, many of the initial premises remain.

Like the driver, trained safety experts and design professionals are also subject to variation in opinion about what may constitute acceptable or unacceptable risk. Their opinions are supposedly better formulated by education, training, analyses, and experience. Individually or together, committee members are likely to have a range of experiences and individual biases that may find a way into a manual or guideline. For this reason, several aspects of the manuals may therefore be viewed as a consensus among engineers for imposing risk on some road users rather than a predetermined measure of road safety.

Decisions used to establish design, control, and maintenance manuals of today continue to be a composite of opinion, and in several instances may lack definitive data or policy statements indicating the level of safety provided. Even so, it may be held that standards generally achieve an acceptable level of safety for public roads. On the other hand, some individuals involved with road safety believe that road design may be a factor in many causal chains leading to collisions.[13]

Through this process, the standard for the provision of road safety has been determined solely by experts. The public has had little direct or indirect input to that process. In this regard, it can generally remain unknown to what level of public safety those developing standards collectively hold themselves and whether that level may be different from what public opinion deems acceptable. At the very least, experts' standards printed in manuals may be questioned because they exclude portions of the driving population. Although injuries resulting from deviations from the standards may be low, at the same time, the risk of injury arising from a facility constructed according to the standards is ever present. Even more relevant is the issue of whether the level of safety provided by the standards is sufficient in the context of the engineering mandate to consider public welfare (and safety) as paramount.

In my personal experience and opinion, the extent of concern for public safety represented in manuals is a function, to some extent, of the members sitting on the committee panel. Manuals formulated at the national level, by committees whose members are academics as well as practitioners, tend to gravitate toward higher standards of performance. Committees that are homogeneous in composition or dominated by special interests are less demanding of performance and more forgiving of the providers of the facility or service. In a similar vein, activities that require more human inputs, such as maintenance, also tend to be more demanding of the user and less demanding of the provider.

9.7 Beyond the Design Standards

Due to the inability of design, traffic control, and maintenance standards to encompass all possible circumstances, engineers must rely on other means to provide transportation facilities for a wide range of users. For example, some road design manuals have little or no content related to the design of bicycle or pedestrian facilities. With the intensified interest in cycling in recent years, engineers have had to reference other sources and to apply the principles of engineering in combination with professional judgment. In doing so, several practices—good and otherwise—have been developed and the related transportation facilities constructed. However, once again, the extent to which these practices satisfy public welfare may not have been tested.

An example of one practice in highway design is the tendency to diverge from the key design criteria respecting the design speed of the facility. The design speed, which is typically higher than the posted speed limit, is used to determine the visibility conditions available to drivers along the roadway while providing some forgiveness for drivers who inadvertently or intentionally exceed the posted speed limit. By dropping design speeds in specific locations on a facility, sight distances for stopping and collision avoidance are reduced. Where there is a hill located near a Stop-controlled intersection, the design speed for the hill may be reduced from that cited by the design criteria. In this instance, designers assume that all drivers will slow on approach to the intersection; therefore the posted speed limit is not changed.

However, Stop signs may be hidden by a hill, covered with snow accumulation, obscured by vegetation, or drivers may be delayed in detecting them under many reasonable circumstances. When this occurs, drivers are not provided with the same circumstances for stopping that is assumed by the overall design criteria. In another example, traffic engineers tend to accept that 85 percent of drivers are encompassed within the operational conditions of design and control elements. The results of this type of reasoning remain self-evident for the remaining 15 percent of drivers. In the assessment of collisions, it is reasonable that some individuals consistently (or occasionally) fall into this group of system users and thus are excluded from the protections offered to the other 85 percent.

While it is possible that these approaches to problem-solving in transportation engineering are consistent with a need to consider public welfare as paramount, the effects on some individuals may be catastrophic. To determine if such actions are satisfying the public demand for acceptable safety, it is appropriate for this type of reasoning to be tested through litigation. Thus, it is reasonable for the settlement cost of claims brought by those excluded from the design conditions to be accounted as part of the transportation system's life cycle operating cost.

9.8 Example of Regressive Standard and the Need for Forensics

Developing standards is a move to garner consistent performance of system users incorporating some threshold level of public safety. Those charged with the responsibility of determining standards almost invariably do so knowing the requirement for public safety. Over the years, changes to national and local standards are common. Changes are typically made because of thorough research and commiseration among learned individuals who have the public's best interest in mind. However, standards do not unequivocally hold public safety as paramount. Almost all transportation engineering standards provide some consideration to the interests of facility providers. In allowing this flexibility, a balance is presumably struck between the need for public safety and the needs of the travel authority.

However, the committees developing standards sometimes shift the balance in the direction of safety or in the direction of the owners' interests. This appears more likely when those in charge are less trained, are homogeneous in their makeup, and are without an appropriate range of stakeholders. Even so, once the committee approves the standards document, it becomes a standard for the industry. Challenging an established balance of public safety and owner preferences can be an expensive and arduous task. The opinion of the author is that such committees should include professional engineering associations as full and voting members, because their mandate is to ensure that public safety is paramount. In addition, committee composition may include eminent academics, other nonbenefiting stakeholders (such as insurers), and possibly some system users (such as automobile associations) if they are not adequately represented by others on the committee. In the absence of such participation, the author suggests that standards should be subject to public scrutiny through court proceedings or other proactive means for establishing acceptable public safety.

For many years, Ontario has established its own standards for traffic control devices and roadway maintenance via multiple volumes of the *OTM*.[14] Each volume is assembled through a committee of representatives from road authorities in the province. It would appear that as of 2012, the committee making changes to the standards in the traffic signals manual had fourteen members—five from the province and nine from municipalities. Five of the fourteen were licensed professional engineers—required to consider "public welfare as paramount"—but not identified as such on the committee list. The status of the others in this context remains unknown, and the workings of the committee remain unknown. It is left to the reader to determine the reasonableness of the actions of this committee in review of the following example, which follows the justification for installing traffic signals since 2007 and into the present day.

The traffic signal justification analyses used prior to 2007 were created at a time when the province contributed to the cost of installing traffic control signals. (At the time they were referred to as warrants in Canada and the US, but Ontario adopted the term "justification" in 2007. The US continued to reference warrant analyses.) As municipalities frequently requested the installation of signals, the province and other authorities used a threshold system encompassing traffic operations for an extended daytime period and a separate independently evaluated collision experience. The system could be used to deny signal installation as well as encourage it. As the warrant system was based on counted traffic, it examined the immediate need for signals rather than the longer-term need. While the specified requirements established a threshold for installation, it was (and remains) a standard of practice for routine justification but does not prevent the installation of signals based on other considerations.

The requirements reflect only the existing operating conditions evaluated through counting traffic at existing intersections. When all specified traffic volume thresholds are satisfied, the installation of signals is typically approved, although installation may not occur for some time. The original analyses used an eight-hour period for consideration, in which all eight hours had to satisfy a specific threshold of traffic volume. This procedure was widely used throughout the US and Canada, providing some consistency between authorities as to when traffic control signals were to be installed.

As traffic volumes on any highway can vary substantively during an eight-hour period, it has long been recognized that some intersections will not operate effectively for periods within the eight-hour envelope. In the 1980s, engineers forecasting traffic for new development determined the future need for traffic control signals premised on only four hours, and funding could be arranged for installation at a future time. Indeed, municipalities required this analysis as a condition of approval. However, the presence of pronounced peaking can occur almost anywhere in an existing network. The peaking of traffic volumes can be more severe at intersections serving land uses with pronounced arrivals and departures, such as those near industrial sites, parks and festival venues, or commuter parking facilities. Where traffic volumes exceed capacity for even short periods, drivers may become impatient and assume greater risk in completing traffic maneuvers.

In recognition of this phenomenon, the US Federal Highway Administration (FHWA) identified the need for signals based on shorter time periods—two peak hours and a four-hour period—in its requirements (warrant system). The standard was presented in the 1988 edition of the US *MUTCD*. Nineteen years later, the need for signals to service four-hour periods was recognized by Ontario but not the need for signals to service situations extending over shorter periods. The manual set out a four-hour requirement for use in the province.

The thresholds and text of the 2003 edition of the *MUTCD* (US) describing their four-hour warrant standard are functionally characteristic of that used in the 2007 edition of the *OTM, Book 12, Traffic*

Signals, regarding signals justification standard. The charts appearing in the US manual appear replicated in the 2007 Ontario manual. Its application was not discretionary, with the *OTM* indicating "the need for a traffic signal must be considered if an engineering study indicates" that conditions are satisfied for the four highest hours of an average day. As the requirements analyses were based on eight-hour counts from which the four-hour warrant could be quickly assessed, all such evaluations reflected a typical traffic engineering approach to the issue. Thus, there was no discretion in that the standard was clear, the data was inherently obtained in data collection, and analysis was required when other justifications were being evaluated.

As of 2012, the *OTM* had modified its text indicating that the Ministry of Transportation did not use the justification, and additional text was added to indicate that "some jurisdictions may consider the Justification applicable for limited specific situations."Thus, there was a significant divergence in the application of the previous and new manuals, making the application of the traffic peaking justifications a discretionary decision. This change also constituted a significant variation from the application of warrants elsewhere in the US and Canada, though the reason for the change is not discussed in the manual.

Removal of the justification as one of the four primary determinants for traffic signals allows the underlying operational issues prompting an examination to persist. Therefore, some locations can continue to be problematic for drivers or otherwise accumulate a greater collision experience due to the discretion the manual allows. In this way, the standard has shifted from recognizing a proactive industry standard and an acknowledged road authority responsibility to requiring accumulated harm before any action need be considered. That harm is evaluated in the *collision justification* for establishing the need for traffic signals.

As a side note, while the manual cites specific locations where the justification may be applicable, it is reasonable to conclude that any location satisfying the justification would benefit from the signal installation, not just those having the locational set specified. The results of making this change could have dramatic effects on provincial and municipal traffic operations, safety, and, perhaps most significantly, authority budgets.

The eight-hour vehicular volume justification is intended for application at locations with a high volume of traffic over a significant part of the day. The analysis curtails the impact to which brief, significant peaks in traffic can prompt the need for traffic signals, and traffic volumes in off-peak hours are key to satisfying the warrant. The four-hour vehicular volume justification is applicable where the operation of traffic on the minor street is the principal reason to consider installing signals. The factors leading to the need for an evaluation can encompass congestion, risk taking, delays, and queuing. Thus, signal installation is more likely to be recommended before collisions accumulate to the point where they would justify the need for a traffic signal. Signal installation based on shorter-period traffic volumes could be expected to prevent or limit the severe collisions applicable in the collision justification. Consequently, locations with significant peaking during a few hours of the day but that operate well at other times become candidates for signals.

Accepting the results of four-hour justification analyses can precipitate a need for signals at locations where they would not have been required based on the eight-hour justification. The effect is that the introduction of the four-hour justification to the warrant system could significantly increase the number of locations in need of signals, leading to ramifications for road authority responsibilities and spending. One means to avoid this fallout would be to not evaluate the warrant as a matter of discretion or formal policy in considering the need for signals. In effect, the discretionary use of the justification, as introduced in 2012, allows it to be excluded as a valid reason for signal installation, contrasting with the 2007 edition of the manual.

The full justification analysis is an important step in understanding the traffic operations occurring at any intersection because it evaluates the more intense operating conditions of the day. This information is key for decision-makers to exercise engineering judgment in whether to install signals or not. Thus, completion of the shorter-period justification is reasonable whenever other warrants are evaluated. Finally, the 2012 *OTM* does not even identify a need for traffic signals due to extreme hours or the two-hour peak hours of traffic operation during the day, as the US *MUTCD* does.

The 2012 edition of the manual expanded the limiting list of locations where the four-hour justification applies. However, evaluating the justification for *all locations* where traffic signals may be needed would allow its intended benefits to be realized across the entire service area. Evaluating the four-hour justification should not be limited by locational conditions. Therefore, it is appropriate to assess the justification as a matter of policy alongside the eight-hour justifications to provide decision-makers with a full range of information.

The justifications can also be used to deny "unwarranted" signals that have been requested by the public. Removal of the shorter-period justification from consideration increases the opportunity for denying the benefits attributed to signal installation. Alternatively, the justifications or previous warrants have never prevented the installation of signals where other factors may be considered, such as traffic operations during shorter periods; ease-of-access benefits for private development, municipal works yards, and commuter parking lots; visibility conditions; operational improvements; and engineering judgment.

The preceding discussion presents a rather obvious example of how some committees can alter the balance between road authority objectives and safety considerations of the traveling public. This ebb and flow in the provision of standards illustrates why forensic transportation engineers must consider both past and present versions of manuals.

The genesis of this transformation of the manual indicates a bias in which the frequency of traffic control signal installations can be reduced by the standards, enabling a potentially significant benefit to road authorities while moving away from proactive collision prevention. The bias moves to a threshold of accepting collisions at locations where a significant potential for collisions exists according to the traffic data. At the same time, the changes transfer the onerous burden of managing traffic operations at difficult intersections to the system users.

It is relevant to review these types of decisions in the context of the Professional Engineers Act and accompanying regulations. The engineering practitioner's code of ethics indicates that they should consider their duty to public welfare as paramount.[15] This terminology or similar is included as a directive in the legislation and/or code of ethics for many engineering associations provincially, as well as for national institutions, such as Engineering Canada and the National Society for Professional Engineers in the US. Several associations explicitly identify public safety along with public welfare, thus making it an integral part of the mandate to engineers and the transportation industry.

In Ontario, the definition of professional misconduct includes "failure to make reasonable provision for safeguarding of life, health or property."[16] Professional misconduct is more serious than breaching the code of ethics since a breach of the code of ethics alone—without other behavior meeting the definition of professional misconduct—cannot be referred to the Discipline Committee. Only allegations of professional misconduct or incompetence may be referred for discipline.

The Professional Engineers Act also establishes the principal object of the Association of Professional Engineers of Ontario as one to regulate the practice of professional engineering and to govern its members, holders of certificates of authorization, holders of temporary licenses, holders of provisional licenses, and holders of limited licenses in accordance with this act, the regulations, and the bylaws, in order that the public interest may be served and protected.[17] Thus, it is possible that an engineer on the committee supporting the *OTM* amendment as of 2012 may have been in breach of the code of ethics.

In the opinion of the author, the terminology change within the manual was a crucial shift in road authorities' required standards of care and a significant move away from safety. While the voting record of the committee is not available, the change leads to serious questions about the role of the committee members effecting the change. At least five of the committee members should have been opposed to the change, as it ran contrary to engineering ethics.

If the five engineers on the committee were opposed to the change, then the update in the manual came about because the committee structure did not support the pursuit of public welfare and safety. Either the votes cast or the composition of this committee was therefore instrumental in moving the standards of the industry away from safety. For this reason, it is appropriate to question whether the makeup of such committees responsible for public welfare can truly represent those interests and, more particularly, public safety.

A colleague suggested that the phrase indicating welfare as paramount may be interpreted less rigidly, which can certainly infer that there is more to consider than safety. Indeed, many transportation-related manuals have accepted the practice of balancing safety with other public welfare criteria, including financial, cultural, and environmental concerns. This is often done by survey methods and adopting conditions serving 85 percent of the population. Furthermore, many instances in manuals cite exceptions to overarching standards where the cited standard may be difficult or expensive to attain. However, such provisions pave the way to allow the exception to become the standard. The 2012 manual certainly paves the way for road authorities to abandon the four-hour justification.

In such cases, it is important to consider both sides of an issue. First, if the professional engineers had intended a more moderate interpretation of safety provisions as a subset of public welfare, the phrase should have been modified to "a high regard" or something similar. However, using only "a high regard" for safety would devalue the principle for practitioners and damage public confidence in all engineering matters. One can appreciate the public outcry if structural, chemical, or electrical design required only that public safety be held "in high regard." One might argue catastrophic failures resulting in significant injuries and/or loss of life due to engineering failures are completely unacceptable. Transportation design, operations, and maintenance typically do not expose the public to single-event catastrophic failures encompassing a high count of fatalities or injuries. Yet some may argue that the standards of the ground transportation systems may precisely allow that to happen one incident at a time but spread over vast geography and long periods of time.

Failures in traffic operations and maintenance elements can occur many times, in many ways, and in many places, resulting in a disconnect between the event and the systemic failure. Injuries and fatalities occur as isolated events and even rare events spanning decades and over thousands of kilometers of road sections and intersections. To use the vernacular, the catastrophic event in transportation facilities occurs by thousands of tiny cuts over the span of decades rather than a singular spectacular event. Consequently, in the absence of explicit assessment, it is not possible to suggest that a tempered interpretation of the phrase should be applied to transportation engineering. Therefore, engineering associations' standard to consider public welfare and safety as paramount must be upheld by the transportation industry.

COPING WITH HAZARDS

This chapter examines the nature of hazards associated with the roadway system. While the roadway system has been a principal focus over many years, readers should recognize it is just one of the several critical systems presenting hazards to travelers. Due to its central role in providing service to various travel modes as well as the frequency, severity, and often dramatic nature of mishaps, the methods for recognizing and dealing with hazards related to motorized vehicle travel is certainly the most well developed and exercised. On the other hand, hazards, whether new, emerging, or long-standing, exist across many travel systems, as exemplified by the more detailed discussion of sidewalk-related risks.

Providing facilities that promote the efficient movement of people and goods requires the explicit consideration of time and motion. And engineering premises and methods that are inherent to roadway systems, including design, operations, and maintenance, are also applicable to other modes, such as bicycle facilities. The design must accommodate actions required by participants, and the control system must tell them how to use it. All systems are subject to wear and tear over time that bring about the need for reevaluation. While this discussion focuses on the road system, the reader is encouraged to relate that discussion to whatever travel system they may have concerns about. For example, if in-service patrols or inspections are relevant to the road system, those same principles for hazard detection can be applied to sidewalks, bikeways, pathways, and more.

10.1 Identifying Hazards to Improve Road Safety

In the broadest sense, a hazard is any variant in the roadway condition in which drivers are required to perform certain actions to avoid collision. Many years ago, Olson and Dewar provided insight into the nature of a hazard in considering human factors:

> A hazard is an object, condition or situation that tends to produce an accident when drivers fail to perform successfully. Successful performance [to avoid the hazard] is dependent on the ability of a driver to detect the hazard, recognize the threat imposed, determine an appropriate action and finally act on that decision.[1]

This description is valuable. First, hazards need only have an enhanced tendency to produce collisions. Inferred is that a multitude of drivers may be able to successfully pass by the hazard without incident. There may be only an extremely small chance that the hazard will precipitate a collision with any one driver. Olson and Dewar place no limits on this tendency. The second inference is that successful performance is dependent on the time required to come to a reasonable decision and to execute that decision. Both conditions are highly relevant to winter weather events and maintenance.

As of 1982, the Institute of Transportation Engineers identified three categories of engineering studies to evaluate transportation safety:

- the before-the-fact preventive approach,
- the alternative approach, which seeks to reduce collision severity, and
- the after-the-fact approach.[2]

The latter has more recently been expanded to include the concept of network screening, in which a collision database is used to identify hazardous locations. An inherent issue with these types of analyses is that the collision experience at specific locations must often surpass some frequency threshold to be noticed. More explicitly, the location would have to be recognized as an outlier relative to comparable locations. That determination can take several years to develop. Even then, interpretation of the data may be required, leaving open the possibility of subjectivity in the assessment.

Focusing solely on the network screening approach in road safety engineering can create an imbalance in hazard detection, as obvious hazards may go undetected for extended periods if there is no incident attached to them. Network screening is a reactive evaluation method. Fatalities, injuries, and property damage must accumulate before an awareness of the hazards is developed. This approach to safety is often at odds with public expectations that hazards should be addressed *before* the harm occurs. The idea that harm thresholds must be met before taking action does not sit well in public discussions. In my community, politicians have used this notion to bypass technical assessments to determine when and where to implement safety improvements needed or not. Either way, network screening is used as a defense against claims but can contradict common sense in addressing specific hazards.

Some road authorities may prioritize network screening over more proactive means of identifying hazards within the system such as regular inspections. The network screening study is a clinical approach that relies on accumulated knowledge. This systemic method is capable of efficiently analyzing many locations, provided the data is accurate. The process requires no prior or intimate knowledge of the road system or potential hazards. With this approach, the transportation authority might claim a lack of prior knowledge about the conditions at locations where a serious collision occurred and where significant contributing infrastructure hazards were present. Finally, network screening requires no specific knowledge related to potential geometric design, traffic control, or maintenance conditions that may present a hazard to road users. Unfortunately, it often fails to identify some obvious hazards. This is especially the case for facilities serving a low number of recurrent users who may adapt to known risks. Problems can arise when new and unfamiliar users encounter these hazards.

For many years, the need to examine noncollision sites as part of systemic analysis has been encouraged. In developing a procedural guide to risk management, Datta recognized that roadway sections with severe defects but no recorded crash history may be as risky as other locations with recorded collisions.[3] In such locations, the rare or unique combination of hazard, road, human factors, and vehicle circumstances generating a collision event have simply not occurred. Therefore, the common expression related to a "collision waiting to happen" has engineering relevance.

The case of the open gate illustrates this point. A large municipal park was accessed by way of a gated service driveway for employee use. The gate was constructed using two steel pipes about 30 cm (12 in.) apart, oriented horizontally and joined at the ends. The very wide gate was a dark color and located in close proximity to an arterial road. From time to time, the gate would swing out onto the road when park staff failed to properly secure the gate upon their departure. When the gate was found to have swung out over the road, municipal staff would typically close it, but securing it remained a problem. Road patrols of the municipality had noted the problem previously, but no enduring repair was made and no effective protocol put in place to address the issue. It was only a matter of time before the right combination of events occurred, resulting in a fatal spearing of a driver who was not expecting an open gate and did not notice it in time to avoid collision.

Network screening could not have identified the hazard in advance, yet the gate was an obvious major road hazard to drivers, as noted by inspecting staff. It was fixed only after a fatality occurred. In this matter, a *sense of urgency* to effect the repair or protocol was missing, which allowed the hazard to intermittently exist for some time. Indeed, network screening would consider the location to be safe until the fatality occurred. Of course, the gate was an obvious hazard to every driver passing by when it had swung out over the road.

Accident prevention by seeking out road hazards has been implemented for a long time as an industry practice. The concepts identified in 1982 by the Institute of Transportation Engineers, whereby engineers conduct audits or reviews to identify situations that may contribute to collisions, are still being used today. The process is routinely completed during the design stage but is also pertinent for in-service facilities. Prior to the current audit and review processes being used, road authorities conducted assessments of roadway operating conditions in the field using design standards to identify deficiencies before upgrading facilities.

Proactive means for identifying hazardous locations have been developed and are widely used today. These approaches include the techniques involving positive guidance, which emerged in the early 1980s and are now supported by the traffic control manuals.[4] The road safety review (or audit) is a relatively inexpensive tool that can lower the risk to system users once the collision experience is noticed, or, alternatively, before collisions occur. This type of process was certainly enabled in 1994, when the Professional Engineers of Ontario indicated that safety problems could be identified through traffic safety reviews.

10.2 A Sense of Urgency in Dealing with Hazards

In transportation systems, collisions are infrequent events that occur with predictable frequency. The aftermath of such events falls to emergency services—police, paramedics, and so on—not the service providers, to manage the event and often the cleanup. Those responsible for operating transportation systems can often carry on with little or no connection between the routine operations of their system and the lurking hazards present.

The cause-and-effect relationship between managing the system and collisions arising from it can routinely be absent. The result can be losing a *sense of urgency* in attending to critical, emergent, transient, and even long-term hazards. On the other hand, the survivors of collisions may experience a lifetime of anguish involving mental, physical, and financial hardship due to this lack of action.

As indicated in the case of the gate, two circumstances are possible: In one, those responsible for the care of the facility did not assess the likelihood of the hazard to cause a collision. In the second, there can be a belief that their facilities are sufficiently safe without intervention to ensure acceptable performance.

Consider the situation in which personnel did not recognize the critical hazards of the gate. They may think: "Someone left the gate open, but it is not my problem" or "It is open now but not obstructing traffic, so I can leave it," as opposed to "Someone left the gate open, and unless dealt with now, someone may be injured." In not attending to the open gate, the potential for serious consequences arises when the hazard presented by an open gate is not properly evaluated, as in, "I will leave the gate unlatched since I am coming back this way in a little while and it is more convenient for me if I leave the gate unlatched until then." These types of rationalizations for nonperformance can be reinforced by blaming a presumedly inattentive driver. Blaming the driver enables those responsible for the gate to disassociate from the event. Cognitive dissonance kicks in, and a service provider believes they are not part of the cause of a serious collision event.

A lacking sense of urgency in dealing with seemingly innocuous hazards can prevail at any level in a bureaucracy, even among those whose primary responsibility is roadway safety. In one instance, an old rural roadway in hilly terrain was rehabilitated in the fall, while a directional dividing line (yellow line) was planned to be installed in the spring. This decision left an exposed hazard unattended for some time, which led to very serious consequences for several people.

The roadway passed through a series of crest and sag vertical curves. At the top of one such curve, the ditches were eliminated and the backslope brought in close to the pavement as the roadway passed through a cut section of one hillside (see Image 10.1). The roadway was not narrowed but was confined by the adjacent terrain. A lateral shift in the horizontal alignment at the top of the hill likely came about to reduce the extent of the cut at the hilltop. The unmarked road ahead would appear straight to a casual observer nearing the crest curve (see Image 10.2). The road was surface treated but left unmarked with no directional dividing line. The vertical curve at the hilltop was very short and not compliant with current standards.

Image 10.1: Crest vertical curve shown from a distance showing right curve in directional dividing line near the top. The directional dividing line was not present at the time of the collision. (Source : Gilchrist, July 9, 2009)

Image 10.2: Crest vertical curve shown on approach to the top with change in direction of roadway not visible. The directional dividing line was not present at the time of the collision. (Source: Gilchrist, July 9, 2009)

Two vehicles approached the top of the hill from opposite directions, with one encroaching in the other's lane as they neared the crest. The young person driving one of the vehicles swerved, resulting in a serious single-vehicle collision, injuring all four people in the vehicle. At trial, the road authority indicated that this roadway was added to the list for line painting to be completed in the next year. However, industry standards as set out in construction guidance and traffic control manuals indicated that the line markings were to be installed before opening the road to traffic. This lack of urgency in attending to a critical task resulted in the largest payout ever awarded to plaintiffs in the province.

In a third case, involving a lack of urgency in winter maintenance, there was an ongoing winter event of low snowfall intensity. Temperatures were cold with moderate to gusting winds, and a light snow continued after roadways in the area had been attended to early in the morning. Due to the cold temperatures and wind, the roadway servicing was short-lived because of the continued light snowfall and blowing snow later in the afternoon.

In town, roadways were partly snow-covered due to the movement of traffic and winds, and multiple witnesses indicated that rural roadways were slippery and treacherous. A collision occurred when a young lady entered a low-level but dense snowdrift shortly after leaving an urbanized area. In examining the winter servicing record, the vehicle operator responsible for servicing that roadway was found to have spent more than three hours that afternoon in the shop, ostensibly washing the vehicle. The lack of a sense of urgency in this matter cost the road authority millions in this single-vehicle collision, as the driver incurred catastrophic injuries.

In the above examples, a sense of urgency was missing on the part of the road authority in dealing with these hazards. The acceptance of risk in the presence of these hazards likely involved a belief there would be no consequences, such as collisions, and no financial impacts, so those responsible traded off the costs of dealing with the hazards in a timely manner with a loss of safety for road users. These circumstances were likely enabled by the *expectancies* of the involved staff who had put off fixing a problem in the past without consequences. Hence, a human factor widely known to affect drivers may also be present in road authority personnel. Road authority personnel may also conveniently but wrongly expect drivers to perform as a homogeneous population, assuming that if some drivers can cope with the hazardous situation without incident, all drivers will be able to.

Whatever the case, a lack of urgency in servicing the public need is simply one of rolling the dice and playing the odds that nothing will happen. It may work most of the time, but a time may come when it is necessary to pay up, and those consequences can be very expensive.

The absence of a sense of urgency can exist at any level in the hierarchy of authorities responsible for the operation and maintenance of transportation systems. Those responsible for prompt action are often disassociated from the consequences of failing to act. When operations are going well, complacency can also creep in at the management level, with respect to their need to identify potential hazards.

Now consider the case where there is a belief that their facilities are sufficiently safe without intervention to ensure acceptable performance. Some may assume there is little need to recognize the safety performance of the system under varying situations and conditions. A field supervisor in charge of winter maintenance may fail to call in equipment operators early, instead allowing them to come in at the usual time. A low-volume road may be deemed to require less maintenance than other roads within the system. Construction inspectors may allow hazards to be present since the construction activity will be completed in a short time. A supervising engineer may set aside a report rather than taking action on recommendations (see Section 2.1). To limit these types of occurrences, a sense of urgency in attending to hazards must be instilled in the organization from the top down. Furthermore, a system of checks and balances is required to ensure that individuals are fulfilling their responsibilities in an ongoing manner.

10.3 A Special Case: Children as a Traffic Hazard

In understanding the expected performance of young pedestrians, industry personnel recognize that the behavior and capability of child and adolescent pedestrians are different in important ways from that of adult pedestrians. The traffic engineering profession has recognized that children and adolescent pedestrians cannot be considered "small adults" regarding their behavior and skill sets as pedestrians. The following section uses several common references in the 1992 *Traffic Engineering Handbook* to identify expected behavior of children in traffic.[5]

To cross a road safely, a pedestrian must first look for oncoming traffic in both directions. If traffic is present, the pedestrian must then estimate the distance and speed of approaching vehicles to estimate arrival time. The pedestrian must then determine how long it will take to cross the road, then judge whether or not the gap in traffic is sufficient to permit a safe crossing. Research has shown that the ability to cross a road safely develops with age. With increasing age comes increased exposure to traffic, increased understanding of traffic's potential hazards, increased experience in making the required judgments about speed/time/distance, and increased exposure to traffic safety education.

A child's concept of safety is poorly formulated, and their schema for critical behaviors such as crossing the street are not well developed. Published research indicates that the pedestrian collision rate is a function of age. The five- to fourteen-year-old population represents the largest group of pedestrian accidents and "has over double the number of accidents of any other age group."[6]

The reasons for the relatively high accident rate among young pedestrians are varied. Avery found that a child prior to a certain age cannot adequately perform the human functions required to cross a road.[7] Similarly, Sandels examined the behaviors and cognitive capabilities of children and suggested that they reach the necessary degree of maturity for safe road crossing behavior between the ages of nine and twelve.[8] This is not to say that such skills are fully developed by age twelve. A study by Connelly and colleagues found that only some of the eleven- and twelve-year-old children tested were able to make safe decisions.[9]

It is also important to consider the speed with which the young pedestrian can perceive and react to potentially dangerous situations.[10] Visual reaction time decreases with increasing age in children by a factor of about three between the ages of four and seventeen.[11] Auditory reaction time is also slower for younger children. Attention spans are shorter for children and adolescents than for adults.

A related skill, which also develops with age, is the ability to scan the visual environment for information. Finding relevant information in a complex environment is difficult for many adults and even more so for most children. Difficulties with visual tasks for children appear to be a function of limitations in speed of eye movements, attention, and memory, rather than visual acuity.[12] A related limitation for children is that they are less able than adults to detect peripheral movement. Studies have shown that inadequate visual search is the most frequent error children make in assessing road crossing situations. Malek, Guyer, and Lescohier found that 39 percent of children did not search at all before crossing, and 60 percent did not see the vehicle that hit them.[13] Malek and colleagues also noted that the impulsiveness of children is a major problem leading to poor visual search behavior.

Reiss examined knowledge and perceptions of young pedestrians in a survey of 933 school students aged five to fourteen.[14] It was found that children's inclination toward "risk-taking (taking the shortest route, crossing in middle of the block, running across when there is a break in traffic, running into the road) increases with age." Boys are more likely than girls to think it is safer to run than to walk across the street when there is a break in traffic, and to indicate that when a child is struck "nothing happens to them." As compared to rural or suburban school children, more urban school children would "run out into the street if no cars were coming or if cars were moving slowly."

Zwahlen examines the difficulty children have with judging the distance of vehicles and found that children are far more variable in estimating distance than adults.[15] Zwahlen also found that children in the age group six to thirteen have not yet reached a high degree of consistency in making distance judgments. A study by Connelly and colleagues found the distance a vehicle needs to be away from a pedestrian crossing location to be considered safe to cross was judged by children to be constant regardless of vehicle approach speeds.[16]

Hoffman, Payne, and Prescott found that a child's ability to estimate the arrival time of oncoming vehicles improves with age.[17] However, even the oldest children tested—nine- to ten-year-olds—did not reach the level of performance of the eighteen- to twenty-five-year-old young adults who were tested.

The ability to accurately judge the size of objects independent of their distance from the observer is also known to develop with age as children learn to interpret different environmental cues. Young children have been shown to have relatively poor size constancy, suggesting that they could easily overestimate the distance of vehicles, which look relatively small when they are far away.

In addition to accurate distance perception, pedestrians must properly judge vehicle speed using auditory and visual cues. Salvatore, in a developmental study of speed perception, found that children rely more on auditory cues and vehicle size than visual cues.[18]

Pedestrians also often make assumptions about what drivers can see and do in a conflict situation. Children often believe that adults will always be kind to them, so they assume drivers will be able to stop instantly if a child is in danger. Their perception of driver behavior and cause and effect is not well developed.[19]

There is a tremendous amount of information related to children of all ages making the trip to school. Good information is typically available online from school boards and municipalities. In addition, extensive information is available from sources dealing specifically with children as well as many transportation agencies and institutions, such as the US Federal Highway Administration, Institute of Transportation Engineers, and Transportation Association of Canada.

In designing transportation facilities, engineers acknowledge a site's specific operational requirements. Further, traffic engineering recognizes a variety of user performance capabilities. For example, where there may be a high number of seniors crossing roads at signalized intersections, signal timing for pedestrian activity may be adjusted to accommodate slower walking speeds. Similarly, where there is known to be child or pedestrian activity, designers may specifically accommodate their needs or at least ensure that facilities provided for children's use comply with the policies of the road authority and the accepted standards for geometric design, traffic control, and operations, as well as maintenance requirements.

DISTRIBUTING THE COST OF NON-PERFORMANCE

11.1 Who Assumes the Cost of Collisions?

Road authorities often monitor the condition of their existing roadways to identify opportunities for improvement. This is typically done through annual capital facilities programming as well as road needs studies every few years. These programs are supported by routine and special initiatives to ensure that travel infrastructure is maintained to some threshold level of performance. Where deficiencies are found, road authorities have established methods to manage the deficiencies on a temporary basis until they can be fully addressed and removed.

These methods may include warning devices to inform users of hazards or rendering an element of the system out of service. In the case of roadways, partial or temporary remediation involving lower-cost physical improvements, along with traffic control device application, may be used to enhance safety for an extended period. Ultimately, complete reconstruction may be required.

All these efforts involve an expenditure of funds. To justify not proceeding immediately, especially where there is a safety issue, the transportation authority may reference an inability to cope with the great financial burden. Alternatively, they may argue that there is a diminishing marginal return on prospective safety enhancements and therefore some may be left uninstalled. Such assessments involve formal or intuitive cost-benefit analyses. Hence, safety enhancements may be considered but not constructed. The transportation authority is thereby able to reduce its construction, operating, or maintenance costs. However, in doing so, the hazards identified (or not) but not remediated could be expected to cause mishaps and injuries.

The cost savings from not installing specific infrastructure elements or undertaking specific action are a trade-off with the cost of mishaps arising from them. In delaying actions, the transportation authority simply passes this cost to users of the system in the form of harm incurred. On this basis, there is a rationale for including those collisions in the operating cost of the system since they were considered but then passed along to other parties. In other words, the payout arising from specific incidents can be enfolded in with other expenditures as part of the cost of doing business.

Unfortunately, the cost to the individuals experiencing a harm arising from such rationale can be substantial. In the absence of appropriate compensation by whatever means available, there is a transfer of a portion of the facility operating costs of the travel authority (for not installing features) to others, including individuals and both private and public institutions. Those transferred expenses are assumed by the involved parties, insurers, the police, health care, and the judicial system.

When judgments are levied against transportation authorities as a result of a harm incurred by the infrastructure, the cost of the judgment can far exceed the savings related to a design feature left out or a task left unfinished. In one city, inspections were terminated on certain local urban streets to save money and simplify the inspection process. All was fine until a sign that had been missing for several months contributed to a pedestrian collision. The settlement payout in that case would have paid for maintaining inspections for many years.

For those experiencing harm, the path to appropriate compensation can be an emotional one, as well as stressful, expensive, and time-consuming. Many opportunities present themselves for the effort to be terminated due to financial or technical constraints. Finding technically capable companies and engineers with the experience and background to properly investigate issues can be very expensive. Specifying the appropriate documentation with some precision may be required in both requesting and producing information. If this process is terminated at some point due to plaintiff constraints, the travel authority can assume significant savings.

In speaking with a state-level bureaucrat on one occasion, I was informed the agency had a three-step process for dealing with inquiries from outside sources, including the public. Step one was to blow them off using generalities and platitudes on the first contact and hope they would not return. The second step was to provide some generally available summary of information and hope they would not return. Only on the third step would they begin to pay attention. Of course, legal counsel can help to circumvent this protocol, but that requires an investment. With this type of protocol in place, it is simply "good business" for transportation authorities to oppose all actions against them, whether or not public welfare and safety are principal issues.

11.2 Facility Inspections and Road Safety

I have often been contacted by legal counsel requesting a list of questions for lawyers to use during the discovery of transportation personnel. Discovery involves asking defendant authority employees about what they know related to the scene of a collision before trial. In response, I prepared generic questions and identified specific types of documents that the travel authority may or should have in its possession. These included past studies, justifications, policies, procedural protocols, design documents, safety reviews, internal specifications for various elements, standards used by the authority, and more, according to the expected type of failure that may have occurred. I also supplied specific questions related to the incident itself, including information that could (or should) be available but might not be due to lapses in documenting procedures and recordkeeping. However, knowing what information is *not* available can be just as important as knowing what information is available, as it determines the authority's knowledge base at the time of the incident. The knowledge base includes what they did know or ought to have known as a transportation authority. With these questions in hand, legal counsel can decide for themselves which questions to pursue.

The American Association of State Highway and Transportation Officials (AASHTO) has stated that for maintenance programs to be effective, they must not only be considered during the design and construction phases but should also include inspections of the operational highway system. The primary purpose of inspections should be to ascertain the safety readiness of the roadway features and to alert responsible personnel to needed corrective actions. Inspections are also used to identify features that do not meet current standards, features that are no longer warranted, and problems that may warrant further attention.[1]

Ineffective inspection programs can transfer the cost of nonperformance to other parties as hazards remain undetected. Hence, there is always a tug between what the transportation authority should have known and acted on and what items they could not reasonably detect. In reviewing inspection standards, it is necessary to consider whether the travel authority imposed constraints on the standards or protocols, which may limit their acquired or documented knowledge. In this respect, items may intentionally or inadvertently be missing from the standards. Some hazards can remain for extended periods because inspection protocols do not identify them as such. This type of protocol allows the travel authority to have no knowledge of potential problems or defects. System users are at a disadvantage when elements necessary for good maintenance are missing due to limited inspection protocols or when standards for repair are set at a low bar for performance. Once again, these types of circumstances are appropriate for judicial assessment and commentary on behalf of public welfare and safety.

Road authorities have employed patrols for many years to inspect their roadways in all seasons. To ensure this task was undertaken in Ontario, the Municipal Act regulations of 2002 were established to mandate patrol inspections as long as the road authority adopted the regulation. The regulation established minimum limit standards for inspection, which could be biased in favor of either the facility user or the road authority, thus placing doubt on the effectiveness of this means to identify and report hazards. For example, if inspections are required only during daylight or normal working hours, nighttime hazards such as sign visibility or overnight frost accumulation can be missed.

Furthermore, patrol inspections can be limited by the extent of training, experience, regulatory environment, or inspection methods the patrol has. For example, the view of a driver of a large truck or pickup truck will be different from the lower view of the driver of a small vehicle. This can result in some hazards being determined insignificant or missed. Pedestrians and cyclists who use single-track vehicles are likely to encounter many hazards not relevant to dual-track vehicles. Further, effectiveness of the task depends on the comprehensiveness of the guiding documents. If safety-related matters are not included in the guiding document, policies move in the direction of providing more protection to road authorities. For example, the Ontario regulation does not include consideration of intersection sight lines and several perishable winter hazards.

As stated, road patrollers performing the inspection task can also lack specialized training in design, traffic control, and maintenance. Therefore, hazards not satisfying minimum limit standards may go unrecognized, and some elements could be ignored. Such is the case where inspections examine the road condition but do not specifically include bicycle facilities.

Hazardous conditions can also continue to exist simply because they were present before the current patrol personnel assumed their responsibilities. If a situation or condition went undisclosed by the previous patrol, then it can mistakenly be considered as not in need of repair. For example, on finding a commercial advertising sign obstructing sight lines, a new patrol is likely to notice the sign the first time they encounter it, but thereafter assume it is not a problem because the previous patrol did not deal with it. A patroller using a pickup truck may miss the sight line obstruction for smaller passenger vehicles. Furthermore, the gradual infringement of vegetation growth in obscuring sight lines occurs and may be repeatedly missed, being less distinctive as it develops over time. Nevertheless, the vegetation can present a visibility obstruction to the same degree as the commercial sign.

Some inspection manuals or regulations may provide guidance only on hazards of an obvious nature and relate only to routine maintenance. Hazardous conditions related to the geometric design or traffic control are not always as obvious, particularly where sight lines are involved. If there is any doubt, these conditions need to be verified via on-scene measurement conducted by knowledgeable personnel. To complete meaningful assessments, those individuals inspecting conditions need to place themselves in the position of the various facility users under the conditions experienced by those users, reflecting time of day, season, traffic flow, and more.

Perhaps most importantly, there is normal variation in the way system users will respond to situations or conditions. At issue is how much of the tails of a normal population are to be encompassed within the inspection program. For example, it can be expected that with vegetation creeping out to obscure signs, there will be an ever-growing number of drivers who will miss the sign.

11.3 Acceptable Safety for Transportation Facilities

Several terms are used to describe the extent of safety that transportation facilities provide. Manuals including standards and guidelines are typically believed to provide an abundance of safety when, in reality, they only provide nominal safety in determining the minimum limits for design and control elements. To that end, many manuals do promote the application of enhanced design, control elements, and maintenance to enhance safety, but because these elements are described using nonabsolute terminology, the recommendations can appear informal, not as a requirement.

However, providing transportation facilities involves a conglomeration of assembled elements from various sources of disciplines. Therefore, the adherence to safety as a paramount issue can become tenuous, especially when it is based on consensus where specific safety advice may be lacking. As new modes of transportation become mainstream, there is no absolute knowledge about how they will function or be used. This further complicates the issue of encompassing safety into standards, protocols, and policies.

Variant terms such as "acceptable safety" or "reasonable safety" have become common in transportation engineering, but their meaning can remain vague. Still, some practitioners may define acceptable safety as that provided by the design standards. Nonpractitioners can maintain a completely different view. With the proliferation of social media, the voice of one person or a few people can become the new narrative or the dominant public opinion and then be used to precipitate change, regardless of the reality.

Public officials are loath to stand up to such narratives, as they become pivot points in career management. In some cases, documented evidence that is contrary to the narrative can be unwanted, unappreciated, labeled as highly biased, or simply ignored by decision-makers if it creates conflict. Consequently, change can be initiated with little knowledge of the true safety-related impacts. As the knowledge of safety is not absolute and difficult to measure, decisions made in the name of safety are unlikely to be challenged regardless of the reality. Reasonableness in both the provision and use of facilities is often opinion and subject to bias accumulated over a lifetime of involvement. For example, drivers will travel at a speed at which they feel comfortable. In many jurisdictions, a driver's speed will typically exceed the legal speed limit by 10 to 15 km/h (6 to 9 mph) without fear of consequences. Such speeds are considered reasonable by users, while enforcement efforts imposing penalties for minor infractions of the speed limit are viewed as unreasonable predatory police actions. Observation suggests an ascending creep in the operating speeds of some roadways over time, possibly enabled by an absence of law enforcement. An absence of collision experiences individually or collectively suggests such a trend is considered reasonable by many drivers.

The design professional has traditionally been the first—but not the last—individual in a transportation authority to be concerned with unnecessary hazards in travel. Even so, there is no assurance that facility hazards or safety have been explicitly considered throughout the life cycle of transportation facilities. Designers simply assume the standards provide safe roads. Beyond the initial design, others involved in operations and maintenance activities can hold differing perspectives of safety and willingness to act, depending on the appearance or severity of hazards. Long-standing hazards left unchanged may not be explicitly considered by those recently hired to assume responsibility for safety matters. Thus, acceptable safety can become obscured over time as more people become involved with facility operation and where maintenance manuals offer less definitive direction than design and control manuals.

The overall collision experience on our roadways reveals the extent of safety current standards provide, combined with the operating and maintenance practices of the travel authorities. This is particularly relevant in determining the safety of specific facilities due to the overlapping nature of these activities. Under these conditions, identification of the extent of safety may be difficult to assess when only an overview of the collision experience is available. Some hazardous situations or conditions can exist for a long time without being reflected in a collision experience. This is particularly possible where the usage is low, in the case of low-volume roads, or where regular users of the facility have adjusted their performance to deal with the hazard.

However, those unfamiliar with the hazard may not assess the situation or condition in time for successful avoidance. In this context, the fact that many individuals may be exposed to a hazard over a long time without incident does not mean that reasonable safety is present. It only means that appropriate site conditions and use conditions have not come together due to the rarity of occurrence. Therefore, the transportation facility may still play a role in causing harm, and it is appropriate to examine any questionable or even all features of the site.

Transportation authorities are not the sole arbitrators of safety in the systems they operate. Many groups or individuals have an interest in defining *acceptable safety*. These include engineers, road safety professionals, politicians, the media, neighborhood and community associations, the legal community, the police, advocacy groups, and any other individuals. All have a different perception of the extent of safety, and they all maintain different views with respect to the extent of safety necessary. Furthermore, many individuals within these groups are drivers with vast experience using the road system. Thus, when they sense that some feature of the road or travel experience is unusual or has a problem, their sense of acceptable safety is activated. However, their description of the problem may be unfocused, confused, or unable to identify the real hazard. Forensic evaluation of any transportation facility conditions must therefore be sufficiently broad to identify and assess all hazards present but not reported by an individual group.

With this array of interest, we might expect that transportation facilities are subject to the scrutiny of safety at any time. In this operating environment, it can be worthwhile to inquire if a facility satisfied acceptable safety at the time and location a harm was incurred. The issue of acceptable safety may ultimately be determined by the judicial system on a location-specific basis. In that process, transportation professionals simply provide information and opinion from which those representing a broader segment of society may come to a finding about whether the location provided acceptable safety. When someone is harmed and acceptable safety is determined not to be present, an explicit or composite system hazard contributed to the harm in a meaningful way, even if the location provided nominal safety.

By their nature, transportation facilities for public use require applied science in their design, operation, and maintenance. However, the practice of transportation engineering extends beyond the physical attributes of facilities to also include human factors and socioeconomic considerations. Due to the complexity of these systems, explicit accommodation of all system users' needs, not only the needs of predominant users, must be encompassed within the life cycle of facility development and operations.

As established in codes of ethics, those providing engineering services for transportation facilities must consider public welfare as paramount. However, such vague terminology provides latitude for interpretation. Intuitively, one may expect that this direction to engineers may ensure a high standard of safety is entrenched in the design, operations, and facility maintenance. Almost all our built, operated, and maintained transportation facilities reflect this approach. Yet there is opportunity in the provision of public facilities to draw attention and funding away from those elements that effectively contribute to the safety of transportation systems.

Hence, when a user experiences harm, it must be expected that evaluations of acceptable safety may occur at any time over the life cycle of a facility. When this occurs, the concept of acceptable safety relevant to that time and place plays a crucial role in assigning damages.

MAINTENANCE ISSUES

By its nature, the maintenance of roadway and related systems can be much more challenging than the design and operations of these systems. Some authorities service a full scope of paved, urbanized streets, and freeways. Other authorities may have almost completely low-volume, unpaved roadways. Differences also appear in capabilities for generating revenue for maintenance, levels of training, and levels of resources to put to the task. Some authorities have a large dedicated professional staff, while others may have a single experienced supervisor directing a couple of employees who have little formal training. Some areas receive high accumulations of snow over the winter, while others receive none.

For these reasons, developing a single or a few maintenance manuals to be used by all jurisdictions is challenging. National or state/provincial standards tend to provide selective rather than comprehensive advice related to system features.

In the view of the author, the challenge of putting together a comprehensive standard that all can use has led to substantial variations in how maintenance is undertaken across jurisdictions. Many road authorities have had to find their own way. Even where a minimum limit standard has been developed, road authorities with high-volume, high-speed, multilane facilities can find their facilities demand more than the minimum for reasonably safe operating conditions. Likely for these reasons, the author has found a great amount of forensic analysis is directed toward maintenance issues. Therefore, much of this book examines maintenance issues and, in particular, winter maintenance issues.

Collisions occur because of a series of events encompassing the driver, the vehicle, the road, and the environment. If one of the elements is modified, the collision fails to occur or occurs with a different outcome.

Take, for example, the matter involving an irresponsible young driver who had just recovered his license after a suspension. He was driving his mother's vehicle with three passengers. He was traveling in a remote rural area well over the maximum speed limit in the early hours one fall morning, so there was little traffic on the roadways. For some "fun," the driver passed through several Stop-controlled intersections without slowing on one long, straight roadway. He came to a third Stop-controlled intersection on the same rural road where there was a low rise on approach, limiting his view beyond the Stop-controlled intersection. He ascended the grade to pass through the intersection, still at a high rate of speed. Unfortunately, on the other side, a ditch and cornfield brought him to an abrupt stop, and a passenger was severely injured in the collision.

In accordance with the sign manual, a large checkerboard sign was required on the opposite side of the crossroad. The positioning of the sign required it to be located directly in line with the errant driver's travel lane. No such sign was present. Post-collision, a sign was installed, which was visible from more than 1 km (0.6 mi.) away. While the driver was highly irresponsible, he had no knowledge that the road ended at the intersection. Had the sign been present, it would have disrupted the series of events, and there was a high probability to certainty that it would have changed his driving behavior, preventing the collision.

While the road authority was less than diligent by failing to provide the sign, it could be argued that the failure of the road authority was also simply irresponsibility in dealing with this situation as a maintenance issue. The location had undergone a multitude of maintenance inspections without detecting the missing sign. Like the driver who was trained in the driving task but failed to conform to the required performance threshold, the road authority staff are trained in their task to provide for reasonably safe travel by way of the signing manual but failed in their duty of reasonable performance.

12.1 Standards of Care

For roadway design, traffic control, and maintenance, standards of care are found in a variety of source documents and industry practices. Source documents may be issued by all levels of government as well as standards-issuing agencies such as government departments, quasi-government institutions, professional organizations, and interested agencies. The documents may consist of manuals identified as policies, standards, or guidelines for maintenance. In the provision of maintenance, there are also widely accepted industry or in-house practices that may not be found in manuals.

For example, one prominent practice that does not always appear in the advice or instructions offered by manuals is the need to actively monitor weather conditions. This should be done as a routine activity, but that is not always the case when not specified in a manual. Explicit practices in this regard should appear in manuals. Both specified and nonspecified activities such as routine or rules of thumb compose the standard of practice that the operators of transportation systems use for the maintenance of their facilities.

Other routine activities or rules of thumb may be widely practiced by individual road authorities. Yet these activities may also not find their way into any manual. One example, the concept of attempting to "melt" snow from the road using salt rather than by removing it using mechanical means, is a poor maintenance activity that was practiced despite knowledge of it as a poor and archaic method. Fortunately, this practice has been discontinued in most jurisdictions. To know whether or not such practices satisfy the currently accepted standards of the industry requires that maintenance personnel remain current in their training.

In the matter of designing roadways at all levels, there is almost universal uniformity in the acceptance of geometric design standards. While details may vary, the fundamental concepts are derived from science or research. Only rarely are the standards specified in these manuals incorporated into legislation or regulation. Such actions can restrict the flexibility of industry personnel in their application. However, maintenance standards and guidelines are not so uniformly applied.

Maintenance standards can have a fundamental premise of providing a defense against claims in addition to providing the service. To illustrate this, during the 1990s in Ontario, maintenance practice was guided by an organization of municipalities. The organization attempted to issue guidelines to establish some minimum uniformity in maintenance practices. However, the listed practices were viewed by some road authorities to be onerous, while claims against the authorities for their maintenance practices was a growing concern. In response, the municipalities convinced the province to regulate the minimum limit of maintenance as a means of defense against claims.[1] While one can respect the issue of claims as a key determinant of the protocols, a potential pitfall with providing a defense by this means is failing to ensure that the safety of the road users is adequately protected and that the legislation is not simply an exercise in constructing barriers to confound claims.

In this context, it must be shown that legislation has considered roadway safety in a substantive manner and not simply referenced safety as a catchphrase to encourage acceptance by the litigants. Substantive safety is founded on an identifiable and established relationship between the intensity or type of maintenance and collision experience. Only when the needs of road users are recognized and included within maintenance procedures can a balanced program be identified to create an acceptable standard of practice.

12.2 A Fundamental Service for Travel

Transportation facilities are intended to move people and goods with reasonable safety from one location to another. Facility maintenance is necessary to allow the elements of a facility to retain their design capabilities in serving system users. At the operational level, maintenance keeps trains on the rails, vehicles on the road, cyclists on their bicycles, and pedestrians on their sidewalk or path, as well as keeping all these users from bumping into one another. Maintenance keeps those who need to travel moving when they need to do so. An absence of maintenance allows features to deteriorate, resulting in lost productivity as well as a decline in personal well-being and the broader economic health of the community served. A host of information sources has specified the importance of maintaining transportation facilities, and one only has to spend a few minutes online to understand how important proper maintenance is for transportation facilities.

As stated previously, collision events arise because of the interaction of four active elements: the driver, the vehicle, the road, and the environment. The driver controls the vehicle based on their knowledge of the driving task, their recent and distant history of experience, and immediate information received while performing the driving tasks. The ability of drivers to anticipate the conditions they will encounter and relate those conditions to their driving experience will affect their ability to perform successfully. The vehicle responds to the control—acceleration, braking—and guidance—steering—inputs of the driver.

However, the vehicle's performance in responding to the driver's inputs is limited by the physical constraints and the roadway condition, including surface friction. The successful completion of a task is time dependent. The roadway condition is affected by the physical geometry, including grade, crossfall, and radius of curvature; environmental conditions such as temperature, wind, cloud cover, and precipitation; and the road authority's maintenance efforts. Roadway features related to alignment and cross section may allow vehicles to slide off the roadway during periods of low friction.

The road condition is not static, and infrastructure changes occur because of many influencing factors. Wear and tear, along with weather conditions, can affect the roadway surface, producing potholes and rutting. Intensity of use can accelerate or slow the polishing of pavement or snow coverings. Seasonal growth in vegetation can obscure important signs. Extreme winds and rain can blow away signs or wash out sections of roadway. Cold weather contributes to the breaking up of road surfaces or introduces a slippery pavement condition that drivers may be unaware of, as in the case of a transparent frost coating. High temperatures can buckle or burst pavements. All these elements can affect driver performance and produce catastrophic events if drivers are not able to detect such problems in a timely manner.

Due to the range of problems that can arise, the preparation of maintenance manuals can be complicated. While the design of roadways can be a one-time activity, maintaining roadways is an ongoing, ever-present problem. Furthermore, as changes can happen incrementally over a period of days, months, or years, it is much easier for those casually inspecting roadways to miss minor issues that then grow into significant hazards. To avoid this kind of misstep, vigilance and a *sense of urgency* is required.

For example, a pavement crack on a bicycle route may take several years to widen to the point where it entraps the cyclist's tire. Inspectors monitoring the crack may not do anything about it during the initial stages. When a change in inspectors occurs, the crack may be deemed as acceptable over time without explicit consideration.

In another example, a visibility triangle installed to ensure there are adequate sight lines across the corners of intersections may become overgrown and dysfunctional over time. It can take several years for vegetation growth to obstruct the sight lines, and the issue may remain undetected during seasons when the vegetation is not in leaf. Casual routine assessments are prone to miss this type of problem. Inspectors can even rationalize a tolerance for hazards or defects in the absence of a collision experience.

Maintenance activities can also induce roadway defects. In one instance, winter salting operations overlapped a pavement-to-gravel transition of the roadway, inducing a long section of potholes on the gravel section when the surface was thawed. The resulting washboard effect caused a loss of control and serious injuries in an ensuing crash by an unsuspecting driver.

All infrastructure maintenance requires an ongoing expenditure of funds. Funds are allocated annually for maintenance through the preparation of a budgeting process. However, for many years now, a recurrent theme among some maintenance personnel is that they are under pressure to do more with less, effectively blaming higher authority for things not getting done. Engineers and maintenance professionals are proud of their efficiencies in completing the maintenance task. However, when operations are efficient, reduced funding does not make sense and can lead to a decay in the safety of street operations.

These issues become more critical in the cases of seasonal variations or extreme weather. In temperate and northern climates, the onset of cooler weather combined with moisture in the air mass will certainly produce slippery roadways when they become covered or partially covered by ice and snow. Hence, the changing environmental conditions should alter drivers' expectancies with respect to vehicle operations and the roadway, but they may not. As part of the change in conditions, roadway friction is reduced from that of a typical wet pavement, which is the metric typically used for design purposes in determining horizontal and vertical alignment as well as some elements of traffic control. Thus, with reduced friction, design elements may not perform as intended. Furthermore, changes in driver expectancies are not adjusted by means of spontaneous insight. Driver assessment of the road condition takes time and can be delayed for an extended period if there are no defining triggers.

Weather that brings about reduced levels of friction is expected during the frost months. These events and the subsequent road conditions are highly predictable, with forecasts available to both the public and to road authorities by commercial weather services. Today's weather forecasting services can provide reliable predictions of coming frost, snow, and other forms of precipitation by time of day and for small subregions. National forecasts are routinely made available for locations encompassing two or three counties. This basic information can be supplemented by a wealth of local knowledge available to road authorities, attained through frequent travels by inspection and maintenance personnel on roads during the winter season. The combined knowledge and information acquired enables road authorities to anticipate road conditions with reasonable accuracy throughout their road networks.

Regardless of weather events, people and goods will be traveling at all times of the day. While the extent of travel may be curtailed by inclement weather, it is simply unrealistic to expect that travel or goods movements would be canceled or delayed until roadway conditions return to a "wet pavement" condition. The public and businesses expect winter maintenance operations to be responsive to the weather and environmental conditions. In this context, the winter maintenance of roadways is fundamental to maintaining economic activity.

Due to the predictability of weather events, road authorities may prepare for these events in advance with reasonable assurance. The road authority can then execute an action plan during and after the event, according to a schedule of activity.

As a task subject to the limitations of human decisions, the successful completion of winter maintenance, like the driving task, is dependent upon human performance. Due to the intensity and duration of winter events, road authorities may plan their operations ahead of time but must also adjust their operations to ongoing conditions. Thus, the task of providing winter maintenance is not straightforward. In this respect, winter maintenance is subject to errors in judgment, like the driving task can be. To cope with variations in weather, a flexible schedule of activity is required. To reduce the frequency of inappropriate decisions in winter maintenance, decision-making personnel must be properly trained in the task.

12.3 Maintenance Standards

Maintenance information tends to be specific to facilities or elements perhaps because development of a comprehensive manual is problematic. For example, the Transportation Association of Canada (TAC) has produced many standards on a wide range of subject matters but has never produced a general maintenance manual. On the other hand, it has produced some excellent materials related to generalized winter maintenance technologies.

The US Federal Highway Administration (FHWA) has produced a maintenance manual that is somewhat strategic in its presentation rather than setting out specifics. However, the FHWA has also produced some worthy publications dealing with specific elements of maintenance, such as gravel roads. It has also been found that various departments, institutions such as the Salt Institute, and private entities have produced some relevant materials. The generalized information these sources provide is often converted to an operational protocol at the local levels of maintenance provision. Still, some travel authorities whose primary focus is not the roadways, such as conservation authorities, have no manuals, are vague in their treatment of maintenance, or have ill-founded maintenance practices.

That is not to say that maintenance information is not readily available, and certainly some very good information may not be widely distributed. Some upper-tier road authorities have developed a good general maintenance manual for their staff and contractors. These manuals set out specific requirements for staff and actions to undertake with regard to roadway defects. However, defining specifications for repairing roadway elements may be missing, which leaves substantive discretion to the operations personnel on whether to act or not.

Acceptance of defining manuals by lower-tier road authorities tends to be constrained by the level of effort and cost implied by adhering to the manual. Beyond general purpose manuals, road authorities may produce and maintain several detailed manuals, such as ride quality specifications and pavement condition management, drifting snow management, pothole repair, gravel road maintenance, access management, and more.

Interestingly, some manuals have a life cycle that fades into the background as common elements become standard practice or as staff changes. Old versions of manuals can be discarded as updated manuals become available. Thus, ways and means for handling maintenance issues may be lost, resulting in limited knowledge or restricted capabilities among current maintenance providers. For this reason, finding manuals that may provide insight to maintenance issues at the time a harm is experienced is important. In some cases, manuals and practices have not been produced for trials by road authorities, possibly due to a lack of awareness by staff because the manuals have faded from current use as new employees are trained in the field.

In the absence of widely adopted standards, many travel authorities cobble together a set of standards they can apply in their maintenance practice. Some of the standards are well formulated, while others tend toward being self-serving. Such standards appear with limitations or caveats specifying related conditions that will be tolerated before or after maintenance operations are completed.

It is common in forensic engineering to simply indicate whether the threshold values of a standard were satisfied or not. Affirming the standard was met should not immediately translate to a finding of no contribution by the travel authority. Indeed, while system users may believe that an adequate standard of maintenance has been satisfied, those same standards may actually contribute to some harmful events. In some instances, it is appropriate to consider the implications of the standards' effects on both system users and facility owners. While some standards may appear comprehensive, this does not ensure that they provide a reasonably effective product for system users.

The following sections are intended to illuminate what the standards mean for those applying them and those experiencing the effects of their application. While the discussion focuses on one set of standards adopted through provincial regulation, it is hoped those who assess harmful events will consider other standards in a similar way to determine if system users are adequately accommodated.

12.4 A Threshold Maintenance Standard

Defining a threshold standard provides insight into whether a facility may be considered nominally or acceptably safe. It does not ensure absolute safety. Consequently, defining a benchmark or standard may be considered from two perspectives: the level of safety to be provided to system users and/or the level of maintenance to be provided by the authority.

While the former seeks to maintain system safety as paramount, the latter seeks to manage resource allocation. On the other hand, all standards set by national agencies or local institutions reflect collective preferences in defining a nominal level of safety, whether or not that level of safety is acceptable to the broader public. Many threshold standards in the design of roadways, traffic control, and roadway maintenance are based on engineering or learned judgment, reflecting imprecise knowledge derived from experience and available studies. While the extent of safety a standard provides may not be explicitly known, there may be a generally held belief that increasing or reducing a parameter's value will improve safety. Such is the case with maintenance. In addition, the extent of safety related to benchmarks is likely to be incremental in nature.

For example, increasing the grading frequency of rural gravel roadways will not make a roadway safe but will likely increase the safety due to the more frequent removal of potholes and washboard conditions. Further, it is well-known that standards providing performance benchmarks cannot envisage all conditions in the field. For this reason, in applying almost all—if not all—standards, experienced or informed judgment regarding public safety is needed.

12.5 Examination of a Defining Regulation (2002)

When reviewing legislation and regulation, government agencies formulate laws to meet their own needs, of which safety is one consideration. However, due to the nature of services offered by states, provinces, and local municipalities, certain common threads should run through these laws. Ontario's Municipal Act (OMA) in 2001 described the requirements of road authorities in maintaining roadways in their jurisdiction in the following manner:

Maintenance

44. (1) The municipality that has jurisdiction over a highway or bridge shall keep it in a state of repair that is reasonable in the circumstances, including the character and location of the highway or bridge. 2001, c. 25, s. 44 (1), v1.[2]

The definition of a highway includes all the lands between the property lines and thus includes all the services within the right of way provided by the municipality. Some legislative bodies have attempted to exclude the areas outside of the traveled way from critical maintenance issues by disallowing claims involving roadside hazards. Further, it may be argued there is a shared responsibility with utilities within the right of way and therefore the municipality does not have absolute control in some matters.

In one instance, a newly constructed roadway underwent a safety review, but the built facility had utility poles installed near the bottom of the ditch line in several locations. As such, errant vehicles entering the ditch would be directed into the utility poles. Upon inquiry, one engineer with the municipality indicated the utility company had installed the pole line post roadway construction and the municipality was not involved in establishing the location.

Despite its inherent vagueness, the above definition of maintenance was likely considered overly onerous by some travel authorities. To reduce their burden, legislators imposed several caveats, allowing for a defense in the event of some liability claims. An example appears below:

(3) Despite subsection (2), a municipality is not liable for failing to keep a highway or bridge in a reasonable state of repair if,

(a) it did not know and could not reasonably have been expected to have known about the state of repair of the highway or bridge;

(b) it took reasonable steps to prevent the default from arising; or

(c) at the time the cause of action arose, minimum standards established under subsection (4) applied to the highway or bridge and to the alleged default and those standards have been met. 2001, c. 25, s. 44 (3).[3]

This legislation was supplemented with a regulation providing Ontario's minimum standards for maintenance. As of November 2002, Regulation 239/02—Minimum Maintenance Standards (MMS)—was enacted.[4]

With the above reference to the repair of the road—although it could also relate to sidewalks, bike facilities, or other infrastructure elements— the character and location of the roadway or bridge must be considered. The character of the roadway or bridge includes the operating characteristics such as speed and traffic volume and other parameters arising from the design or traffic control. The location of the roadway or bridge considers the effects of an urban, suburban, or rural setting, in addition to surrounding terrain such as hills, valleys, or nearby bodies of water. For example, ice can form in shaded locations or on hills or bridges before other sections of the roadway.

Such provisions raise an important question: If the road authority did not know about a problem, *should* it have known? This issue can be complex, as any further assessment requires a knowledge of the inspection procedures inherent to the standards. The requirements for inspections reflect the extent to which road authorities preparing the manuals are willing to pay for a service related to the public good. Standards that favor the municipal budgets have reduced inspection frequency, restricted inspection times, or restricted inspection conditions, such as only during daylight hours. Standards that reflect a greater concern for public safety consider these issues within a more reasonable context.

The effectiveness of standards in serving the public good is a matter of public concern. Whether the protocols for maintenance have been adopted as a matter of public policy is relevant in forensic assessments, as those that are not made into policy under civil authority may be applied at the discretion of maintenance staff. In some jurisdictions, decisions related to protocols not adopted as policy are likely not considered actionable, while discretionary decisions are actionable. Even so, where the maintenance practice exceeds the direction provided by standards—whether policy or discretion—the road authority's actions are likely to be more defensible in both matters of litigation and in serving the public good.

This brings to light a question of whether the standards themselves are reasonable, particularly where they have been developed locally, and whether they have a foundation in broadly held maintenance practice. In my experience, the suitability of documented maintenance standards is rarely challenged even when they are poorly formulated. A challenge of that nature can be an expensive venture due to the amount of time and research required to expose the nature of vague or inane reasoning. However, road authorities can also be reluctant to have such information presented in a public forum and may well be inclined to avoid the cost of a challenge to their established routines.

In one case, I was asked by a plaintiff lawyer to evaluate the standards for winter maintenance. The assessment was extensive, and the findings presented many problems with the standards. The defense retained the services of an engineer to rebut my report. I then provided a rebuttal of the defense report, which was not only critical of the standards but also the means and methods presented. I was asked no questions pertaining to the actual standards. The discovery was abruptly terminated, and shortly thereafter the defense terminated its reliance on the standards, though the reasons were never specified.

The following sections discuss the provisions of the Minimum Maintenance Standards (MMS) from a perspective that considers their application.

12.6 Development of a Regulation

Prior to the development of the new MMS, a responsible roads organization had published their view of reasonable maintenance standards for municipalities to adhere to, if desired.[5] The ultimate value of the standards was to provide a common framework in practice and law for the delivery of service across jurisdictions. The initial version of the guide provided twenty-two service standards for roadway maintenance over all seasons. There was a specified minimum level of service while also detailing a desirable level of service. In the preamble, the guide provided some well-considered reasons for setting out minimum standards for maintaining municipal roadways.

In summary, the manual indicated that a common standard establishes a practical lower threshold for the provision of maintenance services across all municipalities. Also, road authority personnel can enjoy a feeling of fulfillment when the task is completed to a threshold that is better than required by the minimum. There is an inherent understanding the service is delivered according to an effective cost base. On inquiry, the public can be informed that strategic maintenance objectives have been met. At the same time, the road authority establishes a defense against liability claims. Finally, the public is more likely to acknowledge that servicing has realized acceptable safety requirements according to social expectancies.[6]

In the 1995 manual, substantial emphasis was placed on the relationship between roadway maintenance and litigation. Interestingly, identifying a social context suggests there can be an expectation by the public that is independent of the perspective of road authorities. In other words, the reference to a social context documents recognition that the public's concept of service and safety may not align with those of some service providers but is more likely to when there is a standard in place.

Thus, the nominal safety of a minimum standard cannot be automatically validated as acceptable safety, even by some road authorities. This is borne out by the guide's provision of desirable standards being more demanding and separate from the minimum. Some road authorities could set the desirable level of performance as their policy standard of care, thus providing some contingency relative to the minimums. This opens the door for testing differing levels of service and safety through litigation. It was an important issue with the municipalities at the time and one that continues to the present day, as shown by an extract from a posting on the road association's website:

Municipalities are often on the hook for extravagant financial payouts through lawsuits and settlements spurred by those who are injured on their roads—even if they bear very little responsibility for the incident.[7]

While road authorities see this as an unfair burden, in the opinion of the author, the position of the organization is a one-sided narrative. Of course, trial lawyers have a different perspective, whereby vulnerable people using travel facilities owned by municipalities should be reasonably protected from harm in using the facilities. Furthermore, some trial lawyers have pointed out that municipalities are provided with significant legislative protections not available to other types of defendants such as manufacturers. The Ontario Municipal Act (the Act) imposes several limitations related to procedural matters—shorter than typical periods for making a claim—and eligible infrastructure—municipalities are typically not liable for the roadside condition. At the same time, parties to the collision are not limited to municipalities and can include individuals, land owners, corporations, and government agencies. Limiting the liability of municipalities alone potentially shifts the burden for redress to other parties. Thus, releasing municipalities from this burden would set them apart from other parties while removing incentives to do the task well and opening the door for poor performance.

All provinces in Canada have joint and several rules in common law. In the US, there is a mix of joint and several liability, modified joint and several liability, and several liability alone. The modified variations limit liability in some cases, while some maintain exclusions for specific types of cases. In considering the payment of personal injuries for those engaged in travel, there is an aggregate amount required to satisfy those harmed. It would seem that the argument for or against joint and several liability is one of "who pays the bill." One can appreciate that those experiencing harm through no fault of their own should be made whole in some manner through litigation. If the courts fail to provide this, then the victims carry a grossly unfair financial burden, or else the funds must come from other sources.

While municipalities believe they can pay an unfair share, their involvement in litigation would seem to be rare when there are sufficient funds available through other parties, even when the infrastructure may have played a role. Indeed, some safety professionals believe that the roadway plays a role in most collisions. For example, the crossfall of the pavement for drainage directs vehicles off the road and toward the roadside when not countered with steering. While the cause of a collision may be assigned to inattention, the vehicle may well not have moved off the roadway to strike a pole had there been no crossfall. Yet, contributions of the infrastructure are unlikely to find their way into litigation due to regulatory restraints and the additional technical challenges. Municipalities may well experience a financial benefit in being absent from most litigation involving the right of way. Such an absence would also appear to be a function of some lawyers being reluctant to examine the infrastructure related to collision events—possibly because of the cost. There have been many times when I was asked to evaluate the infrastructure only as a last resort to secure appropriate funds necessary to satisfy the need of a harmed traveler.

In the assessment of liability, defining the contributory elements related to individual parties can be a daunting task and is likely to result in some parties believing they are unfairly burdened with financial settlements.

While this may seem unsympathetic, those providing any technical service, including infrastructure, have a liability exposure. Therefore, they should have risk management programs in place as part of the cost of doing business. Maintenance activities are included in road authorities' budgets and are subject to financial pressure when authorities push to reduce costs. Certainly, one means to reduce municipal expenditures is through limiting the quality of services while reducing the cost of outlay through litigation.

While the guide presented a thoughtful and effective policy for roadway maintenance, the municipalities appeared to desire more protection from claims through enacted regulation for maintenance practices. Also apparently, the guidelines were not as widely accepted as hoped; some authorities viewed several of the provisions as overly onerous and/or costly. Consequently, they worked with the province to develop a regulation determining threshold maintenance practices. The move to a regulation was initiated to determine minimum maintenance standards for all municipalities and as a means to circumvent litigation. As the standards were determined through a committee of municipal representatives, the initial standards were limited in scope. The development trail of the regulation is not available for public scrutiny, so the development process remains in a black box.

When issued, its writers did not insist that the regulation be adopted as municipal policy. Municipalities with their own documented practices could continue with those policies, while some municipalities were already providing services beyond the minimum standards. Even so, all municipalities could rely on the protections that the new standard provided. The regulation was enacted as the Minimum Maintenance Standards (MMS) of 2002.

By their nature, maintenance standards or regulations can be formulated in a way that provide substantial protection both to the public travelers and/or to the municipalities regarding liability claims. For this type of policy development, a committee of municipal representatives will often retain the services of a consulting firm to draft the initial standards, which the committee could then modify as appropriate. If the consultant is an engineering firm, they are held to consider public safety as paramount. One can argue that an engineering firm is required to put the package together, as roadway kinetics and kinematics are an important consideration in systems maintenance. The requirement of the committee in this regard is not as clear. To develop a broadly based public policy or regulation that ensures the public good, stakeholders are often asked to comment, although the committee usually determines the final product. Due to the nature of maintenance activities, engineering input is highly relevant.

The research materials and discussions of formulating the MMS of 2002 are not part of the public record. Therefore, depending on one's views, the balancing act of safety versus liability may be weighted toward public service or a liability defense, particularly in dealing with winter maintenance. In the case of the MMS, the regulation has been gradually advancing toward a more comprehensive level of maintenance since 2002. The regulation has gone through multiple revisions over the years that place additional burdens on the municipalities while improving service to the public. These changes appear to arise from the effects of litigation. Whether that is the case or not, the changes have shifted the regulation toward much-needed enhanced public safety, in the opinion of the author.

The MMS presented *outcome-based* maintenance standards. This approach established the condition of the roadway when the servicing or the repair was completed. The standards described the condition and provided a timeframe to get the task completed. The reasoning for taking this orientation is not apparent in the document. The following sections describe how the approach is applied and its effect on system users.

12.7 Roadway Classification

The 2002 MMS Regulation provides for maintenance based on a roadway classification system, set according to a table with ninety-eight combinations of traffic volume and statutory speed limit. Within that array, there are six roadway classifications. Roadway function—arterial, collector, local—was not included as a defining property. Roadways with the highest traffic volume and highest speeds were designated as Class 1 roadways. Those with the lowest speeds and lowest traffic volume were designated as Class 6 roadways. The classification of roadways is then used to identify the level of maintenance to be provided for all-seasons maintenance. The classification system for the 2002 MMS appears in the following table.

TABLE: CLASSIFICATION OF HIGHWAYS

Average Annual Daily Traffic (number of motor vehicles)	Posted or Statutory Speed Limit (kilometers per hour)						
	100	90	80	70	60	50	40
15,000 or more	1	1	1	2	2	2	2
12,000-14,999	1	1	1	2	2	3	3
10,000-11,999	1	1	2	2	3	3	3
8,000-9,999	1	1	2	3	3	3	3
6,000-7,999	1	2	2	3	3	3	3
5,000-5,999	1	2	2	3	3	3	3
4,000-4,999	1	2	3	3	3	3	4
3,000-3,999	1	2	3	3	3	4	4
2,000-2,999	1	2	3	3	4	4	4
1,000-1,999	1	3	3	3	4	4	5
500-999	1	3	4	4	4	4	5
200-499	1	3	4	4	5	5	5
50-199	1	3	4	5	5	5	5
0-49	1	3	6	6	6	6	6

Table 12.1: Revised statutes of Ontario for classification and maintenance of roadways. (Source: Ontario Regulation 239/02[8])

The traffic volume criteria for the classification system reflects a transportation engineering concept referred to as the Annual Average Daily

Traffic (AADT). Due to the temporal variation of traffic on roadways, this is an estimated quantity. For nonlocal roadways, traffic estimates are obtained by seasonally conducting traffic counts via automatic recording devices over several days. Due to land use and transportation system changes over time, the AADT changes year to year. It is therefore appropriate to identify the AADT with the year of data acquisition, for example, "AADT 2004."

Changes in traffic volume can result in the migration of roadways to different classes, although having six classes is likely to promote some stability regarding the designated class of a roadway. The migration of roadways between classifications is more likely to occur where the categories define small ranges of traffic volume rather than in areas undergoing land development that produces major changes in traffic volume. Thus, whenever maintenance is premised on a classification system this detailed, it is appropriate to regularly verify the classification of roadways in assessing maintenance performance.

The estimation of traffic for classification purposes can be problematic. While funding for count programs in larger urban and progressive jurisdictions may be available for their arterial roadways (and possibly collector roads), traffic on a local road system is rarely counted. Many rural municipalities lack any regular count programs and must estimate traffic volume. In some lower-tier road authorities or for local roadways, estimates of traffic may be derived from a single short-duration count or determined through speculation. In such cases, these traffic volumes cannot be referenced as an AADT. Thus, there can be uncertainty associated with the designated class of roadway. The classification of new or improved roadways, particularly in developing areas, can remain unknown for some time.

The decision to use a classification system for maintenance is an extension of the concepts used for roadway design. In design, the facility's geometry is set according to kinetics and the operational context. For example, roadways with higher speeds require larger radius curves to keep vehicles on the road. Pavement widths are set to service the volume of traffic and vehicle type. However, there is a significant divergence from that context in matters of maintenance. In maintenance servicing using classification systems, roadway classification is used to set the priority and intensity of service. Consequently, the classification system identifies which roads are more important from a servicing perspective. Those higher in the classification system are then designated to receive servicing first and more frequently, with possibly enhanced servicing technologies, such as in winter maintenance servicing.

The rationale for defining classification presumedly sets up a structured protocol to manage limited personnel and equipment. This is achieved by establishing a lag time to commence servicing on specific roadways while indirectly managing the potential frequency and severity of collisions due to maintenance issues. Collisions involving higher speed have more severe outcomes. Therefore, if these roadways are tended to first, the overall severity of collisions experienced in the system may be reduced. However, the approach also reflects a belief that roadways with greater traffic volumes are likely to have more numerous collisions.

Therefore, in the application of the table for prioritizing road servicing, by prioritizing facilities with higher speeds and higher traffic volumes, collision frequency and severity are presumably minimized. However, that result is wholly dependent on the number of personnel and quantity of equipment allocated to the task. Thus, the approach sets the framework for establishing maintenance levels in a manner that can minimize road authority expenditures. One notable outcome of this reasoning according to the table is that some roadways with high speeds (but lower traffic numbers) can be provided with lower levels of service than roadways with the same or higher speeds.

As of 2002, the classification system defined the required servicing of municipal roadways according to ninety-eight combinations of speed and volume[9] relative to the provincial classification system, which had only five combinations. Consequently, unlike the upper-tier system, the municipal system has a potential to yield significantly different servicing requirements for roadways with similar operational characteristics.

Limiting the combinations of speed and volume enables more consistent servicing for roadways over a wide range of traffic volumes while being less dependent on smaller variations in the speed limit.

However, in considering the speed issue, individual drivers traveling at 80 km/h (50 mph) and entering a curve on a roadway serving ten thousand vehicles per day or one thousand vehicles per day are likely to have similar probabilities in losing control on a roadway that is snow-covered regardless of the depth of snow. Thus, under similar driving conditions, all drivers have similar probabilities of losing control, but drivers traveling on lower-volume roads with higher speed limits are disadvantaged in terms of the servicing they encounter. For this reason, having more than one classification for roadways with the same operating speed does not consider the safety of the public as paramount but does consider the road authorities' resource limitations in servicing the public need. As such, these policies effectively limit the safety provided by roadway maintenance.

As of 2018, the classification of roadways set out in the MMS regulation had been modified substantively, adding several stratifications for roadways with more than fifteen thousand vehicles per day (vpd). With this change, several high-volume roadways had dropped out of the level 1 and 2 classifications into the levels 2 and 3 classifications. At the same time, key roadways having traffic volumes in the four thousand to eight thousand vpd range were dropped from level 3 to level 4. This change is significant because many minor arterial roadways and collector roadways have traffic volumes in this range. The maintenance requirements for these roadways drop significantly as a result of the change, and the number of roadways involved in the change is likely to be quite large. In total, nine of ninety-eight stratifications had their maintenance requirements lowered by way of regulation. In this way, the committee of municipal representatives in charge of establishing regulations moved the maintenance practice away from the direction of safety. Such measures have an aura of a self-serving bias.

With the trend toward making streets more active transportation friendly—more usable by pedestrians and cyclists—many municipalities are lowering speed limits on both urban and rural roadways. An interesting outcome from this is that lowering speeds on roadways can coincide with a drop in the roadways' classification ranking. Consequently, the road authority can anticipate a generalized reduction in their maintenance burden. This brings to light an ethical question about reducing speeds on some roadways where there is an absence of collision experience or where there is interaction between vulnerable road users and traffic. An ethical approach to this dilemma may be to keep the maintenance classification for the previous legal speed limit.

In addition, the large array of classification by speed and traffic volume in this standard complicates the ability to create rational maintenance routes for winter maintenance. Where servicing routes are determined by geographical location and independent of field conditions, there can be a combination of roadway classes on any one servicing route for equipment or road. To service these integrated routes and roads, it is necessary to adhere to the requirements of the higher-priority class. However, it can effectively diminish the servicing provided to the highest-priority class if roadways are improperly grouped for servicing. Consequently, combining roadway classifications on single routes for winter servicing can temper or reverse the intended effects of prioritization.

12.8 Application of the Standard

The following provides commentary related to the application section of the maintenance standard discussed in this section. Three phrases appearing in the regulation as of 2002 are examined in the following:

Application

2. (1) This Regulation sets out the minimum standards of repair for highways under municipal jurisdiction for the purpose of clause 44 (3) (c) of the Act. O. Reg. 288/03, s. 1.[10]

This section of the act identifies a need to recognize the location and character of the highway, meaning the classification system as set out encompasses only a portion of the requirements of the Act. The two parameters—speed and traffic volume—do not inherently recognize the character or location of the highway. For example, many serious personal injury and fatal collisions occur on low-volume rural roadways with speed limits of 80 km/h (50 mph) and typical vehicle operating speeds that are perhaps much higher. Using only two parameters does not recognize the situational or conditional effects that contribute to preferential icing near streams and hills or washouts on steep grades. The notion set forth in the Act identifying location as a consideration enables and possibly requires the migration of roadways to a higher-priority classification based on problem-causing roadway settings. However, in its current form, the standard does not recognize the importance of locational attributes of roadways as required by the Act.

> **(2)** The minimum standards of repair set out in this Regulation are applicable only in respect of motor vehicles using the highways. O. Reg. 239/02, s. 2 (2).[11]

This exclusion would appear to be directed at those on-roadway facilities designed and constructed for automobile use. It removes bike lanes separated from travel lanes by a lane edge line, cycle tracks, sidewalks, and multiuse pathways. With the advent of active transportation promoted to improve health and reduce energy consumption, there has been a dramatic increase in cycling that includes all-season commuting as well as recreational travel. In response, road authorities have constructed bicycle lanes and bikeways for use by cyclists as well as designating bicycle-friendly roadways. Travel speeds of cyclists can routinely exceed 30 km/h (19 mph), and in some circumstances can be well over 50 km/h (31 mph). With the advent of e-bikes, speeds of 30 km/h (19 mph) or above can be expected to become increasingly common.

The vulnerability of cyclists makes them more prone to crash and injury as roadway and bikeway surface conditions deteriorate. A bicycle is defined as a vehicle by the Highway Traffic Act. Yet this provision of the regulation seemingly allowed the road authority to abandon the maintenance of these travel facilities. Roadway defects such as pavement cracking, potholes, and depressions easily traversed by most motor vehicles can cause serious problems and crashes for cyclists and others. In view of the government encouraging the use of such facilities, excluding specific users from the protection of a standard is counter to the consideration of public safety in any form. However, it is friendly to municipal budgets and the related litigation defense fund.

In the case of bike paths and bikeways, these facilities are public rights of way providing transportation service. Whether or not they are considered roadways is perhaps an open issue in some jurisdictions. Traffic engineering requires that the design and traffic control of these facilities be consistent with that of roadways for motor vehicle use. This is common sense since bicycle facilities must accommodate rapid motion and human factors.

Finally, it is relevant to consider that where a municipality has bylaws requiring businesses and residents to remove snow and ice from adjoining public sidewalks and pathways, there is incentive for the municipality to maintain these facilities in all other locations, particularly those under municipal jurisdiction such as parks. Yet this transfer of public responsibilities to property owners seems to have almost universal acceptance.

In considering winter maintenance, the exclusion could allow road authorities to use commuter bike lanes for snow storage. The consequence of this is that, during the winter months, the bike lanes cannot be used for their designed purpose, and cyclists are either forced off the road or must operate in mixed traffic, contrary to the capital expenditure of constructing the bike facility in the first place. Pedestrians can experience similar conditions with snow-covered sidewalks. Such measures place these and other road users at risk and move the maintenance provisions away from safety.

Sixteen years after the original regulation was prepared, winter maintenance provisions for bike facilities and sidewalks were added (RSO. Reg. 239/02, amended May 2018). Still, the revisions have some interesting caveats. For instance, 2.5 to 10 cm (1 to 4 in.) of snow is allowed to remain on bicycle facilities. The reality of cycling is that just about any amount of snow on a bicycle facility presents a hazard to cyclists and thus the facility is unlikely to be used. Further, there is no provision for icing on bicycle facilities. Any amount of ice in areas where bicycles must turn presents a significant hazard.

As a last point, when a significant weather event is announced by the municipality, servicing needs only be done if deemed necessary. The use of the terminology requiring a "significant" event is important because it is open to argument and proactively establishes a defense should the travel authority experience a claim. Surely, these types of provisions pay lip service to these facilities in winter maintenance but are more about protecting the road authority from claims and reducing the winter maintenance budget than considering public safety as paramount.

There were also other significant exclusions in the regulation, such as the following:

(3) This Regulation does not apply to Class 6 highways. O. Reg. 239/02, s. 2 (3).[12]

Class 6 roadways have speeds of up to 80 km/h (50 mph) and traffic volumes of up to forty-nine vehicles per day. Roadways with speeds of up to 80 km/h (50 mph) and fifty vehicles per day are Class 4 roadways. Consequently, a difference of a single vehicle per day precipitates a substantial difference in the minimum maintenance required. In a similar context, roadways with volumes of forty-nine vehicles per day and a posted speed of 90 km/h (56 mph) have a Class 3 designation.

The concept of allowing a road authority to abandon the maintenance of public roads because they have a low traffic volume is irrational. By their nature, these roadways are likely to have a combination of poor geometrics and, in some cases, limited or neglected traffic control devices. Yet any of these roadways may be used from time to time by unsuspecting motorists who are unfamiliar with the road and may encounter defects without warning. At speeds of 50 to 80 km/h (30 to 50 mph), during the fall-to-winter transition season before roadways become impassable, the results of unexpectedly encountering a hazard or defect can be catastrophic.

While the preceding discussion focused on winter maintenance, the regulation applies to all-season maintenance. Whether traveling in the frost-prone months or not, there is always a possibility for road users to crash or become marooned because of roadway defects. For example, gravel roads and shoulders can experience washouts of the surface, fallen trees can obstruct passage, or heat-generated pavement heaves in warmer climates can suddenly appear. Low-volume roads need to be formally closed to public use if they are not maintained.

In the view of the author, these types of rationalizations for the provision of maintenance have no technical merit for support. The provisions are arbitrary and self-serving for road authorities. In the absence of a more rational classification system, attempts to establish appropriate classifications for specific roadways are compounded by uncertainty in the daily traffic estimations and open the door for bias toward lower classifications. A more reasoned approach would be to use only a few speed categories for classification, recognizing the commonly cited safety mantra that "speed kills." Alternatively, and perhaps more appropriately, the common engineering classifications of arterial, collector, and local roadways may be used for the allocation of equipment.

The very concept of having constructed a roadway for some purpose and then abandoning its maintenance because of low traffic volume is simply a rationalization based on cost or level of effort. The collision experience of roadways with low traffic volumes, which typically have less forgiving geometry and/or fewer signs, have been a concern to transportation professionals for many years.[13] However, the approach to the provision of maintenance of the regulation codifies the concept that where traffic volumes are sufficiently low, the road authority should have no exposure to liability for sections of roadway irrespective of the road condition. This type of provision moves the regulation in a direction away from safety. Where no maintenance is provided, rights of way should be closed to public use.

With these types of provisions for maintenance established within a regulation, it is difficult for the public to evaluate maintenance practice. Consequently, the public may have little knowledge of what to expect from transportation authorities in the maintenance of facilities made available for their use. In Ontario, claims against road authorities are heard in superior court by a judge alone. Further, while cases are open to the public, the public is not informed of these cases. Also, it has been the experience of the author that the defendant road authorities will move to have the public excluded from the court, thus further limiting potential public scrutiny of these types of problematic standards and the issues arising from them.

12.9 Facility Inspections and Road Safety

The American Association of State Highway and Transportation Officials (AASHTO) has stated that for maintenance programs to be effective, they must not be considered only during the design and construction phases but also during operation of the highway system. The primary purpose of inspections should be to ascertain the safety readiness of the roadway features and to alert responsible personnel to necessary corrective actions. More directly, inspections are used to identify features that do not meet current standards, features that are no longer warranted, and problems that may warrant further attention.[14]

Road authorities have employed the use of patrols for many years to inspect their roadways. Requirements for road patrols may be driven by rules of thumb, regulation, or policy. Regulations effectively establish minimum limit standards for inspection. However, the effectiveness of this means for identifying and reporting hazards can be limited by the extent of training, experience, regulatory environment, or inspection methods used by those managing the task or completing the inspections.

Hazards identified by patrols may be of an obvious nature and relate only to routine maintenance. However, hazardous conditions related to the geometric design, traffic control, or maintenance are not always as obvious, such as situations involving the long distances of sight lines. For example, during winter months, sight lines can be obstructed by snow windrows and stored snow. Roadway cracks or edge drops in bicycle facilities may grow over a period of months or years before they become a problem.

It is important that patrols be cognizant of the link between facility defects and injury-causing events on roadways, bicycle facilities, and sidewalks. A patrol sitting high in the cab of a single-unit truck may not see the problem experienced by the drivers of small cars or motorcycles or problems present in a bicycle lane. These drivers high up in a cab also have a different view of the road ahead compared to those lower down or to one side of a roadway. Still, patrollers must acquire knowledge of the potential for collisions to occur. For example, at intersections and driveways near hills, drivers who are unfamiliar with the location and have lower eye height could have difficulty properly assessing appropriate sight distance or sight lines. Similarly, during the winter, the drivers of some vehicles may not be able to see over top of stored snow at the side of the road. Individuals riding motorcycles or bicycles can be using the right side of the lane or a bike lane, which affects their visibility conditions.

While most drivers may properly assess a hazardous condition, some may not, most notably when there is a time constraint. *Capturing only one system user in a defect can be proof of the defect, regardless of the fact that thousands passed by without incident.* Such conditions need to be verified by on-scene observation and measurement by knowledgeable personnel.

To complete meaningful assessments, those inspecting conditions need to place themselves or at least think of themselves in the position of the various road users under the conditions drivers and others experience, reflecting time of day—light and dark—seasons, traffic flow, and more. Therefore, it is not reasonable to assume that digital monitoring via weather reports or looking out the window of an office can replace the need for inspections in the field.

For example, utility poles can be a particular problem. In one instance, an errant vehicle sheared off a hydro pole midblock. The utility company came out to repair the pole and put in place temporary conditions at the site of the pole without regard to the rest of the roadway. It took several hours to complete the repair. Meanwhile, the utility company repair work had darkened an intersection with traffic control signals, including the overhead intersection illumination. The road authority was notified of a power outage in the area but did not inspect the location, as it was some distance away from the location where the patroller was located when the call was received. During the outage, a serious collision occurred. Had there been an appropriate inspection and action, this collision likely would not have occurred.

The prospects of individual or shared responsibilities are likely best left as a legal issue, while it is sufficient to indicate that there may be several agencies in play. However, this example does point to a need for diligence and a sense of urgency in attending to potential problems, which requires that appropriate protocols and communications between agencies be established and utilized.

THE WINTER DRIVER

13.1 A Context

Literature examining collision experience during the frost-prone months reveals that collision frequencies are substantially higher relative to summer conditions. Much of this information has come from the review of routinely collected collision data showing seasonal variation. These statistics have been used to support efforts to improve winter maintenance practice and technologies while highlighting the need for new equipment technology and servicing methods. There have also been significant efforts in developing winter maintenance management systems and decision-making models.

However, little research has focused on the dilemma drivers encounter via hazards during the frost-prone months. These hazards may be continuous, as in the case of snow-covered roadways, or intermittent, as in the case of drifting snow or situational icing as occurs on bridges. Cues indicating the presence of hazards such as a slippery condition may be difficult to detect or not noticeable enough for drivers to see. Further, the mechanisms by which drivers cope with hazards of longer duration are largely undocumented.

In many collision reports prepared by responding police officers, the cause of the collision would seem self-apparent. Drivers simply ignore the reduced traction of roadways with frozen precipitation on them. While the cause and effect of winter collisions may seem readily apparent, the reports reveal little about why these collisions occur. Indeed, while great effort has been expended on improving the winter servicing technology, little research has been done regarding the dilemmas and uncertainties drivers contend with during winter weather conditions. Improved understanding of the driver experience by those who perform winter maintenance operations may assist road authorities in determining how to manage response time issues and the need for ongoing operations. Understanding both the roadway and driver needs are important in developing an effective winter maintenance program directed toward the safety of the road user and to encourage a sense of urgency and confidence in winter maintenance personnel.

13.2 Winter Collision Experience

The Transportation Association of Canada (TAC) has provided some basic information about the collision experience arising from winter weather events. Citing the work of several authors, the TAC Salt Management Guide reveals a long history of understanding in Canada considering the winter collision experience as of 1999. While the numbers may have changed somewhat since then, the basic message is just as valid today. Since this information has been known for such a long time, the winter maintenance industry should be well aware of the critical importance of winter servicing to drivers.

The following summarizes some of the information in the publication:

- Snow and ice on the road was a major causal factor in an average of 222 fatal and 11,837 injury accidents per year between 1990 and 1997.

- Snowfalls of 5–10 mm (0.2–0.4 in.) result in accident rates that are 3 to 5 times greater than under dry conditions.

- The risk of collisions is 25 to 35 times greater under icy road conditions relative to dry road conditions.

- An estimated 11 percent reduction in collisions may be expected when salting previously unsalted roads.

- An estimated 26 percent reduction in accidents may be observed when comparing salted versus unsalted roads.

- Salting has a greater effect on reducing the number of collisions on roads where the speed limit exceeds 70 km/h (43 mph).

- Salting reduces accidents more on roadways with poor horizontal geometrics than those with good horizontal geometrics.[1]

There is a general belief that drivers experience collisions far more in the frost-prone months than during the summer months. This is partially borne out by reported collision data. Examination of five years of data (2006 through 2010) reveals some important characteristics of the winter driving collision experience,[2] and this information is still relevant today.

The data shows the share of collisions during the four winter and the four summer months to be surprisingly close. The share of annual collisions during the four winter months (36.3 percent) was only 5 percentage points higher than during the four summer months (31.2 percent). Further, the share of fatal collisions was substantially lower during the four winter months (28.7 percent) relative to the summer months (39.5 percent). The data is suggestive of there being less energy involved in winter collisions, possibly because of lower travel speeds. This is also supported by the share of annual personal injuries occurring during the winter months (31 percent) relative to the summer months (35.8 percent). Of course, with fewer travelers and/or reduced travel distance during the winter, a portion of the nearly 5 percent difference was likely to be related to decreased exposure to travel facilities.

However, the trend was dramatically reversed in the case of property damage collisions, with the number of these being far greater during the winter months. There was a 7.7 percent increase in property damage collisions during the winter months (37.6 percent) relative to the summer months (29.9 percent). Property damage collisions represented, by far, the greatest number of collisions in both seasons.

The important takeaway from this information is that the five-year data shows that during the winter months, the *frequency* of collisions increased while the *severity* of collisions decreased. This would seem intuitively consistent with more slippery roads, resulting in more vehicles sliding off the road but at lower speeds and, therefore, softer landings.

Exposure is a measure of the amount of travel being undertaken. It is reflective of both the frequency of trip making and the distance traveled. Typically, exposure increases during the warmer months, when more of the population is on vacation and traveling. Including the effects of exposure would likely enhance the seasonal variation discussed previously. Further, the frequency of unreported collisions may be higher in the winter months, as drivers sliding off the road recover their vehicle without police involvement.

Finally, during the winter, roadways or most sections of roadways can be in good condition for long periods due to effective winter maintenance and good weather. This would be a bare and dry condition. Typically, only during winter weather events and for a relatively short post-event period is the winter driving experience a problem.

To put this into perspective, precipitation levels were compared for the four winter months and four summer months in four Ontario cities (Windsor, Hamilton, Kingston, and Ottawa). The information was assembled using the seasonal normal reporting of Environment Canada for the four cities.[3] The data was generally consistent for all four cities, showing that during the winter months, the four cities have approximately fourteen more days of very small amounts of precipitation than during the summer. Of the 121 days of the four winter months, precipitation is greater than 0.2 cm (0.08 in.) during about half of the days. While the number of days with only a small amount of precipitation during the winter months is significant, servicing may be required due to slippery conditions. Only eight days with significant snowfalls of more than 10 cm (4 in.) occurred during the winter.

The duration of winter precipitation events can extend from several minutes to several days depending on the location and nature of the event itself. For example, a frost-covered roadway may form anytime overnight and quickly disappear in the morning. A brief snow squall can place snow on the road that may quickly disappear with daytime heating or endure for several hours depending on temperature and sunlight conditions. The seasonal data also shows that major snowfall events where the plowing of all roadways may be necessary can occur relatively infrequently, especially where permitted accumulation thresholds in winter maintenance standards are set relatively high for some road classifications before plowing is required.

Depending upon one's interpretation, the weather data may suggest that the conditions enabling winter collisions are rather limited, which in part may explain why the share of winter collisions do not exceed that of the summer collisions by a greater amount. An alternative interpretation may be that the winter collision experience is surprisingly high, considering the limited number of enabling events arising from the weather.

Of course, this data applies only to the region in which these four cities are located. However, due to the importance of tracking events, there is typically a wealth of information available related to seasonal weather conditions. The information contained in the preceding discussion was assembled and examined relatively quickly. It can be useful for determining when to expect the first frost, when winter servicing needs to be ready to go and maintenance budgets estimated. For non-frost-prone months, the information can provide insights into the frequency and timing of extreme weather events such as dry spells, hurricanes, and heavy rain. For a better understanding of weather patterns, similar cross sections of normal weather conditions are likely to be available for any transportation authority (and forensic analysis) for any region on the continent. All one has to do is search for it.

13.3 Collision Inferences

In assessing the actions of drivers involved in winter collisions, there is a tendency for institutional reporting to focus blame on the driver. This information is tabulated in motor vehicle accident/collision reports. The reasoning is that if the driver lost control, they must have done something wrong or otherwise not adjusted to the winter conditions in an appropriate manner. This facet of collision reconstruction is heavily subject to hindsight interpretation and bias.

The process is also enabled by motor vehicle accident (MVA) reporting. The reports inherently point to winter driver error as proximate to the cause of the collision by the provision of checkboxes dealing with the driver's condition and actions. In considering the driver action, a common reference is that the driver was traveling too fast for conditions. A less direct but still accusatory statement is that the driver "lost control." The inference is that if drivers sufficiently reduce speed or otherwise exercise better performance, no loss of control would occur and, likewise, no collision. Thus, the errors of the driver are effectively recorded on the form, while the roadway servicing circumstances are not.

Most forms also have a checkbox indicating the driver was traveling normally, but this is typically reserved for the victims of at-fault drivers. I have not come across a situation in which a driver who was known to be exceeding the speed limit was considered to be driving normally, or, in other words, reasonably. But this is an important issue. If the operating speed of traffic is moving at or above the posted speed, maintaining pace with other traffic is a safety-conscious decision since speed differentials are a factor in many collisions. Whether a driver should maintain the pace of traffic or slow on encountering less-than-ideal conditions is not a clear-cut decision. However, the following sections provide some insight into reasonable or at least expected behaviors with winter conditions.

Of course, not all police officers simply complete the forms and carry on. A more complete description of conditions may be found in duty notes or in police reconstruction reports of *serious* collisions. Perhaps more so in recent years, there appears to be more extensive documentation in duty notes that summarize driving conditions prior to the collision event. Some reports are even critical of the winter maintenance activities.

Typically, police services identify only the road condition, whether slippery, icy, or snow-covered. The police do not identify issues with respect to roadway servicing. If the road condition was not bare and dry, it can inherently be the police position that it was the involved drivers' responsibility to identify the problem and modify their driving accordingly. Yet again, there is an assumption of driver error. On the other hand, there are several reasons why a normally skilled, normally alert, and normally prudent driver may lose control without committing a definable driver error—driving reasonably if not normally.

A few of these reasons are:

- On freeway trips, drivers can travel long distances without performing actions, such as light braking and minor steering corrections, that would alert them to changes in road surface conditions.

- The roadway surface condition changed suddenly because of isolated effects, such as altered servicing, landscape setting, and subtle changes in weather.

- A driver attempts to adjust to the road condition by undertaking a precautionary response such as braking, throttling, or steering but fails in the execution of the task due to weather.

- A driver's response to other traffic such as approaching vehicles or disabled vehicles.

- A driver inadvertently wanders outside of narrow vehicle paths or wheel tracks on a partially snow-covered roadway due to centerline visibility issues.
- Vehicle instability occurs as a result of wind conditions, wind gusts, or large passing vehicles.

In the first two situations, conditions change without the driver becoming aware of the change, and previously successful driver control actions result in a failure and loss of traction. In the last four situations, the driver attempts to do what is right for conditions, but a loss of control is the result of a minor over- or underestimation of available friction. The only difference between success and failure is a modest difference in the order of magnitude of the driver action.

The fact that the driver may not have known precisely how slippery conditions were or may have been attempting to determine the extent of slippery conditions may be considered irrelevant by some investigators in defining the proximate cause of collision. This information may be important to determining contributory elements and should be revealed during an investigation. On the other hand, the trauma of a collision can produce gaps in memory. Still, the forensic information is sometimes able to identify clues on this matter as part of collision reconstruction.

13.4 Trip Planning and Travel

In today's economic environment, travel is necessary at all times of the day. Many of these trips are nondiscretionary, such as travel to work, to acquire a needed service, or to transport goods. Other trips are discretionary, such as those related to personal business and recreation, and may be canceled during inclement weather. In either case, during winter events, those traveling have assigned a greater need to the benefits of the trip than to the risks and possibility of a failed experience based on perceived travel conditions and past successes (expectancies).

In balancing the risk of collision with the benefits, trips are likely made under an expectancy that roads will be (or should be) serviced within a reasonable time and that making a reasonably safe trip is possible during a winter weather event. Due to the nature of nondiscretionary travel, authorities may expect system users on all facilities throughout the day, even if there is some variation in volume from the norm. In undertaking nondiscretionary trips, those moving goods and providing services are likely to be somewhat inflexible in the time at which they can start or finish a trip. That same sense of urgency should be just as applicable to those servicing the roadways in order to keep them as safe as possible.

During the frost-prone months, decisions about whether to travel are likely considered to some extent before getting into a vehicle. These decisions relate to what may be known of the road condition, for example, using a bare driveway to decide. In some cases, a driver may consult weather data. Others may simply look out the window. These actions create expectancies about the trip rather than provide defining information for the decision. At the trip origin, frozen precipitation on the road may not be present or considered likely during a trip. On the other hand, frost-covered roadways may be encountered intermittently throughout a trip. Consideration of these possibilities and other travel risks may not be inherent to the original expectancies of system users. Road authorities cannot assume that drivers will universally consider how conditions may change, what hazards to expect, or where the winter hazard-prone locations may be.

Decisions related to planning for a trip are also likely to include expectancies such as consideration of successful experiences of making trips in good or poor weather. If the route has been traveled without incident in previous winter weather events, the driver will likely have less trepidation about completing the trip in spite of currently poor weather conditions. Other factors affecting the decision are likely to include familiarity with the route, the availability of alternatives and alterations once the trip has started, the expected delay because of congestion or potential incidents, the duration of postponements, and finally, the expected winter servicing of the roadways. If the outcome of these considerations is that the trip can be made with reasonable safety, drivers will likely make the trip.

The variability in these decision processes results in some drivers making the trip despite the weather event or expected winter servicing. Road authorities must therefore anticipate that travel will take place at all times of the day on any day of the week. Thus, standards that limit servicing days or times are not in the interests of the traveling public but rather favor employee schedules.

13.5 The Winter Driving Task

Traveling on a snow-covered roadway requires decisions related to both the control and guidance functions of the vehicle. The control functions relate to use of the steering wheel, throttle, and brakes. Manipulating these control devices typically takes precedence in the driving task. Guidance refers to the process of selecting a path and managing related decisions, while control focuses on adjusting vehicle spacing. Therefore, when traveling on a snow-covered road, drivers are making decisions in response to their visual and tactile senses related to speed selection and path. Changing road alignments, traffic control devices, and operating conditions, such as leading vehicles and approaching traffic, can prompt reevaluation of previous decisions made during the trip as new or emerging information becomes available. However, this type of reassessment takes time and may not be completed before encountering hazards, potentially leading to a mishap.

For example, when traveling on a bare, seemingly dry road and approaching a snowdrift, drivers will first receive visual information about the drift—detection. The next step is to determine the extent of the threat—identification. The decision must account for the size, shape, extent of road coverage, density, and more, leading to a prediction that the drift may cause a loss of control. This assessment takes time. The driver then determines a course of action—decision response—and finally, they take action—volition. Some drivers may react instinctively while others may not even initiate the process before encountering the hazard. Conditions can be exacerbated by lighting or visibility conditions, roadway geometry, and variability in roadway friction.

If a snowdrift is sufficiently visible far in advance, the driver may visually acquire a sense of the drift related to the depth of snow, the length along the road, and the path of other vehicles through the drift. Even so, the full extent of the hazard can remain unknown during the approach. The unassessed hazards on approach to a snowdrift could include the slipperiness of the road surface, the depth of snow, and the extent of hydrostatic drag in passing through it. While the driver may have some expectancies, these can only be fully assessed after entering the drift, since every drift can be different.

Further, a driver may exit the drift before important knowledge is acquired. The extent of that knowledge, or lack thereof, can be crucial to safe performance on encountering the next drift. Therefore, these conditions create uncertainty and a dilemma for drivers in determining speed and path selection. Such conditions can dramatically extend the response time for drivers, which can vary widely. The actions of drivers in leading vehicles of a platoon—a moving queue of vehicles or convoy—can affect the performance of those following, leading to success or failures in the driving task. Due to changing conditions, prior knowledge or successful performance in navigating previous drifts may not enable safe performance on encountering the next one since conditions can change.

A snowdrift is used in the preceding discussion because it is a clearly definable winter hazard. The same evaluative processes are likely to be present with other hazards, such as encountering an icy section of roadway that has been serviced or is experiencing intermittent whiteouts. These clearly definable hazards have a beginning and ending location.

However, the process is also applicable to less definable situations, such as driving on a partly snow-covered roadway or following the wheel tracks of previous vehicles. These situations are likely to provide few defining cues about the conditions, thus opening the door to a much longer period of assessment, misinterpretations of the information, and judgment errors. These considerations are important in determining whether an individual's actions were normal or reasonable and are also applicable to situations in warm and temperate climates when considering driver reactions to environmental hazards such as heavy rain, fog, dust, and more.

13.6 Driver Loss of Control Due to Frozen Moisture on the Road

In roadway design, the amount of friction assumed for vehicle operations is substantially less than what is typically available from most roadway surfaces. It is not uncommon for roadway design to assume a friction of 0.24 to 0.30 g—a dimensionless quantity but stated as a share of the force of gravity—for a wet pavement. On the other hand, roadway friction levels for dry pavements can be in the range of 0.70 g to more than 1.0 g. Consequently, the difference between what design assumes and what is typically available provides drivers with substantial latitude in driving performance without sliding off the road under normal operating conditions. Current and past driving experience provide latent expectancies for drivers about how much friction may be available and needed for normal driving tasks. Some drivers inevitably may have little knowledge or experience in how much friction is available during a winter weather event.

In the case of frozen moisture on the roadway, friction levels may be as low as 0.10 g for slippery conditions or as high as 0.40 g for some snow-covered roadway conditions. Available friction can therefore fall below the bounds used for design. Consequently, speed limit signs, which typically provide drivers with a benchmark for speed selection, may no longer be appropriate. Drivers must choose a speed according to some intrinsic assessment of a safe traveling speed.

Complicating matters, friction can vary according to winter servicing methods or roadway setting, and can change over relatively short periods or be different in different locations. Water draining across the roadway in shaded areas can offer wet pavement friction during the day while washing salt residue from the road. As the temperature drops or the salt concentration becomes more diluted, slippery/icy conditions can develop on an otherwise dry road. Further, drivers may encounter some conditions infrequently year over year, depending on the type of weather systems affecting an area or the extent of trip making by a driver. A driver's expectancies can be much less finely tuned to the amount of road friction available and required for vehicle operations when less frequent winter weather events are present.

13.7 More on Response Time

A design response time for drivers on approach to a hazardous condition can be as low as one second for traffic control devices or as long as 2.5 seconds for an emergency response to a single stimulus such as a stopped vehicle on the road. The American Association of State Highway and Transportation Administrators (AASHTO) points out that with more information to consider, drivers' response times can double.

In considering the response times of drivers to various conditions, AASHTO provided some consolidated insights, as of 2001:

- Drivers' reaction times increase as a function of decision complexity and the amount of information to be processed.

- The longer the reaction time, the greater the chance for error.

- With unexpected events, reaction times increase by 35 percent.

- A complex decision with several alternatives may take several seconds longer than a simple decision.

- Long processing times decrease the time available to attend to other tasks and increase the chance for error.[4]

Of course, these response times commence after detection. When conditions change gradually over a long distance, or otherwise in situations where changes in conditions are not noticed or expected, drivers can travel long distances without detection. Then, detection may occur only when a control or guidance maneuver is required, at which point it is too late.

In the case where a winter driver must select an appropriate speed and path, the decision is complex since at least two control devices must be manipulated, but the magnitude of response is to be determined as well. Where an initial cautious response does not provide the necessary effect, an adjustment or alternative control device must be used. These choices can extend the decision-processing time, and in some situations, by a considerable amount. A response involving unexpected conditions and six information bits may take 4.5 seconds for a typical driver. However, to encompass 85 percent of the driving population, as much as 8.0 seconds may be required.[5] Once again, the full extent of the hazard can remain unknown until a driver has entered the hazard area, which can be several hundred meters (yards) long in the case of a drift. At that time, there are several decisions for a driver to inherently or explicitly consider in attempting to manage speed and maintain directional control.

Several of these decisions, which are likely to be implicit rather than explicit, are:

- Should the driver slow or coast through the drift?
- If coasting, will it allow the vehicle to pass all the way through?
- Should braking or steering be done to test for slipperiness?
- If slowing by braking or coasting is to be done, what speed is appropriate?
- Is traction better in the wheel tracks or in the untracked snow beside the tracks?

- Will the depth of drift outside of the wheel track destabilize the vehicle motion?
- What speed is appropriate for any of these decisions/tasks?

Again, drivers must use both visual and tactile means to make a decision—evaluating, prioritizing, and acting on sensory data. The time requirement to complete these assessments/tasks occurs during a period when the driver is stressed and the opportunity for collision is enhanced due to the presence of hazards. Whether or not these decisions are made and executed successfully can be dependent on the time available.

Again, using the snowdrift example, a driver moving along at 50 km/h (30 mph) upon entering a snowdrift will travel about 28 m (92 ft.) in 2 seconds or 68 m (223 ft.) in 5 seconds. This range in time may be considered reasonable for some to respond, but at the same time, there is likely to be more opportunity to lose control and enhanced potential for collision. However, conditions may be poorly discernible due to lighting, windshield clarity, translucent ice and snow on the roadway, and more. Information related to decision sight distance situations can provide some insight here. These are situations that may be difficult to perceive or require complex reactions such as a speed, path, and/or direction change, resulting in much longer response times. The response times for these situations can be very long, up to 14 seconds or more for a complex situation on an urban roadway.

By the end of the response period, the loss of control may already have occurred. If the drift is visible beforehand, a driver may have sufficient visual information to select a correct course of action before arriving. If there is blowing snow or a vertical curve in the roadway surface, a driver may have little time to select a course of action before entering the drift.

The driver may need to alter their initial decision after entering a longitudinal drift if the results of the initial decision were poor. The driver would then reassess based on the new information. Within the drift, slowing from a speed of 60 km/h (37 mph) to 40 km/h (25 mph) by braking can take 2 seconds, while slowing by coasting can take as long as 11 seconds. Braking carries with it additional risks for loss of control. For larger drifts or snowy, slippery roads where the driver also needs to respond to wind conditions, a depth of snow cover, and wheel tracks through the drift, an extended response time may be expected. Drivers may take a relatively long time to adjust to any change in the roadway condition. Even then, drivers may continually reassess and make changes to their driving actions as they pass through a drift.

While the preceding discussion has used the example of a driver entering a snowdrift, there are many winter driving conditions where similar decision processes may be involved. These can include changing conditions at the beginning of a snowfall, traveling from a serviced to an unserviced area, traveling from an urban to a rural setting, turning onto a different roadway, and more. They can also include changing environmental conditions such as fog, rainfalls, whiteouts, and smoke.

13.8 Driver Response to Winter Conditions

The following identifies some of the available research from the turn of this century encompassing driver response to winter weather conditions. Research was conducted in Scandinavian countries in response to the development of new winter maintenance practices. Subsequent research in the US and Canada confirmed much of the earlier findings, summarized below. Older reference materials are relevant today because they state what has been available and known to the maintenance industry for a long time. This information can assist in establishing maintenance practices and a sense of urgency in operations.

As of 1997, Wallman and colleagues initiated research directed toward a winter road maintenance standard for Sweden, including an understanding of driver performance during winter conditions. Not surprisingly, they found a high proportion of crashes occur on wet, snowy roadways because of reduced friction and/or reduced visibility. Importantly, drivers are more likely to misjudge prevailing friction conditions during winter weather events.

In summarizing driver response to winter weather conditions, several performance-related human factors were noted:

- Driving speeds on winter roads vary widely.
- Drivers travel at 75 to 90 percent of their normal driving speed.
- To maintain stopping distances, drivers should be traveling at approximately 50 percent of normal driving speeds.
- Drivers have trouble judging friction levels, and the difficulties increase as the roadway becomes more slippery.[6]

Wallman found a wide variability in speed reduction for drivers responding to slippery winter road surface conditions based on a perceived appropriate or safe speed. We would expect that half of drivers would indicate that the adjusted average speed was too fast for conditions, while the other half would indicate the speed was slower than necessary. What one driver (or witness to collision) sees as too fast or too slow can be viewed as entirely inappropriate by another. In the preparation of collision reports, "too fast for conditions" is typically unchallenged since the collision is seen as proof of that.

Yet that is a subjective and conveniently unbounded threshold for the determination of cause. The errant driver may have been traveling along with other traffic, well within the speed range of the 85 percent of drivers the industry considers to make reasonable decisions. While half of drivers would likely assume the errant driver's speed was too fast for conditions, perhaps the errant driver simply undertook a corrective driving action, such as braking, with an unfortunate result. In essence, drivers have no benchmark guidance to identify an appropriate speed because the legal speed limit is set for different conditions, and snow-covered roads and/or slippery conditions are encountered relatively infrequently while offering a variety of traction capabilities.

Also, one observer's assessment of an individual's travel speed as being too fast may be expected to carry with it significant personal bias and not be representative of a suitable sample of drivers, particularly in response to collision events. It is important to consider the performance of most drivers at the time if a prudent, normally skilled driver is to be identified, not just the few involved parties. Consider a crash on a partly snow-covered road involving multiple drivers, while some other drivers were able to avoid the crash. About all that can be concluded from this is that one hapless driver lost traction at some time and in some place. That circumstance is just as likely as not to randomly occur with any driver performing a needed task. The crash may be reflective of a changing environmental or road condition producing either a precipitous or unintentional driver action. The errant driver may simply have been moving along with traffic at the time, at a speed that many drivers believed was sufficiently safe for conditions.

In 2001, Andrey and colleagues prepared a wide-ranging summary of the effects of significant weather events, including winter weather, on driving performance.

Several key findings of their review are:

- There is evidence that as a behavioral response to weather events, drivers make adjustments just before and during trips. Driver adjustments include increased concentration, alertness, and caution, manifested as increased following distance or greater care in turning/cornering maneuvers.

- Minor adjustments also dominate decisions by drivers during travel in storm events. Speed reduction is the primary adjustment, and estimates of the reduction vary substantially from 15 to 50 percent of usual driving speed during intense precipitation.

- Snow, drifting snow, and blowing snow can obscure the road conditions ahead while reduced contrast in the field of view makes viewing more difficult.

- Wind can make steering difficult. While passenger vehicles are less susceptible to lower wind speeds, wind can be problematic for vehicle handling in snowdrifts.

- Drivers are already stressed and wary of driving in poor conditions.[7]

Andrey and colleagues' research shows that drivers respond to winter weather conditions in a multitude of ways, only some of which may be visible to a casual observer. Minor adjustments, which include speed and path selection, dominate driver actions. The research also recognizes that drivers must consider and react to more than simply a slippery road condition. Drivers are less likely to be inattentive or distracted when facing winter conditions. Further, their commentary shows that drivers are dealing with multiple concerns and decisions during a trip. Blowing and drifting snow can obscure lane alignments as well as details of snow hazards that may be found on a roadway. Obscured hazards can include defining wheel tracks through a drift, the depth of snow within a drift, or even the road alignment. Additional hazards arise from making adjustments to path and speed selection at any time during a trip on snow-covered roads, whether traveling on tangent sections of roadway or through curves. A loss of traction may also occur due to wind gusts or large passing trucks.

Several researchers have examined the effects of winter weather on travel speeds. Norrman and colleagues concluded that drivers are not adept at adjusting the speed of their vehicle to the prevailing road conditions.[8] In examining snowfall impacts on a state highway system, the analysis of Qin and colleagues inferred that drivers may typically not slow sufficiently.[9] Kumar and Wang completed an assessment of the impacts of weather on highway operations, finding that drivers reduced operating speeds on rural highways only by a range of 10 to 18 km/h (6 to 11 mph) due to snow events.[10]

Olson and Dewar state that several problems can arise when driving in conditions of reduced visibility, including snow.

These include the following:

- Poor distance estimation
- Speed selection beyond available visibility
- Variation in speeds and headway
- Overresponse to variation in vehicle speeds
- Indecision in lane selection, vehicle speed selection
- Degraded depth perception and perception of details
- Reduced peripheral visual information leading to an underestimation of vehicle speed
- Increased response times to signs[11]

Principal among the above list are the items concerning speed selection. Drivers operate with uncertainty when encountering unusual conditions. In this regard, the dilemma of speed selection is likely not static.

In summarizing the above research, one may conclude that drivers are not well suited to driving during winter weather conditions. More specifically, there can be a significant disparity between the perception of risk and actual risk in the winter driving experience as shown by the wide variance and indecision drivers display in speed selection. On the other hand, the frequency of collisions during winter weather events continues to be rare relative to the total distance all vehicles travel. Therefore, drivers' subjective evaluation of the risks is likely appropriate—a high proportion of drivers successfully complete their trips during a winter weather event, and lower injury and fatality rates occur. Given these circumstances, it is not possible to define whether the drivers that fail in their assessment of conditions—collision or not—did so inadvertently or were willing to assume greater risk.

An important message for those responsible for winter maintenance operations is that drivers will overwhelmingly respond to winter weather conditions by driving at speeds that do not fully recognize the extent of reduced friction available. As the collision experience related to individual weather events is likely to be time dependent for drivers, a sense of urgency and a timely response to winter weather events by road authorities is important.

13.9 Travel Speed

The results of the more recent research regarding drivers' actions in slowing when encountering snow on the roadway is reasonably consistent with Wallman's older report. Most drivers will slow to speeds of 75 to 90 percent of their normal driving speeds. Yet the mean travel speed on roadways commonly exceeds the legal speed limit by 10 km/h (6 mph).[12] Studies have noted that 45 percent of drivers have exceeded the speed limit by 20 km/h (12 mph) in the last thirty days, while 35 percent of drivers have exceeded the speed limit by 10 km/h (6 mph) on residential streets.[13] As most automatic traffic counting programs collect speed data, calibration of this information can be tailored to specific locations.

In assuming a generous condition that the mean operating speed on the highway is consistent with the legal speed limit, a speed for a normally skilled, alert, and prudent driver may be identified. On snow-covered freeways with speed limits of 100 km/h (62 mph), speeds in excess of approximately 90 to 100 km/h (56 to 62 mph) would be considered imprudent, as illustrated by the actions of most drivers. Travel speeds of 75 to 90 km/h (47 to 56 mph) would be considered reasonably prudent. Speeds less than 75 km/h (47 mph) are more cautious than most drivers would consider.

These findings were generally borne out in the author's personal observations for selected highways on March 1, 2014. The posted speed limit was 100 km/h (60 mph). Over a two-hour period of driving on four- and six-lane freeways, there was light to moderate snow, with moderate winds producing a partly snow-covered to track-bare roadway condition. Traffic was light due to the location, the day of week, time, and weather conditions. The author was operating a vehicle at a steady speed—the control vehicle—and recording the passing and passed vehicles. While traveling at a running speed of 80 km/h (50 mph), the control vehicle was passed thirty-two times while passing only two vehicles itself. Traveling at a speed of 90 km/h (56 mph), the control vehicle was passed thirty-two times while passing only eight vehicles.

Thus, these observations support the research that most drivers do not slow sufficiently for snow-covered roadways. Indeed, most drivers would willingly operate at speeds considered imprudent for the road conditions, according to friction research. However, that is really no different from many, if not most, drivers exceeding the posted speed limit during good weather and dry or wet road conditions. Once again, since most drivers consider these speeds to be reasonably appropriate, the importance of a sense of urgency in maintaining roadways during the frost-prone months cannot be overstated.

13.10 Winter Tires

The use of all-season tires for winter driving conditions is common in many locations, particularly where there are infrequent snowfalls. The Traffic Injury Research Foundation reported that in 2008 (and again in 2011), only 43 percent of Ontario drivers used winter tires on their vehicle.[14] In this respect, the actions of a driver in Ontario using all-season tires are consistent with the actions of most drivers who may be considered normally skilled and prudent. Yet winter tires provide a significant benefit in areas with longer winters, when there are frequent storms and greater accumulations of snow. Still, one can appreciate that if the tire companies rate their tires as all-season tires with the M+S (mud and snow) designation, vehicle owners will be disinclined to pay extra for tires that can realistically benefit them for a few months of the year.

This brief discussion is important from two perspectives. The first is that most vehicle owners are considered reasonably prudent, reasonably skilled drivers. Whether or not they have snow tires on their vehicle is a discretionary decision. The simple fact that a vehicle does not have snow tires during a winter event does not point to abnormal or negligent behavior where a significant portion of the vehicle fleet of the area also does not have snow tires. The second point is that winter maintenance practice must recognize that vehicles will have variable capabilities in coping with snow, and a sense of urgency in maintaining winter roadways is of paramount importance.

13.11 Variable Environmental and Road Conditions

A loss of traction can occur due to braking, acceleration, or steering effort that demands more friction than what is available from the road surface. A loss of traction can also be caused by a specific road condition—snow depth, ice, slush, surface discontinuities, ponding water—or environmental effects—wind, large vehicles—or some combination of these. The reasons for the loss of control in a collision will frequently remain unidentified. The driver may have responded to a condition on the road or conditions ahead and undertaken a typical acceleration, braking, or steering action consistent with successful travel up to where the loss of control occurred. However, the same action proved unsuccessful due to a change in road condition, such as a somewhat more slippery road than previously encountered.

In traveling over longer distances in the absence of stop-and-go conditions, some drivers may not experience sufficient feedback from the roadway and vehicle to realize that conditions have changed. Road conditions may also change dramatically due to weather and/or roadway setting. As drivers can be expected to select a speed based on known conditions, speed selection may be premised on a false sense of the road condition. One such situation is the intermittent accumulation of transparent ice or frost in low-lying locations. When collision occurs in these circumstances, the contribution of the driver and roadway must both be considered, and roadway servicing can be expected to be a substantial issue.

13.12 When Collisions Occur

In considering the road surface condition where collisions occur, there is rarely information to indicate whether an errant driver evaluated the slipperiness of the road surface pre-collision. This information will typically come out as witness evidence and may well be affected by hindsight bias. Furthermore, road conditions can change dramatically over a short period. Scene information during winter crash events can be highly perishable according to temperature variation, lighting, daytime warming or evening cooling, wind in combination with terrain, and other setting characteristics.

Conditions appearing in police photographs may not adequately present the road conditions at the time of collision. Thus, it is necessary in examining some collisions to shift the timeline back from the time of police photography to the time of the collision. Activity in the collision scene photographs can provide clues. Footsteps in the snow, snowfall accumulation on debris, or snow present underneath involved and uninvolved vehicles stopped at the scene all provide insights to conditions at the time of the collision and will help to indicate the nature of changes that have occurred since the collision. Furthermore, the rest position of the vehicle can be a substantial distance from where the loss of control occurred or where a driver detected the hazard. It must be considered whether the loss of control occurred at a more hazardous location or time than was found elsewhere during the day due to the roadway setting, environmental conditions, or even road servicing. Roadway setting in particular can reveal much related to the contributory elements.

13.13 Uncertainty in Speed Selection

As previously stated, during winter weather events, a usual benchmark that drivers may use to set their performance is the legal speed limit. However, this is likely to be a poor reference since it is associated with dry road or damp conditions. In the presence of significantly less roadway friction due to liquid or frozen moisture on the roadway, drivers appear to be generally aware that slowing is necessary to manage the risk of travel. However, without a reliable benchmark, they are left to their own interpretation of an appropriate speed, and studies have shown a wide variation in opinion. Therefore, witness information providing an opinion related to speed must be considered with significant caution.

The speed individuals choose during a winter event is likely the result of an intuitive assessment or at least partially based on the speed other drivers select. As noted by Andrey and colleagues, there is an uncertainty associated with any speed or path selection. Consequently, drivers likely make ongoing adjustments to speed in response to the road condition, or, alternatively, to the choices that are made by other drivers around them. The results are a wider variation in speed than may otherwise be apparent and the likelihood of more conflicts between drivers than may otherwise be observed. This leads to an ongoing dilemma related to whether the driver should modify their performance or not.

13.14 Winter Maintenance Implications

A loss of control can arise from several sources related to the vehicle-roadway interaction. Indeed, in the event of collision, the driver is likely to remain unaware of what guidance or control activity may have precipitated the loss of control, if any did. As such, the driver may have done nothing different at the time the loss of control occurred compared to their actions at other times during the trip under similar conditions. Alternatively, the driver may have performed as other drivers who successfully completed their trip. This being the case, driver error cannot be assumed central to the cause of individual collisions during winter weather events.

In considering the implication for road authorities, the issue of response time is a human factor that is not likely to change. However, some aspects of performance may be modified over time, such as that of speed selection during poor weather. Changes may be brought about by awareness and educational programs. Still, driver changes to better manage winter conditions may be slow at the start of the season and progress thereafter from learned experiences over the winter.

Collision rates in Canada have been moderating for many years. The trend is likely to be a reflection of many factors, including education, vehicle technology, roadway safety, and more. Whether or not a portion of the trend may be attributed to winter maintenance is not as clear. Even so, effective winter maintenance operations have been shown to reduce the collision experience arising from winter weather events.[15]

The ongoing technology development trends in servicing will likely provide improvement to the collision experience. Still, winter servicing must recognize the performance capabilities and fallacies as well as the collective behaviors of drivers when encountering the roadway hazards of the frost-prone months. The timeliness of responding to winter weather events is likely to be a key contributor to an effective servicing program.

13.15 The Takeaway for Travel Authorities

Upon experiencing winter weather conditions, drivers are required to make many choices related to speed and path, often in the absence of usual benchmarks and under conditions that may be difficult to detect. The roadway or operating conditions may precipitate or contribute to the loss of control. Consequently, drivers' opportunity to lose control is enhanced.

Driver performance may be improved somewhat with educational and media programs but is unlikely to experience significant change in the foreseeable future. Effective winter servicing delivery programs must therefore recognize these dilemmas faced by drivers and respond to those needs.

The preceding discussion has presented a rationalization of the winter driving experience. Ongoing research is needed to identify drivers' decision processes and to further identify reasonable driving behaviors.

WINTER MAINTENANCE PROGRAMMING

14.1 An Emergency Service

Research has shown that winter maintenance activities provide a safety benefit.[1] More specifically, winter maintenance can reduce the frequency of collisions during and after periods of inclement weather. With the provision of winter maintenance, road users experience fewer injuries and fatalities, and there is a reduced burden on the health-care system, law enforcement, and legal system. However, perhaps most importantly, the effect of reduced collisions is a reduction in the number of individuals and families experiencing harm, from moderate inconveniences to long-term damage to their emotional, financial, and physical well-being.

The nature of winter maintenance has several characteristics similar to other emergency services. With other emergency services—police, fire personnel, and paramedics—the location and type of emergency cannot be predicted. Still, the general type and frequency of emergencies to which they will be required to respond are predictable. These services respond to singular locational events while concurrent events may be active. To do so, they prepare in advance, and their response is typically prompt. These services inherently recognize that public safety is paramount and that reduced response times have significant safety benefits. As a result, there is a public expectation that emergency services will be delivered with a *sense of urgency*. Those engaged in these services fully realize the need for a timely and effective response by the nature of the event and their personalized service involvement. They are fully exposed to the trauma individuals experience.

Of course, for emergency services to be provided in an expeditious manner, the road system must be maintained in a state that will allow responders to perform their task. For this reason, those maintaining the road system are intrinsically bound to other emergency services, particularly during the frost-prone months.

For similar reasons, winter maintenance service also requires a timely response. The sooner services are initiated and properly executed, the more collision potential is reduced. The research of Qin and colleagues found that proactive winter maintenance efforts significantly improve safety; maintenance efforts prior to the beginning of a snowstorm lead to fewer crashes.[2] Further, with better quality and more frequent service, the collision reduction benefits will be both enhanced and extended. Few would argue with the need for the timely delivery of emergency services such as police, fire, and ambulance. For these personnel to do their jobs, winter maintenance staff have to perform their duties, which are best done before other emergency service are required. Therefore, a *sense of urgency* is especially important.

However, with winter maintenance, there is no personalized connection between the need for a timely and effective response and the effects of not performing in that manner. For instance, the equipment operator remains distant in time and space from the trauma of a collision event. In this way, there is no direct connection between the service provided and the benefits derived therefrom or the problems resulting from an incident. This distancing from the trauma of collision events is enabled and extended by the reporting systems of the police and media. Both reporting systems tend to focus on the driver's actions as the cause. The road condition is identified as a scene description rather than a contributory element. By these means, there can also be a significant disconnect with any sense of urgency in performing the winter maintenance task.

Still, since winter events are predictable in both intensity and duration, road authorities have a distinctive advantage over other emergency services. By monitoring weather forecasts, they can prepare for winter maintenance services in advance. This aspect of the service can allow road authorities to manage the servicing of roadways in a more cost-effective manner than some other emergency service operations.

Of course, winter maintenance activities cost money. Due to the potential for a disconnect from the emergency nature of the service, the training of those involved, and perhaps the seasonal nature of operations, there is significant potential for these services to be the subject of intense pressure for budgetary restraint. These pressures appear to be more intense in smaller, less technically advanced road authorities. In this type of financial environment, it is critically important to ensure that winter maintenance is able to provide reasonably safe operating conditions for all drivers, whether they may be familiar with the winter maintenance service of the road authority or not. By this means, it is possible to ensure that budgetary considerations do not become a justification for delayed servicing and nonperformance.

14.2 A Sense of Urgency in Servicing Hazardous Conditions

Collisions occur with predictable frequency, although they are very rare relative to the volume of roadway system use. Still, some responsible for providing these systems at various levels of management may carry on with little knowledge of the relationship between their operations and collision experience. Where knowledge of the relationship is absent, the sense of urgency in attending to transient and long-term hazards can be lost.

However, for road users involved in collisions, dealing with the results can last a lifetime. As previously discussed, the case where an individual was responsible for winter servicing but instead decided to wash the truck contributed to a life-altering injury for one young traveler. While this is most certainly an extreme case, even short delays in servicing can be expected to affect collision experience, as collisions are more likely to occur at the onset of an event, before drivers have had time to adjust.

A case in point is the time of day when winter operations are conducted. It was and remains a practice among several municipalities that winter patrols and/or operations are not conducted overnight. Without inspection, the road authority has no knowledge of the road conditions. This practice is enabled when winter weather collisions are presumed to occur because of the drivers' own errors. Consequently, this type of provision encourages an inherent denial of the relationship that exists between winter maintenance and collision experience.

In some authorities, a road patrol will inspect the system in the early hours of the morning and, if required, call out operators at 5:00 or 6:00 a.m. to attend to roadways. This schedule of activity can be documented in the servicing standards and remains the standard for when to commence servicing unless the road authority is informed by external sources of hazardous conditions. Such practices remove the need for vigilance and enable a culture of denial and delay. In this way, a sense of urgency remains absent from winter maintenance. Beyond that, this type of provision effectively transfers responsibility for locating and repairing defects in the transportation system to unknown third parties who cannot be relied upon to understand the relevance or urgency of attending to the present hazards.

It is often the case that the repair and maintenance of low-volume roadways is not held to the same standard as for high-volume roadways. While better maintenance on high-volume roadways is more likely to reduce the number of collisions, this narrative is irrelevant at the individual level. A vehicle moving at 80 to 90 km/h (50 to 56 mph) that then strikes a utility pole or pothole can expect the same type of injuries and vehicle damage on a low-volume road as on a high-volume roadway. For this reason, blanket statements about the repair of one road relative to others may be considered irrelevant and each case should be examined in the context of its system users.

14.3 Two Approaches to Winter Maintenance

Two different approaches to the provision of winter maintenance are practiced. Some road authorities use an *event-based approach*. With this approach, authorities recognize that the safety of the road system deteriorates quickly with the onset of winter weather events. Where there is a possibility for frozen moisture such as frost to be on the road surface, proactive action is undertaken to maintain the best available serviceability of the road system throughout the event or to urgently return roadways to a defined road surface condition within a specified time.

The method typically strives for a wet pavement condition, which is typically the design condition, but may allow other conditions for low-volume roadways. With current technology, a road authority can begin servicing roadways before the onset of the event and continue using proven methods during and after the event. This approach implicitly seeks to maintain the best possible degree of safety for the road system throughout the duration of the event given the available resources. Notwithstanding that goal, snow and ice may be found on the road during weather events according to the intensity of the event. Standards for this approach relate to the activity to be undertaken throughout the event rather than the road condition. In this way, winter maintenance activities must be fully engaged as appropriate throughout the event.

The alternative is an *outcome-based approach*. This method sets outcomes—qualitative statements—that describe a state of being or condition specification rather than the activities and procedures used to achieve the results. The Ontario Minimum Maintenance Standard (MMS) reflects this approach to all maintenance. The outcome-based approach is premised on a maximum acceptable condition or defect *before and after* servicing rather than some predefined threshold of operational performance. The extent of the potentially hazardous conditions considered to be safe for public use before operations commence and after they are completed is effectively no different. The connection to road safety or specific winter events (or even the operating conditions on the roadway) is not a consideration for initiating maintenance servicing.

For example, snow on the roadway is not sufficient to initiate servicing. Thus, the standard does not explicitly recognize snow on roadways as a hazard. No regulatory-driven servicing need be undertaken with the onset of the winter weather event. The safety of the road system is allowed to deteriorate for some time until conditions are met to initiate servicing. Consequently, a deteriorating/hazardous condition may exist for extended periods. In this way, the approach does not fit comfortably with the Ontario Municipal Act (the Act) or the engineers' code of ethics. In dealing with defaults relative to the state of repair for highways and bridges, the Act requires that road authorities:

". . . took reasonable steps to prevent the default from arising . . ."
(2001 c. 25, S44^3)

On the other hand, the regulation of the MMS infers that the accepted conditions/defects are considered reasonable and that the public should be able to cope with them. Of course, as previously indicated, the reasonableness of the standards depends on the biases and balances of those responsible for their development.

Given the precision with which weather forecasts are issued and the road authority's intimate knowledge of seasonal weather events, it is increasingly difficult to argue that deteriorated or unsafe road conditions may not have been expected. Furthermore, the technology of today's winter maintenance equipment allows many, if not all, road authorities to proactively prepare for the event. At the very least, with forecasts of inclement weather during the frost months, it is reasonable for road authorities to inspect problem-prone locations as a means to prevent a default (according to the Act), such as frost formation, from arising there and elsewhere.

The outcome-based approach to winter maintenance allows a very high bar for claims and a much lower bar for municipal performance. The reason is that reasonable or common-sense winter maintenance practices are unlikely to support this type of policy. Indeed, some municipalities have found it necessary to use an event-based approach for servicing and an outcome-based approach to defend against claims.

Winter maintenance standards written in this manner are typically developed by the road authority or committees representing road authorities. Given the extent of deterioration the policy allows, the road authority can delay servicing and put road users at significant risk while they reside under the protection of legislation. In evaluating these types of policies, common sense must play a significant role, particularly in the presence of the more progressive policies of the event-based approach.

14.4 Defining a Winter Hazard

Given the nature of roadway hazards, there are several aspects to consider. Some hazards are readily identifiable by motorists. Few people would fail to identify an object or deep snow on the road as a hazard. However, the presence of snow sweeping across the road surface is likely to be viewed as offering little inherent hazard, and, therefore, drivers will often not make the necessary adjustments (see Section 13.1). The reason this situation is hazardous is that each passing vehicle packs a little more snow onto the surface, leading to a buildup of compressed snow and ice.

Therefore, those responsible for roadway maintenance must be cognizant of all potential winter hazards, both obvious and subtle ones drivers may not inherently identify or identify in a timely manner. Further, not all hazards that may be a cause for potential harm are on the traveled portion of the roadway. Hazards can also be present along the roadside.

For example, drivers may not notice snow stacked against barriers since it is all well off the road. However, these snow windrows can be compacted by weather and settlement and then act as ramps to launch vehicles over the barrier and into the hazard the barriers were intended to protect drivers from. In such cases, contact with the windrow can be initiated by conditions on the road, while the lack of appropriate winter maintenance has not only nullified an important safety system but has turned it into a potentially lethal hazard. It is therefore worthwhile to set out some common ground for the assessment of hazards.

One manual discusses the nature of hazards and what drivers need in order to safely cope with conditions on the road. The following information is readily available to road authorities through their traffic manuals or texts. In the *Ontario Traffic Manual*, a condition hazard is defined in the following manner:

> Any location where the condition of the highway and its immediate environment needs to be interpreted as a cause for extra caution or a cause to modify speed or path should be considered a condition hazard.[4]

Thus, a hazard need only to elicit a cautious response by a driver. In the case of roadway features such as curves, drivers are informed of how to respond by the presence of warning signs and pavement markings that reveal the location, extent, and degree of hazard. In the case of winter hazards, no warning devices are available. Drivers must visually assess conditions ahead to determine if a hazard is present and how that may affect their travel. The visual cues may be readily apparent, such as a large or deep white snowdrift on a dark pavement. However, in other cases there may be no clues available, such as with transparent ice or frost—black ice—on a dark pavement.

To cope with conditions, drivers must do a perception-reaction assessment to complete a successful maneuver. However, during winter conditions, drivers can travel for long distances without realizing that a hazard is present, and, indeed, may never realize a hazard is present before collision occurs (see Section 13.3). Such could be the case with transparent ice or snow. Drivers would need to experience a vehicle guidance or control issue—steering or braking—to identify this type of hazard. The period of assessment on a hazard of limited length can be very short and not provide the driver with sufficient time to react.

Structures are especially known to be problematic, due to the distance over which identification of the problem must occur and the recurring bump often found at the end of approach slabs. Railway crossings can also pose significant hazards, especially if the crossing surface is rough. In one case during a winter storm, a small vehicle was effectively shredded by a large truck after losing control and experiencing a head-on collision on a rough crossing where the crossing signs had been removed but the rails (and bump) remained (see Section 9.5).

Pavement smoothness testing measures the bumpiness of the road. Where the magnitude of specific bumps exceeds some threshold amount, repairs are programmed. A test was completed of a section of the road including the crossing, and it was found that the location of the crossing exceeded the allowable roughness for that type of roadway. Despite this, the road authority had not determined a planned program for repair. With that lack of initiative, the road authority seemed to be detached from the seriousness of the defect under operating conditions such as ice and snow. Thus, road authorities must be familiar with *potential types of hazards* and manage the servicing of these hazards in a manner that recognizes human failings.

The preceding extract from the manual recognizes that drivers need only to be cautious on approach to a hazard for it to be considered a condition hazard. A caution response may involve precautionary adjustment in the guidance and control of the vehicle or simply acquiring an extra firm grip on the steering wheel. Where speed or path adjustments are necessary, changing the motion of the vehicle may require a significantly longer time where roadway surface friction is reduced by frost, snow, slush, ponding water, black ice, or ice. The driving task adjustment must be completed under a significant time constraint. Over- or underreacting can lead to collision or cause others to crash. The perception-reaction time can be significantly extended due to multiple decisions and uncertainty:

- concerning whether a response is even required,
- the type of response required, and
- the magnitude of response if that action is selected.

The hazards associated with winter weather events may not be recognized as such when they are proximate to the cause of collision. To illustrate a response and outcome of this nature, consider the actions of a driver involved in a collision due to frost. Prior to collision, the driver's selected speed and path are presumed to be appropriate. However, with the convenience of hindsight, an error in assessment is revealed. The driver's action may have been entirely consistent with the actions of previous drivers successfully coping with the hazard, particularly in the case of a moving platoon. Collisions occur due to changing road conditions, with time, traffic volume, tire performance, or possibly a slightly different magnitude of driver response to the road condition. By the time the police arrive, the hazardous condition can have disappeared due to a warming pavement. Consequently, driver error is identified as proximate to the cause and recorded as such by the police. The condition hazard remains unevaluated.

Situational hazards may be considered higher-level hazards and include combinations of conditions that may be fixed in time or temporal because of environmental conditions. For example, a roadway curve with insufficient superelevation is a condition hazard. During the non-frost-prone months, the curve may well satisfy the needs of most drivers who routinely exceed the posted or design speed of the roadway. However, if the location is prone to drifting snow or frost formation, the condition hazard is exacerbated by environmental conditions and is much less capable of serving drivers' expectancies. While the curve radius or superelevation represent hazards of moderate concern, the addition of environmental conditions significantly enhances the hazard.

Even when a winter hazard is obvious, most drivers require several seconds to identify an appropriate course of action and several more seconds to complete the action—and longer if it is an infrequently encountered situation. Response times and distances similar to those of decision sight distance would seem applicable (see Section 5.1). Once the response decision is made, the magnitude of the response may not be evident until the response is partially complete, such as a speed change while ascending a hill on a snow-covered road. At that time, the decision process is reinitiated. Third, the ability of a driver to detect the hazard may be hindered, leading to a delay in responding. Poor lighting, glare, or poorly discernible roadway conditions can lead to detection delays. These types of conditions frequently exist after dark, when headlight illumination may provide insufficient reaction time, especially for poorly visible hazards like drifting snow or black ice.

In the case of roadway traffic operations, an improved response availability is provided to drivers through the installation of retroreflective warning signs installed well in advance of the hazard. For winter conditions, means to advise motorists of a condition or situation hazard ahead are not readily available. Consequently, drivers may be surprised by the condition or situation hazard, particularly if it was created by the winter maintenance operations. In at least three cases examined by the author, snow-clearing operations resulted in a windrow separating the mainline lanes from merging lanes on a freeway. With this occurrence, drivers were confronted with an unusual hazard while accelerating to the speed of highway traffic and approaching the end of the merge lane, which imposed a significant time constraint. The plowing operations of the day had placed a snow windrow between the through and merge lanes. In each of the three cases, one driver's attempt to pass through the windrow at an adequate merging speed to join the mainline traffic led to the loss of control.

The presence of snow or ice on the road due to a storm passing through an area are, without question, easy winter hazards for road authority personnel to identify. However, many other situations or conditions that may not be listed in the manuals need to be recognized as hazards.

Other less self-apparent winter hazards include:

- Drifting snow
- Slippery compacted snow
- Snow deposits on the road from winter operations
- Changes in road condition between road sections due to sunlight exposure
- Residual sand deposits on roadway due to winter operations
- Frost deposits in hollows, near rivers and streams, or in shaded areas
- Unmarked roadway deflections on snow-covered roads
- Ponding water on roadway created by frozen windrows or drains
- Visibility obstructions created by snow storage and windrows
- Snow windrows contributing to drift formation
- Frozen windrows that cause ramping during vehicle excursions
- Improperly set salt-spreading rates

These types of hazards may be created by the environmental elements and terrain conditions or by the road authority's winter maintenance operations.

14.5 Roadway Hazards and Common Sense

Much of winter maintenance is a matter of common sense. Since weather events are predictable, it is reasonable to prepare for them in advance. In the case of winter storms, the amount of precipitation may vary somewhat from forecasts. However, adjustments to planned and ongoing winter operations are possible at any time. Plows can be raised or lowered and chemical treatments adjusted at the touch of a button. Contingency planning allows a road authority to cope with expected occasional equipment failures and employee absenteeism. During winter events, operations personnel can observe firsthand the evolving road conditions. Recognizing these elements and making efforts to accommodate them is a first step toward providing common-sense service.

From a knowledge base of longtime practice, the road authority can predict road conditions that may be generally present throughout the system as well as conditions in key locations subject to more rapid deterioration. These may include hollows, bridges, and drifting-prone locations. For example, one municipality used wood surfaces on pedestrian bridges, which could become slippery, as a telltale sign of slippery conditions on structures with paved surfaces. Weather reporting systems and new technologies such as RWIS capabilities provide real-time information about road conditions in hazard-prone locations. There can be little doubt that the knowledge of the authority responsible for maintaining adequately safe roadways will be substantially greater than that of individual drivers. Therefore, road authorities should not be dependent upon the police, motorists, or other third parties to inform them where road conditions need attention. The application of common sense gained through observation and years of attendance to the road system is applicable. Most importantly, vigilance and a *sense of urgency* is needed, alongside their knowledge.

As winter maintenance reduces the likelihood of collisions during a winter weather event, delays in servicing roadways do not adequately provide for the traveling public's safety. Proactive programs with considered effort before the event are more likely to provide substantive safety. Programs that allow thresholds of road surface deterioration before maintaining them serve only the road authority in defending claims while placing the public at risk.

The outcome-based approach to winter maintenance is at odds with policies citing public safety as paramount. Indeed, most senior-level road authorities understand they cannot reasonably allow certain conditions to be present before taking action. In general, responsible road authority personnel are committed to searching for potential problems, carefully monitoring conditions when there is a potential for lower surface friction, and acting before collisions occur via anti-icing and having servicing personnel on standby.

Perhaps the most important takeaway is this: While many road authorities have adopted outcome-based standards, common sense indicates that they cannot wait until there is 2 to 4 cm (0.08 to 0.16 in.) of snow on the road or until they are notified of an icing problem before servicing commences.

While a disconnect between servicing and collision experience may remain in these authorities, their operational protocols recognize that the safety of the traveling public is cause for early action. Thus, outcome-based standards are irrelevant to their operations. *The practice of these system–user-conscious authorities implies these standards should not be relied upon for guidance in servicing or as a defense against claims*, because common sense does not permit personnel to act in accordance with the outcome-based standards in the face of public safety.

14.6 Training in Hazard Identification

Regardless of the approach to providing winter maintenance, it is important that road authorities search for conditions *that tend to produce an accident* (see Section 10.1). In taking reasonable steps to prevent a default in winter maintenance, it is necessary to monitor conditions with an expediency that is consistent with the evolving conditions, precipitation, and temperature. Of course, monitoring is key to finding any defect or maintenance condition in need of action.

Multiple relevant means are available for monitoring conditions. However, it is the opinion of the author that the most effective method is to be on the road looking for problems, especially in problem-prone locations. That is the task of the winter road patrol. The purpose of their inspections is to maintain the safety readiness of the road system and identify conditions that vary from the usual or expected condition of the roadway.

In view of their frequent attendance to their roads over many years in all types of weather, road authorities have the experience necessary to identify locations likely to experience winter hazards. This wealth of knowledge allows the road authority time to plan a response and enables a proactive response to expected conditions. Drivers, on the other hand, cannot be expected to have a similar knowledge base or experience. For example, drivers that infrequently travel some regions or roadways will have limited prior experience in anticipating hazardous locations there.

Those inspecting roadways must also use precaution and common sense when identifying hazards. The catchphrase protocol is "a cause for extra caution." This phrase is important since drivers cannot be expected to have specific knowledge of potential failure mechanisms on a location-by-location basis, whereas the road authority does or should have that knowledge. The examples of winter hazards in Section 13.3 provide a sample of situations and conditions that can present a hazard to drivers.

14.7 Managing Roadway Operations

As winter maintenance involves an expenditure of public funds, road authorities will sometimes justify nonperformance by suggesting that the maintenance would have been too great of a financial burden on the transportation authority. However, satisfying acceptable safety is simply part of the cost of doing business. Where these arguments prevail, road authorities can realize a significant cost saving. However, in doing so, collision frequency must be expected to increase until the roadway is restored to a normal or wet pavement condition.

The absence or delay of effective winter maintenance trades off roadway expenditures for potential collision experiences and a cost accrual for the traveling public, as well as the ancillary cost of other emergency services (police, fire, ambulances), health-care services, legal services, loss of income, and pain and suffering of the involved parties. In initiating the trade, the expenditure savings for the road authority is a fundamental service simply withheld from the public.

In road safety analysis, safety enhancements, such as increasing the frequency of winter inspections, are assessed along with other operating costs. The enhancements are often accepted or rejected based on cost-benefit analysis. Additional authority services may be accepted where the benefits, expressed as the monetary value of reduced collisions, exceed the additional expenditures required by the road authority by a specified margin. In this way, the monetary costs of certain collisions are legitimately incorporated within the roadway's operating costs.

Over the long term, the savings accrued by the road authority or others is stochastic in nature. The reduced expenditures of not providing the service may or may not exceed the costs incurred by those involved in minor and moderate collisions. Unfortunately, forgoing the inspections/servicing can result in far more substantial costs to the individuals involved in collisions as a result. These costs may far exceed the benefits accrued by the road authority unless those experiencing a harm are successful in having the road authority contribution recognized.

In such instances, the transfer of a portion of the winter maintenance costs to road users through an enhanced collision experience may be viewed as justified from the municipal perspective if they are assigned no liability. Given a low frequency of successful liability claims, this type of decision-making provides a significant financial benefit to the transportation authority. Unfortunately, the transferred costs are borne by individuals in the form of financial loss and pain and suffering, as well as the support systems. These systems include police services, emergency responders, health care and welfare providers, legal and judicial services, and more. In some cases, those costs borne by injured parties may far exceed the authority's savings.

15

ELEMENTS OF WINTER MAINTENANCE SERVICE

15.1 Developing a Suitable Winter Maintenance Policy

The purpose of maintaining roadways during the winter is to extend the duration of acceptably safe travel conditions for people and goods in a driving environment that is not static. This is achieved through managing road friction. With the intensity of winter weather events in the US and Canada, roadways with little maintenance can become impassable or otherwise dangerous during frost-prone months. Winter maintenance returns roadways to conditions that are nominally or acceptably safe for public use. Yet there is an ever-present potential source of conflict between the quality of maintenance provided and the cost to the road authority. To this end, the lower the quality or frequency of winter maintenance that is defined by a policy, standard, or regulation, the less the winter maintenance operations of the road authority will cost. Meanwhile, the road authority maintains some liability protection afforded by the law or regulation when the service is deemed to provide acceptable safety.

| Cost of Service | | | | | Quality of Service |

MAINTENANCE SERVICE CONTINUUM

Image 15.1: Continuum of maintenance service allows resource allocation between the cost of service and the quality of service, including safety. (Source: Gilchrist, January 17, 2025)

Conceptually, a maintenance standard represents a single point on a continuum with quality of service on one end and cost on the other (see Image 15.1). Whether that level of service provides acceptable safety remains an independent issue. The term "acceptable" is a rather vague term and offers no conveniently measurable definition regarding winter maintenance. Indeed, the term is arguable according to whether a stakeholder provides the service or receives the service. What may be acceptable according to one stakeholder may be far removed from what another stakeholder accepts. A misbalance can acutely benefit one group at the expense of the other, according to whether policies and practices become weighted toward improving road safety or reducing maintenance expenditures. While it would seem prudent that the development of standards be ratified by a balanced representation of both the suppliers and recipients of winter maintenance, such an approach may constrain the extent of safety provided.

While a premise of road system design is for drivers to see and respond to hazards, giving them sufficient opportunity for avoidance, these same criteria are not as amenable to winter maintenance issues. Still, the basic concepts remain applicable. Road friction keeps vehicles on the road, whether the road surface is dry and bare or icy/slippery. Consequently, winter maintenance standards must recognize these basic operational parameters where the legal speed limit exceeds some threshold value. As a basic threshold, a speed limiting value in the range of 30 km/h (19 mph) is perhaps an appropriate threshold for winter conditions, as personal injuries tend to be less life-threatening at or below this speed.

15.2 The Importance of Weather Information

Weather forecasts allow winter operations to be prepared in advance of events and for servicers to adjust their operations as required during an event. The weather record indicates what happened, which may be quite different from the weather forecast. The record allows a matching of the winter operations with the weather experienced. Radar imagery is available for forecasting, while past radar images provide tremendous insight to what did happen over large or small areas.

The US National Weather Service produces forecasts at regular intervals. In Canada, general forecasts have been issued in text format about four times daily for many years. Special bulletins can be issued as needed when there are significant changes to a previous forecast. Forecasts are archived and can often be retrieved from the national service for any area upon request, although some weather media outlets may also archive the information. Forecasts are issued for relatively homogeneous weather events and may be referenced according to locational groupings of towns, cities, counties, or regions.

Weather recording locations are often associated with airports, significant landmarks, or population groupings. Typically, airport locations include the most complete set of data, including hourly temperature, dew point, humidity, wind speed, wind gusts, cloud cover, and precipitation, and can include text observations—sun, cloud, drizzle, snow, and so on—and snow depth. Station data may also be sparse for some locations, providing only temperature and humidity.

As an explanatory variable in crashes, weather information can be a powerful tool. Hourly precipitation can be summed to produce estimates of snow or rainfall precipitation at the time of collision. The dew point is an important data element because it can provide an indication of the roadway surface condition—dry, wet, frost—at the time of collision. Frost is a form of ice producing slippery conditions. Wind speeds are important in providing insight to whether snow may be swept from exposed road surfaces. High wind speeds and gusts can contribute to vehicle instability in maintaining a path or losing traction. When weather data is placed in context with terrain information, the likely localized effects of weather on roadway and vehicle operations can be identified.

For those undertaking maintenance, understanding the weather information requires a knowledge of the terminology and the technology. It is worthwhile to have access to a good glossary that highlights the varied forms of weather elements.[1] For example, the term "snow flurries" has different connotations. To some people, it means a very light snow that comes and goes during the day. However, the detailed description of this event describes flurries as precipitation in the form of snow from a convective cumulus-type cloud.[2] Flurries are characterized by the suddenness with which they start and stop, by their rapid changes in intensity, and usually by rapid changes in the sky's appearance. With this type of cloud formation, it is possible to have isolated snow-shower activity delivering a solid cover of snow, which can be expected to provide slippery conditions when the fallen snow is compacted by traffic.

The nature and placement of weather stations can also have a significant effect on some reported elements. As data is collected at about 2 m (6.5 ft.) or more above the ground surface, the temperature at ground level can differ somewhat from the recorded temperature. Also, wind speed and direction may be affected by nearby terrain, vegetation, and buildings. Weather stations at airports tend to be in open-air settings, while temperature information from local reporting facilities may be less well situated.

Accordingly, winter weather events can be localized occurrences dependent on the nature of atmospheric conditions, orientation to major weather-influencing landforms such as lakes and hills, and details of the local terrain setting. Maintenance personnel must be aware of these possible effects since forensic investigations will examine the historical weather records and radar imagery for a geographical area that can be expected to encompass possible variances through the area. Forensic work should consider forecasts for locations within at least a 25 km (16 mi.) radius. However, in areas with fewer reporting locations, weather data for a much larger area is required.

Weather forecasts are produced by some of the most powerful computers available and highly complex algorithms that track evolving and ever-changing weather systems. Forensic meteorologists can provide some insights to the broader weather systems affecting crash sites. However, in most forensic investigations of a crash site, the knowledge of operational personnel in reviewing weather forecasts and actual weather conditions tends to be more relevant to the crash event because it is timely and observation-based. Operations personnel cannot be considered weather experts but can be expected to understand and respond to information available to them as well as comment on what they observe. In forensic examinations of events, a description of the larger weather system that extends beyond the area typically considered by operations personnel is less relevant but can be useful. What is more relevant is the weather forecasts commencing twelve to twenty-four hours before the event and the weather record of the event as it was occurring. This is the information used by maintenance personnel to commence and manage ongoing operations.

While some forecasts pan out exactly as predicted, others do not. Therefore, substantial uncertainty can be associated with weather events and forecasts. While forecasts of temperature tend to be more stable and occur within a few degrees of that predicted, forecasts of precipitation can change hourly. As many media outlets have been providing hourly forecasts for more than twenty years, it is possible to observe how these forecasts may change in the presence of heat and humidity. Within an hour, a forecast of 60 percent chance of rain can change to either clear skies or 100 percent chance of rain. When the dew point and temperature are close, the forecast can change very quickly from dry conditions to frost accumulation on structures or road surfaces. Due to the uncertainty in weather forecasts, during the frost-prone months, operations personnel should closely monitor not only the weather forecasts but the actual conditions on their roadways. With today's technology, maintenance personnel need access to weather forecasts and data 24/7, during any activity and in any location.

15.3 Terrain and Locational Effects of Weather

Terrain conditions can significantly alter the generalized weather that has been forecast. Those in mountain regions regularly experience this phenomenon. However, similar effects may be observed in areas without such extreme changes in elevation. To illustrate this point, the author's region is generally flat to gently rolling, but due to an old fault line, a western part of the area is about 100 meters (109 yards) higher than the rest at the west end of Lake Ontario. As a result, with east winds that usually bring wet weather, the western area receives substantially more snow and cooler temperatures than the rest of the region. Further, the arrival of spring weather is delayed by about one to two weeks. Due to these relatively small changes in elevation, the need for winter servicing of the area can be substantially different from the lower part of the region during the frost-prone months.

In a more localized context, there are many instances where the accumulation of frozen moisture on the roadway can be affected by the terrain encompassing the roadway environment. Many drivers have observed signs near structures that indicate a bridge becomes icy before the roadway or have experienced conditions where there seems to be good traction one minute, and the next minute conditions are icy and slippery. This section provides several instances where local terrain conditions can create hazards not found elsewhere on the road.

Snow accumulation on the road is a hazard for drivers, whether the snow is newly fallen or blown onto the road. Snow on the road surface reduces road-tire friction and increases the likelihood of collisions. Drifting snow, as opposed to falling snow, is responsible for about 30 percent of road maintenance budgets in agricultural areas.[3] In view of drifting snow's impact on road maintenance requirements, road authorities must be just as vigilant in monitoring the effects of drifting snow as new falling snow.

The displacement of ground snow occurs in several ways, including creep, where particles roll along the surface; saltation, where particles bounce along the surface; and turbulent diffusion, where particles are carried along in the airflow without ground contact. Snowdrift formation occurs where the airflow is disrupted. At locations where wind speeds drop, snow particles stop moving or otherwise fall out of the airflow. Typically, wind speeds drop in locations where the moving air mass expands to fill a void. This can occur over very large areas, as in the case of our community, or relatively small areas, such as fill sections of roadway.[4] Other typical locations where wind speeds can drop include ground depressions or low spots such as ditches; along raised features such as fencing, hills, or ridges (including roads); or around woodlots, buildings, trees, and utility poles, to name a few. The change in elevation need not be great to alter the airflow near the ground surface.

As wind speeds increase, so does the possibility of drift formation. The wind speed at which ground snow will begin to move depends on the condition of the snow cover and air density. Fluffy snow will begin to move when wind speeds reach about 20 km/h (12 mph), allowing drift formation. Snow can fall out of the moving air mass when wind speeds drop below about 24 km/h (15 mph). At wind speeds of 35 km/h (22 mph), about 90 percent of snow moving in the air mass remains within 1.5 m (5 ft.) of the ground. With wind speeds of 40 km/h gusting to 50 km/h (25 to 31 mph), conditions become highly favorable for significant low-level ground snow movement and snowdrift formation. While drivers may not reflect on these properties of snowdrift formation, such knowledge is important to those responsible for maintaining safe travel conditions.

The characteristics of drifting snow are very different from that of falling snow. As snowflake particles are transported, their structure is damaged and particle sizes are smaller than falling snowflakes. Drifting snow particles may be infinitely small or as large as about 0.5 mm (0.02 in.). Particles that are no longer flakes become progressively smaller and more rounded due to fragmentation and collisions with the ground or other particles. Smaller, lighter particles are also more easily lifted by the airflow. These properties of drifting snow create very different conditions in snowdrifts from that of newly fallen snow during storm conditions.

As the snow particles in a drift are small, of various sizes, and rounded in shape, snow deposited in drifts is denser than newly fallen snow. For example, the density of newly fallen snow averages about 100 kg/cu. m (6 lbs./cu. ft.), while the density of newly deposited drifted snow may be as high as 300 kg/cu. m (19 lbs./cu. ft.).[5] Additionally, wind-deposited snow particles can freeze together upon contact. The bonds between particles can grow and strengthen through sintering, which involves heating without melting. For this reason, wind-deposited snow becomes resistant to subsequent erosion within only a few hours of deposition.

Based on these properties, the presence of a sizable snowdrift on the road will have a significantly different effect on vehicle operations than loose, newly fallen snow. For example, the densely packed snow of a drift can produce various resisting forces on different sides of the vehicle. Where the depth of snow is greater on one side of the vehicle than the other, the forces can become unbalanced and can affect the stability of vehicle operations, potentially producing a loss of traction and control, independent of any driver action. Due to the density of snow in drifts, some drivers have noted they feel the drift "grab" their vehicle.

In one case involving a snowdrift, the author was asked to evaluate the road conditions and to state an opinion regarding the contribution of the road conditions to a serious collision event. At issue was whether the conditions present at the time of the collision were compliant with winter servicing standards of the day. To the east of the collision site was a wide expanse of open fields that could allow the transport of snow over long distances. The fetch—or distance blown snow can travel—was sufficiently long to produce small particle sizes, low-level drifting, and, subsequently, relatively dense drift formations at the small change in elevation as the wind rose to pass over a roadway. A dense, compacted snowdrift developing from the terrain and wind conditions of the day is consistent with the evidence of the investigating officer, who indicated that he could feel the police vehicle hitting the snowdrifts. That description is also consistent with the evidence of a witness who felt the bump as he was plowing the road.

The open field to the east gently rose as it neared the roadway. This terrain provided a significant opportunity for winds to pick up ground snow upon moving toward the road. As the airflow moved across the rising ground to the east and over the east road shoulder, it would have accelerated somewhat. However, in passing over the road, there was likely a sufficient change in terrain conditions for ground-level winds to slow, which allowed snow particles on the underside of the air mass to fall out. It is also probable the presence of landscape features farther west assisted in reducing low-level wind speeds near the road. These conditions are likely to produce a large low-level drift, which is consistent with the police sketch.

In another case, a wide expanse of open fields to the north of a collision site would allow the transport of snow over long distances, allowing the production of small particle sizes and, subsequently, dense drift formations. The winds of the day were from the west at sufficient speeds to initiate drifting snow. Therefore, conditions were set for snowdrift formation along the road because of surrounding terrain conditions and an elevated road setting. The wind would have blown across a large expanse (fetch) before encountering the rise of a treed knoll. Police photographs show wind-driven snow in the airstream well over a meter in height. Because of the wind speed, direction, and height of the road above the surrounding land, the height of the void on the underside of the airstream as it passed over the road was likely substantial (see Image 15.2). Due to a large void, a sizable component of the airstream close to ground level could slow, resulting in the rapid formation of drifts at the site of the collision.

Image 15.2: Terrain condition showing rise over the roadway at the end of a long fetch.
(Source: Gilchrist, October 19, 2009)

Another important aspect of terrain conditions is that they can produce a change in temperature over relatively short distances. Temperatures close to the freezing point can dramatically alter vehicle operations. In one collision case, the roadway descended a long, low grade from a height of approximately 247 m (810 ft.) on the south side to a low point of 229 m (751 ft.) on a lakeshore, then ascended again on a low grade to the north. A large hill much higher than the roadway was located on one side near where a loss of control had occurred. The collision occurred on the roadway at an elevation of approximately 236 m (774 ft.).[6] The grade of the roadway was measured and found to be approximately 0.035 m/m (vertical meters/horizontal meters, 0.035 ft./ft.), or 3.5 percent, at the location of the collision.[7] The roadway shoulders were flanked by small open drainage ditches.

Collision occurred at a time when temperatures varied between -1 and +3°C (30–36°F) during the day. A reconstruction was done on a day with identical conditions. It had snowed overnight, and a plowing operation had been completed earlier in the morning. At the time of my arrival, the roadway remained bare and wet with track bare sections. Slush was present on many sections of road (see Image 15.3). These conditions were almost identical to those at the time of collision.

Image 15.3: Water is clearly visible draining along the right side of the southbound lane. The photograph was taken approximately two hours after the shoulder plowing operation was complete. (Source: Gilchrist, February 14, 2013)

On inspection of the collision site, a rut in the wheel track was found along the right side of the southbound lane. The presence of the rut was verified using a 0.9 m (2.95 ft.) straightedge. The shoulder was level and did not drain water from the roadway. Draining water from the roadside had collected in the rut from the west half of the road and some portions of the west shoulder and then drained along the right wheel track of the southbound lane. The rut extended from the top of the hill to the bottom. Measurements of the rut showed that it was wide, extending from the lane edge line into the lane a distance of approximately 0.6 to 0.8 m

(2.0 to 2.6 ft.). Repair of the wide, shallow rut was not required by the standards for roadway maintenance.

Several air and pavement temperature readings were taken over the period of collision. In this terrain with the day's weather, air temperature readings were generally in the range of 0 to 2°C (32.0 to 35.6°F), with the cooler temperature locations at the top of the hill. Roadway temperatures were generally -1 to -3°C (30.2 to 26.6°F). The pavement temperatures were consistently -3°C (-5.4°F) relative to the air temperatures at all locations where measurements were taken. Also, it was found that the pavement temperature at the bottom of the hill was consistently -1 to -2°C (-1.8 to -3.5°F) relative to the top of the hill.

It is apparent that with these terrain conditions, while air temperatures were higher, cooler air at ground level would flow down the hill onto the roadway and then descend along the roadway (see Image 15.4). With these conditions, it is possible that a film of meltwater washing off the road along the rut would freeze to create an icy condition in the rut in the lower part of the hill when the rest of the roadway remained well drained and ice-free.

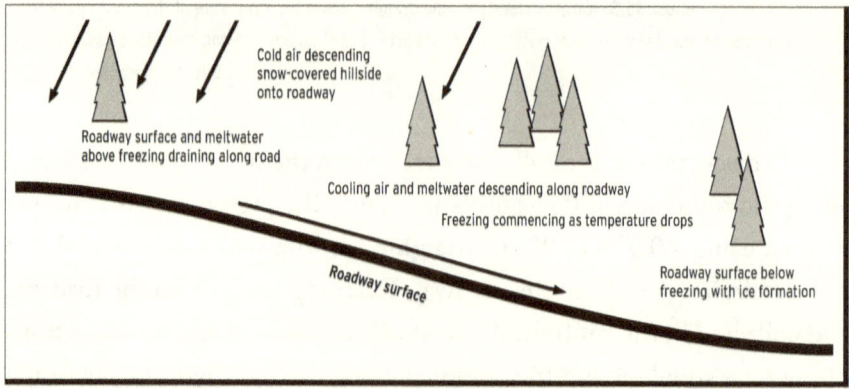

Image 15.4: Colder, denser air descending hillside onto roadway and then down along the roadway. (Source: Gilchrist, January 17, 2025)

This example is a case where the road authority believed that with temperatures above freezing for the day, one servicing of the roadway was sufficient and the warm temperatures would take care of the rest. Unfortunately, the limited servicing and road defect allowed conditions for ice to develop in an area where drivers could reasonably expect a condition free of ice. Thus, an unexpected encounter with ice on a rising grade resulted in the loss of control and collision.

15.4 Radar Imagery

Radar imagery can be used to verify the content of the forecasts with respect to precipitation levels, time of arrival, and the tapering off of precipitation. Historic weather and radar images can often be accessed online. The images record conditions at about ten-minute intervals. Today, radar imagery allows rapid modification of general weather forecasts as it tracks small cells of weather so forecasts can be modified significantly during the day as conditions evolve. Therefore, the precipitation conditions leading up to and at the time of an individual collision can be identified quite accurately, given an appropriate understanding of the weather information.

Still, uncertainty can be present in monitoring weather events. For example, Environment Canada notes there can be differences between radar imagery and actual conditions. Therefore, those providing winter maintenance must recognize these characteristics and set a course of action that is timely, prudent, and in the interest of the traveling public's safety. Thus, responsible road authorities need to have a prudent, attentive, and common-sense approach to winter maintenance to cover the range of possibilities and to safeguard the traveling public to the extent that servicing allows.

The weather images shown on the internet are available from federal weather departments and commercial services such as The Weather Network (TWN). Environment Canada provides past and forecast animations of the radar images spanning a specified period, including the historical images for hours past and forecast images for hours to come. Information available online can present animations extending over several hours of forecasts. The recorded and forecast weather can encompass shorter periods; therefore, the public or winter maintenance personnel monitoring the weather at any time of day can have forecast radar imagery with a good indication of the potential weather and likelihood of precipitation in an area over the next several hours.

These forecasts represent an excellent source of information for nonprofessionals in the planning of winter maintenance. However, electronically monitoring weather conditions cannot reveal the full extent of variation over a winter maintenance service area. Vigilance and monitoring of the conditions in the field is still required.

Examining the imagery and knowing how it affects winter maintenance does require some understanding, as conditions appearing on a monitor can be quite different from those in the field. The radar images record the likelihood of precipitation at an elevation of about 1,500 m (0.9 mi.). Where the images show more intense activity, precipitation is more likely to also be present at ground level. However, the regions around areas showing precipitation in radar imagery can experience quite different conditions due to local atmospheric conditions and terrain. Further, snow generally reflects less radar energy than rain. Consequently, moderate to heavy snow can appear light in intensity. Similarly, light snowfalls may be present when there is no activity identified by radar images. For this reason, there can be snowfalls at ground level exogenous to the area defined by the precipitation intensity indicator of the radar images.

For this reason, Environment Canada's website indicates that:

- Snow generally reflects less energy than rain,
- Moderate to heavy snow can appear light in intensity, and

- Just because echoes appear weak on the screen or do not appear at all does not mean there is not significant precipitation falling somewhere.[8]

In one crash site examined, the radar imagery showed a definitive precipitation event well to the west of the highway several hours before the crash. However, there were sparsely spaced groupings of reflections scattered throughout a large area for many hours beforehand. There was a general movement of these reflections toward the crash site. The radar reflections encompassed the winter operations center and the crash site about two and half hours before the crash. The road authority in this case indicated they saw no significant snowfall activity in the area. However, both drivers at the scene and police reported there was light snow, while photographs of the road condition indicated a thin layer of compacted snow polished to transparent icing. Given the uncertainty of the radar imagery, field inspections using road patrols were necessary to remove the uncertainty and to substantiate forecasts. Still, the radar imagery will assist in how to go about the task of physical inspections as well as winter maintenance.

There can be a significant difference in the way forecast weather and radar information may be considered. It is a misjudgment to consider a forecast 100 percent accurate and invariant at the time that it was issued. In any maintenance protocol, forecasts should be considered in the context that significant variation could occur from one forecast to the next.

15.5 Remote Weather Information Systems

Since the 1990s, the road authorities in the US and Canada have been constructing remote weather stations to create Remote Weather Information Systems (RWIS). Typically, these stations are placed in locations considered sensitive to weather conditions such as near bridges or hills where winter road conditions can deteriorate faster than other sections of roadway. These weather stations supplement winter patrolling activities by providing real-time road and weather data.[9] They can be used by managers to initiate and direct winter servicing operations in real time.

The weather stations include communication capabilities for data transfers from multiple locations to central facilities. RWIS stations measure atmospheric and pavement conditions. Pavement data can include road surface temperatures, freezing point notification, surface condition—wet, icy, flooded—chemical concentration (salt), and subsurface conditions such as soil temperature. Central RWIS hardware and software are used also to process data enabling the production of nowcasts (ongoing weather forecasts). The forecast weather can then be disseminated to road authorities for location-specific information in a format that is readily assimilated by a road manager or patrollers. RWIS data is used by road authorities to support decision-making.[10]

These devices were developed to assist in the monitoring of developing conditions. In this way, the devices supplement the activity of road patrols, allowing personnel to obtain real-time information for several key locations so the patroller can effectively be in multiple places at once. To be effective, the information must be examined in a timely manner to provide a benefit before and during a winter weather event. While management of the systems may be subcontracted, road authorities and related agencies should maintain direct access to the data stream as it is being produced.

An RWIS station is particularly relevant for continuous monitoring at key locations, sometimes known as hot spots, susceptible to rapid changes in roadway condition. Hot spots are bellwether locations since exposure to terrain and atmospheric conditions can produce icing locally and/or before other sections of roadway. Regular or frequent monitoring of the stations can be done by personnel at central facilities or those at yard locations. As of 2004, provincial RWIS stations in Ontario could be accessed directly by individuals with internet capabilities. Given the RWIS stations provide continuous and complete monitoring at key locations 24/7, the information can be used effectively by operations personnel, combined with a working knowledge of their road system acquired over many years of winter maintenance experience. As with any technology, there is a learning curve in becoming effective in application. Operations personnel need to be trained in their use and application and to *make use of them*. Therefore, the road authority should have protocols in place to ensure that the information is accessed regularly.

Some stations may not need to be continuously monitored where they typically have predictive capabilities. For example, some will indicate three levels of snow, and separate ice conditions are available at any given time.

The warning levels of this technology include:

- a "watch," indicating conditions are evolving that contain the possibility of snow or icing;
- a "warning," indicating conditions are evolving that indicate snow and ice are probable; and,
- a "snow and ice" condition that indicates these contaminants are on the road surface.

Thus, even if the radar does not have a strong indication of precipitation, the RWIS station may produce a "watch" and "warning" condition in advance of icing. The station monitoring of temperature and dew point is capable of forecasting when frost may be present in low-lying areas or on hills.

15.6 Anti-Icing

Anti-icing is a practice that was developed prior to 2000.[11] It involves a process of spreading liquified salt on roadways before a winter weather event. The action is carried out when conditions are dry to damp and/or when there may be uncertainty about whether icing may occur, or, more importantly, when icing is more certain. It is also used for low levels of moisture—frost, isolated flurries—while being particularly well suited to locations where terrain, such as hills, and atmospheric conditions can cause road conditions to deteriorate more rapidly than on other parts of the roadway.

Anti-icing gives the road authority time to respond, because if conditions do not require servicing for some time, the salt solution can remain on the roadway for up to three days. In this way, the solution may be installed on the road when driving conditions are good and be there ready to do its task at the right time.

15.7 Equipment Technology and Reporting

Computerized spreader controls for depositing granular or liquid materials on the roadway have been available for many years. The controls can indicate vehicle position, on-off cycles of spinners/augers, travel distances spreading and deadheading, quantities utilized, solid and liquid spread rates, and more. This data is an important source to ensure oversight of the servicing operations. Consequently, the data needs to be retained and properly stored. The equipment can be installed on both owned and contracted service vehicles.

These systems produce a clear record of the activities of vehicle operators once the engine has started. The vehicle location devices record date, time of day, vehicle number, longitude and latitude, travel direction, and travel speed. On patrol vehicles, the information will show where the patrols were being undertaken; if patrols were taken during dry, wet, or snow-covered road conditions; whether key locations in the road system were evaluated; whether the operators were diligent in their duties; and more. When combined with weather and radar data, the usage data can help determine if the patrols were likely to encounter specific weather conditions at key times during the day.

Many systems can plot position information on a map indicating where the truck is located at any time. While travel direction is recorded, it is possible in some instances to determine the lane location of a vehicle on wide roadways. The data will show when trucks were being filled or serviced and when breaks in the servicing occurred for such activities as rest periods, meals, refilling, and refueling. In operations involving spot salting, the data will show when and where the spinners were activated and the spread rates. Summaries are typically provided, indicating material spread and quantity used.

This information can take several forms, including summaries, maps, and line data. A line of data with the above information is recorded whenever there is a change in operations, such as lifting the plow or hitting the blast button of the spreader for the rapid discharge of salt or sand. Hard copies of the data commonly contain tens of thousands of lines. However, the data can typically be scanned and rendered searchable quite easily.

With the location coordinates of the collision known, a precise record of the servicing for a collision site can be created. These records will show how many times servicing occurred pre-collision, the time of servicing, whether the plow was up or down, whether abrasives or chemicals were used, and the application rate. In the experience of the author, on several instances servicing was noted to have occurred several times, but no action was taken preceding the collision.

15.8 Documentation of Winter Maintenance Activity

Preparation for Winter Servicing

The preparatory information for winter maintenance has not typically been an issue in the author's casework. However, it can be. The onset of winter weather is likely to be signaled by early overnight frost affecting specific locations. Establishing a means of treating these locations needs to have some priority because drivers are less likely to be tuned in to these possible conditions than are road authorities. Due to uncertainty of the arrival dates of cold weather, equipment needs to be ready well in advance. Today, these conditions may be best handled using liquid anti-icing techniques. Beyond that, plowing and salting operations need to be ready to go several weeks before the first snowfall is expected. Seasonal weather reporting through several media outlets is capable of providing insights to the timing of these activities.

One element of winter maintenance that is not well documented is the assignment of routes and scheduling of activities. This task is quite difficult to perform, and the personnel assigned to these tasks are often not well trained for it. For state and provincial highway systems, plowing and salting can be relatively straightforward, as vehicles are likely to service a limited number of roadways. However, even with these, the nature of the operation can be quite different from one trip to the next. During winter storms, trips tend to be out and back, keeping the main roadways clear. Still, trucks engaged in plowing and salting typically have different travel speeds that must be accommodated. The circuit times for these tend to be of shorter duration. However, at some point, particularly in urban areas, intersections must be cleared, sight lines ensured, and more, so the circuit time can be much longer. Ideally, it would be appropriate to document routes to accommodate the variation. However, such precision is unlikely to be available in most road authorities.

Event Monitoring

A winter weather event begins when a weather condition that could potentially lead to winter maintenance commences. Typical events bring snow, ice pellets, or freezing rain, but may include frost conditions. Bare pavement is lost when the snow cover on the road has reached an extent where winter operations are required. The timing of starting winter operations is key to the likely success of those operations.

One road authority commences solid salt-spreading operations when there is less than 0.5 cm (0.2 in.) of snow or when slippery conditions develop. While this snow depth may seem slight, traffic can compact that snow, quickly turning it into a slippery condition. It is therefore reasonable that any depth of snow beyond this level can create hazardous conditions. While operations may not be able to prevent slippery conditions from occurring due to temperatures or snowfall or freezing rain intensity, the road authority must be fully engaged in the public interest. As most collisions occur near the start of an event, delays in beginning operations fail to recognize the importance of serving the public

One upper-tier road authority requires that road patrols record when the event began, when an acceptable pavement condition was lost, when the event ended, and when an acceptable pavement condition was regained. Once winter operations commence, it is necessary that the road authority be engaged in those operations continuously until acceptable conditions are regained. The acceptable condition is wet pavement, but this status is not issued until all of the roadways exhibit that condition across the whole width of the road. A wet pavement should not include deposits of slush, since slush is a form of ice and can refreeze. Where removal of all frozen moisture may not be possible due to very cold temperatures, aggregates such as sand should be used to enhance pavement friction.

Road and weather information sheets can be used by road authorities throughout the day to summarize road conditions across their networks. For example, conditions may be bare and wet in some areas while track bare or snow-covered in other sections. Whereas the on-scene reporting of many media outlets tends to pick snow conditions at a single location, this documentation provides an opportunity for the road authority to convey the range of conditions that drivers may experience throughout an area. When information is provided to the media outlets in this form, it would be appropriate to indicate the status of operations, such as continuing and cleanup.

Patrol Reports

Patrol or other monitoring reports may convey the extent of winter weather monitoring before an event until after active operations are completed. Reports should indicate the individual reporting, date and time, equipment used, start time of the patrol, route description, and key points and times while on the patrol, including breaks and related activities. There should be a capability to describe basic weather status, such as temperature and precipitation; the road condition, such as pavement temperature, bare and wet, lightly snow-covered, track bare, and so on; actions taken, such as callouts; and operations underway, such as plowing, salting, cleanup. This documentation should include a capability for notations—responses to collisions, contacts with nearby service personnel.

Winter Operations Record

Winter operations records document the operations of specific personnel and vehicles. This information includes the date and time of callouts for personnel, arrival time for duty, departure times for the yard, route information, activity undertaken, and return arrivals at the yard. For the servicing operations, there should be a description of the route attended, load levels, actions (anti-icing, plowing, cleanup), materials used (aggregates, chemicals, anti-icing), along with spread rates and a concise description of the conditions found while attending to the activity of the time.

WHO WILL DETERMINE ACCEPTABLE ROAD SAFETY THRESHOLDS IN THE FUTURE?

The public is becoming increasingly concerned about the level of safety provided by our road systems and demanding a greater say in how much safety is provided. This is illustrated by an increasing frequency of events where the public has demanded enhanced road safety regardless of the safety currently provided. The public is also acting on their demands through public forums, the political process, the media, and quasi-judicial hearings. Advocating for public safety or safety features is a sure means to garner public support at present.

In these evolving times, nonmotorists using the street have put forward the important ideal that the street ought to be safe for all, including pedestrians, cyclists, and even children at play. People living and working in areas where road users walk, bike, and more have projected a view that traffic service in such areas need not be considered the dominant activity. Other street activities could assume a key role in the identity of living space and the quality of a neighborhood. This section explores some issues and trends in defining the level of safety provided for our road systems and who is the benefactor of those safety initiatives.

Historically, panels of experts preparing geometric design standards and traffic control manuals have determined road safety. However, some traditional standards are now being challenged in public discussions. It is now readily apparent to those who must build or expand our road systems that there is a wide range of road users and an equally wide range in the perception and acceptance of risk regarding road safety. This gives rise to new questions about what is acceptable safety and who is qualified to set standards for road safety. Today, there is an increasing list of participants who will influence future levels of road safety.

The impacts of these trends on the assessment of road safety have a potential for significant imbalance in road authorities' allocation of resources. The ability of the road authority to systematically manage roadway safety in the future will depend on their ability to assemble and assimilate data. However, perhaps more importantly, the ability to allocate resources in an efficient manner will depend on their ability to manage their public relations. Some have suggested that road authorities develop the protocols and procedures to manage their allocation of safety resources in an open and public forum. An important element of that process is to identify the implications of allocating resources in a manner that serves the safety demands of special groups or parochial interests rather than the broader need.

The well-founded theories and principles that engineers and scientists have diligently pursued over many years are becoming increasingly effective in defining the elements necessary for safer roads. In considering the approvals processes for new facilities, these theories and principles are exposed to and evaluated by the public. In these processes, road safety defined by the public can be a matter of perspective and be substantively different from that postulated in the design office. Consequently, design and safety engineers specializing in roadway geometry, operations, traffic control, and maintenance will increasingly be required to deal with the public. Special interest groups may be expected to assume an equal or even leading role in advancing their own safety perspectives. The following discusses emerging trends affecting the role of the public in the design process and assessment of future road safety elements for new or rehabilitated facilities.

16.1 An Example of Risk Tolerance

In the past and in some cases the present, the movement of people and goods on arterial roadways has been a primary function, and thus, accommodation of the motor vehicle has driven many design considerations. The predominance of the automobile in the right of way produced a driving environment that was often insensitive to other users of some roads. On these roads, drivers almost solely interact with other drivers who coincidentally have similar objectives. Exceeding the speed limit is often routine.

Where there is interaction between drivers and other right of way users, often vulnerable road user conflicts can develop. In these locations, the expectations of drivers could differ significantly from other individuals using the street. Still, it has been recognized by the transportation industry and other disciplines that vulnerable street users were not protected by the protective shell of the vehicle and remained exposed to serious injury and death because of some drivers' errant actions. Yet drivers must share these streets with others.

One can therefore appreciate how more vulnerable facility users may harbor very different perceptions of risk related to traffic operations, including speeding, turning, and compliance with traffic controls. These differences in risk tolerance are revealed in complaints to the police or municipal representatives. The anxiety and frustration of these groups in dealing with traffic is frequently expressed dramatically at public meetings or in online discussions. This often results in residents or authorities trying to mitigate risks to vulnerable road users by attempting to exert some control over drivers' risk-taking behaviors.

A good example of the effect of such actions is the application of traffic calming mechanisms—speed humps, curb realignment, and other means—going back to the early 1970s in Europe. By the mid-1990s, the idea was beginning to catch on in the US and Canada. Since then, under public pressure, these trends have evolved into "complete streets" and Vision Zero programs. The former accommodates multiple uses of the street for nonautomobiles, including cycling, outdoor dining, and many other activities. The latter is aimed at zero traffic deaths through design and operations while focusing on enforcement and training in some cases. These programs have gained substantial traction with both the industry and the public, sometimes showing significant results such as a lowering of the base speed limit on city streets by 10 or 20 km/h (6 or 12 mph).

These programs have also met some resistance, which indicates polarized opinions about how much inconvenience and risk may be tolerated. For example, Ontario is moving to control the introduction of bicycle lanes due to the rise in urban congestion as a result of removing traffic lanes. Transportation authorities have now assumed the task of balancing the need for movement for reasonable travel times and the need to accommodate other perspectives and activities in the streetscape. The outcome is that the acceptance of risk is likely to be an individual determination, usually based on the activity desired and perceived rather than real values of risk. As risk is frequently determined subjectively from media sources and experience, a wide range in risk tolerance may also be expected within the traveling population. Further, acceptable risk is unlikely to be consistently applied in time and place. For example, individuals may want drivers to obey the speed limit on their street while they themselves travel at excessive speeds on nearby residential streets.

Given these variable perspectives of roadway safety, there exists a range of acceptable safety within the exposed population. While road safety has traditionally been determined by the experts, the concept of determining acceptable levels of safety may be moving increasingly toward public debate. In an open forum such as municipal council meetings or hearings, the public may simply disagree that the level of safety provided by the experts is acceptable. Pressures placed on decision-makers will not go away. Those pushing for change have developed advocacy protocols to ensure their interest stays in the forefront over time.

In observing social trends over the past two decades, reporting on issues of roadway safety has become a steady source of attention by the media, particularly after serious crash events. Through that process, the public is becoming more concerned about road safety, more knowledgeable, and better organized to develop and promote specific goals. If knowledge is power, the current practice of involving the public in the engineering decision processes will create a technically demanding environment for those seeking road project approvals where there are debatable safety issues. In view of the ever-expanding requirement to inform the public on traffic and transportation improvements, that trend may be expected to continue well into the future.

16.2 The Citizen Safety Specialist

When the risks are considered to be acceptable, there is a tendency for many people to consider the situation as "safe." I once had a childcare worker explain to me in a public meeting that she allowed toddlers to play in the cul-de-sac of a residential street. On the cul-de-sac were half a dozen homes with relatively short driveways. Many children lived in the area, and the smooth surface of the pavement was convenient for sports activity, games, and wheeled toys. Her belief that the cul-de-sac was a safe play space was supported by many others in the meeting. Their argument was that drivers in the area were aware of the children at play and responded by using extra caution (or at least the ones who knew about the children at play did so). As a significant group in a public forum, they appeared to present a compelling argument that was conveniently adopted by the politicians who were present in that public setting.

That being the case, it might be imprudently argued that a driveway would also be a safe place to play since it is even less traveled and further removed from the street. However, anyone who has read the newspaper will know that from time to time, children are struck by vehicles in their own driveway. Such events are possible when a driver is distracted or otherwise backs onto the street without adequate surveillance. In the US, approximately fifty children are backed over by a vehicle in their own driveway every year.[1]

While children continue to play in the cul-de-sac without a collision experience, those experiencing the benefits will likely continue to consider a cul-de-sac to be safe. Why not? There is a history of successful play with no harms to suggest that it is unsafe. Further, should a harm occur, blaming the driver will allow the notion that the cul-de-sac is a safe place to play to move forward unchecked. Who could possibly blame the parent of an injured child, saying they should not have allowed the child to play on the street?

Hence playing in the cul-de-sac or on the driveway has some risk, but the road may still be considered safe. Following a child-vehicular collision, those living in the area may be tempted to reconsider their perceptions based on the reality of a collision experience. In doing so, the cul-de-sac might be labeled as unsafe. However, there was no physical change to the street setting that would render it safe in one instance yet unsafe in the next. Therefore, it is better to consider the street as "less safe" than the untested perception. One may therefore agree with the widely held opinion of road safety professionals that roadways are not and were never "safe" in the context of road safety. As a term of art, "safe" cannot be applied to either the cul-de-sac or the driveway.

The range of opinions related to what constitutes acceptably safe conditions highlights a need to define safety in a way that ensures constancy in the application. Again, students of road safety generally accept that a durable change in safety must arise from a change in the physical or operational conditions of the road, both of which are measurable quantities. For this reason, changes to the roadway physical attributes or traffic control can only render roadways more or less safe.

In considering the opinion of the childcare worker, she was considered knowledgeable in child safety and, by inference, thought to have knowledge of road safety by the politicians who were present. She was a voice of authority. However, almost all individuals hold some kind of opinion on road safety, and in an open forum, each must be given a voice. Even within the transportation engineering discipline, there are widely dispersed levels of knowledge and opinion concerning road safety.

Within the last ten years, research has intensified, which has greatly increased the knowledge of some. However, the dispersal of that knowledge can be limited, making it only available to those who seek it out. There are those at the forefront of the research who have intimate knowledge of an increasingly complex science in road safety. Others simply rely on design manuals to establish road safety. In a public forum, the difference between perception and reality can fade in the face of public narratives.

Attempts to accommodate the broadest range of narrative and opinion exposes the concepts of facility safety to unquantifiable considerations. Increasingly, this range includes the public view, myths, and perceptions of risk held by the public rather than measurable safety as determined by road safety professionals. While designers and road safety engineers may like to ensure that all decision-making is premised on the application of rigorous science and engineering, at least some future road safety decisions are unlikely to be determined in such a clinical environment. It may be expected that special interest groups will use judicial, quasi-judicial, or political processes to advance their view of road safety.

To illustrate this point, a midsized city had installed a comprehensive one-way street system in the 1960s. Fundamental concepts for its installation were based on engineering principles and human factors considerations. The one-way system reduced the number of conflict points for drivers and pedestrians at unsignalized intersections from thirty-two to just five. The reduction in the number of conflict points at signalized intersections was not as great because some of the movements are not allowed to proceed at the same time.

For example, drivers (and pedestrians) did not need to look in both directions to determine whether to proceed from a side street into the main street when crossing or turning. Rather, they only needed to evaluate the speed and arrival time of traffic coming from one direction. Thus, entering or crossing a street was a much simpler process. The system recognized human factors limitations and enabled better coping for system users while speeds could be controlled through signal progression.

With the advent of streets designed for equity among all users, the narrative became centered on slowing down vehicles while every collision was attributed to the one-way feature. This perspective was pitched aggressively by advocacy groups and secured the support of the only newspaper in the city. As a result, the system is undergoing a reversion to a two-way system. In this situation, there is little incentive for anyone to test the collision experience of the two systems since the results may run contrary to the narrative, and no decision-maker wants to be put in that position.

In recognition of the wide range of opinions related to what is reasonably safe, even among road safety professionals, attempts to obtain a consensus on acceptable road safety can be a daunting task. Therefore, it is important that practitioners universally understand and apply road safety concepts. This at least allows the determination of consistent levels of road safety. Whether or not those levels are adopted as acceptable may be debated by interest groups. To establish a basis for describing road safety in the future, it is perhaps worthwhile to recognize how road safety considerations have been facilitated in the past.

16.3 The Highway 407 Safety Review

In Ontario in 1997, the following issues were fleetingly projected from the design office into public view. A proposed new freeway system had proceeded through functional planning and design in the 1970s. Lands had been acquired, and everything sat ready for final design and construction. When the decision to construct was made two decades later, the design update was fast-tracked with little in the way of change.

The roadway was constructed, and in a display of triumph by the government and transportation industry, the Ontario Provincial Police were invited to preview it. The police were very direct in their evaluation of the facility, saying the facility had some unsafe features. Following that assessment, the road was not opened for public use. Some of the highlighted concerns were unprotected high-mast lighting supports and the design radius of inner loop ramps. In response, the province retained the Professional Engineers of Ontario, who assembled a panel of six safety and design experts from across Canada to examine the design of the constructed facility. The panel consisted of both academics and prominent practitioners. The resulting report effectively became a safety audit, possibly Ontario's first.[2] It also exposed a significant failure by the engineers and reviewers in the consideration of public safety at the pinnacle of highway development in the province.

The nature of the police's road safety challenge was unique and very public. Here was Ontario's newest freeway, supposedly designed to satisfy premiere levels of public safety. Police voiced their concerns given their experience, including millions of kilometers of travel, as well as observation of the collision-prone locations and potential hazards within the existing freeway system. Evaluation by the experts echoed several of the police concerns. The road authority did act to diminish the hazards police and experts highlighted. To the benefit of those now using the facility, the expected safety performance of the road was raised with the provision of cost-effective, safety-conscious enhancements. The safety enhancements arising from the challenge would not likely have been implemented before opening the highway unless the police had expressed their views so publicly.

Did this mean there was a shift in who would determine the safety of

Ontario roads? No, but it did illustrate the depth of knowledge the public held when they have a specific opportunity to consider the safety inherent to the design-build industry. The experts' suggestions were returned to the design professionals for consideration. Practically, a decision by the road authority not to support the recommendations of the experts was insupportable. Even so, decisions respecting expected safety performance were effectively removed from the traditional source—the road design professional—and placed in the domain of several safety specialists. The experts moved the facility in the direction of safer operations. The resulting report was again a consensus based on individual experience, bias, and opinion. The implications of this action were far-reaching and effectively changed the design process in Ontario, at least for a time. This event led to the emergence of the road safety reviews as accepted practice in the province.

16.4 Determining the Safety of the Current Streetscape

Road design and traffic control are provided by transportation and traffic engineers and technologists. Current geometric design standards have been undergoing development for well over seventy years. In the early years of standards development, committees of design experts relied on classical physics, preliminary studies, assumptions, analyses, and opinion to establish design standards. These standards aimed to equip design professionals with the tools to create roads they believed would meet acceptable safety standards. These experts recognized that information was inexact and further study was needed. Public agencies adopted the safety standards, and the public seemed to as well. Over the years, the standards have been reviewed, reassessed, and expanded. While much has changed, many of the initial premises remain.

In the 1990s, the collision experience on US and Canadian roadways led a growing group within the industry to recognize that the safety the road systems provided was a significant issue. New concepts for safety assessment were researched in several countries, leading to explicit safety considerations in facility planning, design, operations, and maintenance. The thinking shortly thereafter became consolidated in the concept of design and in-situ safety audits. In design, the audits reviewed geometric elements and recognized the importance of considering safety-conscious elements that could provide improved safety at a reasonable cost. The same process could be applied to operating facilities where collisions were identified as a problem. Several manuals were developed specifically for this purpose. The first Canadian audits that I am aware of were produced by the University of New Brunswick in 1999.[3] The US Federal Highway Administration produced a guide in 2006.[4] A national guide for Canada was issued in 2001.[5]

At about the same time, it was also recognized that the identification of collision-prone locations could be a problem in itself. This led to the development of better systematic analyses and structured methodologies developed to identify those locations in a whole network analysis. In this process, road sections and intersections were grouped according to common characteristics such as traffic volume, road type, and so on, and subject to systemic analysis. Collision experience was identified, including variation over the years, and smoothing techniques were developed to identify an expected collision rate, best reflected in about seven years or more of data. In this way, every road section and intersection in a network could be ranked for collision experience, and black spots—collision-prone locations—could be identified. These black spots could be tested to determine the potential for improvement. Those intersections that ranked high on the list could then be scheduled for safety improvements using a cost-effective approach. The focus and methodology development led to enhanced safety consciousness in the industry.

However, to better assess both design proposals and existing facility safety, the industry required additional tools. Indeed, those key individuals focusing on roadway safety believed that transportation professionals were not making sound decisions because they lacked explicit information of the facility features' effects on safety.[6] From these beginnings, those concerned about highway safety commenced the development of a highway/roadway consciousness. The American Association of State Highway and Transportation Officials (AASHTO) embarked on a major project to develop the *Highway Safety Manual* (*HSM*). This publication provides guidance for well-researched, quantitative safety assessments in the provision of roadway facilities. The first edition was issued in 2010 and has been undergoing refining enhancements ever since.[7]

The *HSM* is a multivolume manual that contains information related to human factors, the fundamentals of traffic safety, safety management and improvement programs, and predictive methods for assessing alternative designs and improvements. The manual informs users about the data required for effective safety management and crash modification factors (CMF). These factors quantify the change in expected average crash frequency because of geometric or operational modifications to a site from the set of base conditions. For example, the provision of a two-way continuous left-turn lane on a four-lane roadway has a modification factor suggesting the post-installation crash rate would be about 0.76 that of the pre-installation rate.[8]

These advancements in the transportation engineering industry are important to the practice of forensic engineering. The history of an injury site is important to what the transportation authority should have or could have had in place at the time of a specific event. If a location was identified as a priority location for potential improvement but no improvements were completed, the reasons need to be stated. The reasons for not having completed improvements can be relevant, even contributory to collision events. Therefore, documentation related to such contributing factors needs to be examined during collision investigations.

Since these types of programs have been developed, transportation authorities are better able to understand the collision experience within their systems and act to the best of their ability. The search for and identification of problem locations, along with an expenditure of resources to remove or mitigate the problem, has been a task of transportation authorities since before I entered the industry in 1974. Therefore, the absence of comprehensive programs in the context of the public concern for safety in this day and age may be considered a failure within the travel authority. Still, to have that type of information is to recognize a need for improvement and an expenditure of funds.

Perhaps for this reason, in investigating the collision experience of a crash site, the authority is often not able to produce relevant information, and I have been referred to the police department's individual collision reports. Like the basis of many maintenance standards/defenses, the authority is not confronted with a liability if it was not aware that the problem existed. It is left to the reader to determine whether the travel authorities should be more proactive in searching for problems.

16.5 Challenging Traditional Design Practice

The road design professional has traditionally been the first and sometimes the only individual in a road authority's facility design and approval process explicitly concerned with road safety. Others involved in the design process simply expect road safety will be satisfied with compliance to geometric design standards. The design professional obtains guidance for a nominally safe design from the design manual. Designers' preferred approach is often to maximize the movement function at minimal cost, which is enabled by the minimal limits set out in design manuals. It is assumed, sometimes incorrectly, that adherence with the manual will produce a safe design.

Given this discussion, there is a growing array of participants who may in the future question the level of road safety provided by manuals. Those individuals include road safety professionals, as well as politicians, journalists, lawyers, and homemakers—in fact, anyone in the public.

Special interest groups have specific goals related to road safety. Their interest in road safety or some other advocacy may arise as a means to promote or protect business interests, to improve the quality of life for those residents living along the road, or to further environmental concerns. Their knowledge can be significant and their influence on the political process and the media substantive.

Such groups are unrestrained by design or control standards or public expenditures. They are free to set acceptable road safety standards as a primary focus—or abandon it—in seeking other goals. Their position may be readily adopted by law enforcement, which is deemed to have significant experience and insight in matters of road safety through their role in enforcement and as collision investigators. Alternatively, politicians may inadvertently set standards by making decisions that move projects in the direction of safety—or away from it—in seeking public support. Other key participants in this process involve investigative journalists and special interest groups. However, anyone may question the extent of road safety and find a narrative to advance their cause.

With this array of participants voicing opinions on the level of roadway safety, it must be expected that from time to time, those design professionals and even road safety engineers will be challenged for control over who will determine acceptable safety. In some cases, the challenge may be well-founded, as it was in the case of Highway 407.

16.6 Emergence of the Safety Assessment Process

Like the driver with a wide range of reasons for speeding, design professionals are assumed to have a broad range of objectives to be satisfied through design. Objectives may include the need to keep traffic moving, to provide property access, to keep construction or operating costs down, to reduce emissions, or to protect the environment. Road safety is just one issue of several for design professionals.

In observing emerging practices where there are competing issues to be resolved, the weight assigned to safety enhancements may be inappropriate if left to the design professionals alone. Processes now used to incorporate safety decisions into roadway design rely on experts to identify issues about the safety of the design. It is then up to the design professional to adopt the expert's recommendations or to defend the safety decisions of the design. By its nature, the process is one that raises questions within the profession about the appropriateness of safety decisions.

As a result of the questioned ability of design professionals to effectively deal with road safety (and other design issues), routine road safety reviews, like that done for Highway 407, have emerged as a subdiscipline of transportation engineering. Ostensibly, the role of the review is to enhance safety, assuming that nominal safety is provided by the geometric design standards. However, standards do not ensure a safe driving experience for all motorists. For this reason, the role of the safety review is directed at ensuring there is substantive safety. If the role of the safety specialist performing the review is to enhance the safety provided in roadway design, it would seem reasonable that others may also be granted a voice in that capacity. In an open process, experience has shown those providing input will not be limited to designers or road safety professionals.

By inference, the process of using a specialist for evaluating road safety can lead to a public perception that design professionals may be less able or willing to ensure adequate road safety. This process suggests that the responsibility for safeguarding the public is either removed from the design professional or that their role in ensuring safety is diminished in some way. Such notions are, of course, inconsistent with engineering practice. Still, the process and the impressions created by the emergence of the road safety review are likely to affect the profession over the long term.

In the emergence of these trends, it is an unsettling thought that design professionals not specifically trained in road safety may be less attentive to public safety than those specifically designated as safety experts. Likewise, it is unsettling to consider that acceptably safe designs will not be formulated unless a safety specialist is retained. Where this process is going is currently uncharted. In a recent situation, after the in-situ road safety review was completed, a couple of local politicians added their own suggestions to trump those of the review.

Based on this process, reasonable questions arise: How safe is "safe enough"? How are safety decisions made? And who should make those decisions? While substantive research has examined how to determine road safety, the implementation of road safety is much less clinical. There is always opportunity for the careful evaluation of systemic safety undertaken during the design stage to fall off the rails during the implementation stages. The benefits of a systemic assessment of road safety may only be realized if the implementation program continues to reflect the same depth of thought and goals. Hence, road safety reviews are ideally conducted at several stages in the design process. It is therefore worthwhile for road authorities to plan for road safety in the context of multistage exposure in a public forum and in the scientific sense.

Considering how everyone has a perception of acceptable risk, everyone also has an opinion about what is adequate safety and what is not. In this context, like the childcare worker allowing children to play in the cul-de-sac, everyone with exposure to travel may be considered a "safety expert." Their opinions are based on a set of experiences reflecting personal bias, adopted beliefs, living environment, and much more. In almost every case, individuals have vast exposure to the road system, geometric design, and traffic control attributes over an extended time. Consequently, within the general population, there is expansive lay knowledge of design and control elements affecting roadway operations. Therefore, those critical of roadway elements generally have some knowledge base for their opinion.

In the case of Highway 407, much of the real decision related to safety rested with the panel of experts, although the panel's suggestions were returned to the road authority for specific action—or not. In retrospect, the process effectively allowed much of the decision-making to be made away from a public forum, but it was representative of a noticeable trend to question the level of road safety. In the end, the experts made their suggestions and the road authority quietly followed through, the public excluded.

In this instance there was a perception of unsafety associated with the new road that was subsequently supported by the recognized experts.

While previously in use elsewhere, the concept of using experts specifically trained in their discipline to assess road safety has caught on as a necessary design activity. Now, finding an appropriate level of acceptable safety performance has become a specialized discipline within transportation engineering. It spawned a whole new consulting industry of preparing road safety reviews. By virtue of the process, retaining the "expert" for a review is likely to precipitate safety enhancements and a better design that will be acceptable to the public.

Still, one must wonder why that objective cannot be trusted to the design professional. After all, engineers are required to consider public safety in the provision of any design. In this process, it would seem that design professionals have systematically failed in their obligation to the public and are now paying the price.

16.7 Desired Rural Road Safety

The second example of challenging road safety thresholds involved a two-lane rural road. The road in this case was formerly a provincial highway and constructed to the standards of a primary highway. Growing traffic volumes and changes in traffic orientation had come into conflict with the desired roadway operations of roadside residents. In 2002, a dramatic collision was followed several weeks later by a second collision with multiple fatalities. While the driver in the second collision had a blood-alcohol level well over the legal limit, individuals living on or near the road stated the road geometry was a significant contributor. Collision occurred on approach to a vertical curve. The opinions of roadside residents were reported in the press, and virtually overnight, the road became a "killer highway." Subsequent to that, or perhaps spurred on by the exposure, a citizens action committee was formed and continued to receive ongoing media attention.

In the year following the collisions, the citizens group received several safety enhancements they had pushed for, including lower speed limits and intensified police enforcement. Two years later, their efforts were widely reported as successful, as there had been no fatal collisions, and total collisions were down by 28 percent over a one-year period.

However, the "killer" adjective continued to be used in referring to the road. Furthermore, the police had issued more speeding tickets on this road than on any other in the city. Staff reports indicated that changes, including extra law enforcement, have not reduced the extent of speeding, with 92 percent of drivers exceeding the posted speed limit, which was reduced from 80 km/h to 70 km/h (50 mph to 44 mph). Travel speeds were not reported by the media, and road authority staff recently recommended returning the regulatory speeds to their previous level.

In response, the citizens group suggested the data collected by the road authority were misrepresenting actual conditions and further pointed out that the unsafe conditions arose from blowing snow, curves, blind spots, deep ditches, and poor visibility. The citizens group secured the support of both area municipal and provincial politicians. Consequently, the city decided not to reinstate the previous speed limits. Since then, the group has developed a list of further initiatives to be implemented, including the installation of roundabouts at intersecting roadways. The citizens group has recently indicated that:

> We're experts on this highway. We see the same issues going on over and over again and we want to add to the expertise the City has.[9]

The actions of the city in response to public demands may well have improved the safety of this road. In this process, the citizens group has used data to advance their goals through public forum. The data the citizens group used is appealing but not necessarily unbiased or correct, and while well-intentioned, may not be in the best public interest. For example, there is heavy reliance on just two years of data, which appears to suffer significantly from problems related to regression-to-the-mean effect and other issues related to statistical inference.

However, the citizens group's information is readily available and frequently repeated and reported by the media. It has in effect become *the* information used by the decision-makers, possibly to the exclusion of even the data supplied by safety evaluators. Politicians hear or observe the data and rely on its inference because it is simple, seems to tell a good story, and may be used to garner political support. Through this process, the group has acquired the necessary political support to advance their goals. On the other hand, the professional staff of the road authority have been discredited and made to appear inept in evaluating road safety. The recent city decision to support the recommendations of the "expert citizens" suggests the road authority professionals have little influence in identifying acceptable safety.

While the actions of the citizens group are intended to enhance the safety of their roadway, the goals of a road authority may not be so singularly focused. It is only through the systemic analysis of the road system that the relative safety performance of the subject road may be evaluated. The cost of substantive police enforcement on the subject road is perhaps drawing important resources away from other policing or roadway enforcement needs. Furthermore, the group's current proposals for safety enhancements have substantive dollar costs attached. While the cost of satisfying the citizens group may have been minimal to this point, the more recent proposals require substantial investment. Among the other initiatives, those proposals call for the installation of several roundabouts. In this regard, the potential for drawing important dollars away from other more critical expenditures on road safety appears more likely.

16.8 Where Is the Safety Bar Going to Be Set in the Future?

The minimum values for design elements provided in geometric design standards may perhaps establish a lower bound for roadway safety. However impractical, one may also envisage an upper bound that includes a full range of human factors—possible driver action, roadway and vehicle operating characteristics, and all the influences from weather and other sources. Between these two limits, for some like the citizens group, there is no predetermined threshold of safety to be satisfied. The safety bar may be set at any height where they call the shots.

The road safety bar will be set according to the quality of information provided and depth of understanding of those making the decisions. Design standards, which provide a reasonable trade-off between safety and other objectives, including cost, traditionally filled the role. This design model is likely to be increasingly challenged in the future. That past approach may be increasingly viewed as secretive, possibly not reflective of public standards for acceptable safety, and perhaps even contrary to public good. Yet, where decisions take place in a more open or public forum, there is opportunity for poorly formulated or unfounded safety decisions, as well as the serious risk of ad hoc safety applications.

In addition, future challenges are likely to question the decision of how safe is "safe enough." The community at large wants to be informed and is increasingly provided means to become involved or otherwise influence public decisions. Unfounded but popular arguments that support safety at a single location may well produce a systemwide safety detriment if safety issues are not dealt with in an even-handed manner. Inarticulate arguments that do not maximize safety may be viewed as simply promoting crashes, a role that most individuals and agencies want to avoid. On the other hand, safety improvements are subject to the laws of diminishing returns. Still, in the face of increasingly less acceptance of risk and higher valuations of personal health and safety, there will likely be a significant move toward safer roads, fueled by sources exogenous to the design profession. For this reason, as previously stated, the selection of acceptable safety may become a daunting challenge.

Just where the safety bar should be set during the design process does not seem to have a ready answer. In the broadest sense of health care, the cost of achieving societal goals through implementing safety enhancements beyond those provided by the nominal safety of the standards may never be known. After all, it is conceivable that, at some point, road safety expenditures are made at the expense of other health-care expenditures. Regardless, improved road safety will reduce the disastrous health and financial impacts of preventable collisions. Furthermore, the cost of safety enhancements considered as a capital or operating expense but left unimplemented simply transfers those costs to the few individuals involved in related collisions, as well as other systems encompassing enforcement, emergency services, the judicial system, and health care. In this circumstance, the collision costs related to some safety enhancements should be treated as part of the roadway capital and operating cost, but they typically remain unassumed by the road authority.

16.9 The Role of the Road Safety Professional

Procedures for evaluating road safety have been around for many years. Many traffic engineering textbooks identify the monitoring of collision experience as an important management tool and specify means to accomplish that task. Many conscientious road authorities have acquired the knowledge and experience to assess road safety in a systematic way. Unfortunately, many road authorities do not manage their road system safety as well as they should. Some do not even maintain copies of collision reports.

In the event of collision, the press will typically seek easily available information from those willing to convey it. Frequently, that involves interviewing police or nearby residents because road authorities either do not have the information or are unwilling to discuss it due to political or liability reasons. In doing so, the road authority excludes itself from a public evaluation process. When the press goes elsewhere for information, implying the road authority has a poor safety record is convenient, impersonal, and frequently directed to reduce the onus on individual drivers involved in collisions. In following investigations of liability, one of the first questions that a road authority may expect is how the collision experience of the road section or intersection compares to others within the network.

A response to these events that can indicate the location exhibited substantive safety or was of low priority to improve relative to other locations can provide an effective first line of defense. Without that information, the basic tools that allow a road authority to defend itself in a liability claim or in planning the safety of a new road are missing. The road authority has no informed or substantive basis for declaring a position regarding road safety issues. When the public demands road safety action, having information available that suggests the location is indistinct from other locations may be sufficient to satisfy those asking the questions.

Given these considerations, one must wonder whether the design professional and road safety engineer will remain qualified in the eyes of the public to determine acceptable levels of road safety. If road safety is unable to be set to some minimally acceptable public threshold, design decisions are unlikely to be enduring. Furthermore, the design or safety engineer will be unable to incorporate acceptable safety into the design. In this event, levels of road safety may ultimately be decided in an open, possibly political forum. Thus, road safety will be susceptible to the biases and opinions of any citizen expert within the public who has a particular view of how road safety may benefit them.

To manage road safety in a meaningful way in this situation, those responsible must provide the appropriate data revealing a full range of benefits and consequences arising from road safety decisions or indecision. The information must be sufficient, well documented, and unbiased.

The role of the design professional and safety engineer seem to be in transition at this time. In the meantime, it is appropriate for the design professional to go beyond the nominal safety provided by geometric design standards. Prudence would suggest that designs will need to ensure substantive safety for all road network users, recognizing the likely significant variation in risk tolerance.

Levels of safety established in this manner may be sufficient to satisfy public demand. When they are not, the design professional must be prepared to identify the consequences of changing design levels of safety for all those exposed to risk. To do so, they will need procedures and protocols capable of revealing the full consequences of decisions in a manner the public can understand.

17

A FINAL THOUGHT

In view of the emerging trends in who will evaluate road safety, a network analysis is unlikely to be sufficient. Rather, the network analysis is only one step. Having accomplished that task, it is important to also have a proactive program of network-based enhancements in place. This requires setting reasonable priorities in a systemic approach to safety. That information must be supported by firsthand knowledge of the geometric design and traffic control elements that have a meaningful effect on road safety.

Perhaps even more importantly, it will be necessary to convey complex road safety information to the public in a concise and understandable way. Similarly, the road authority must have an ability to anticipate and deal with myths, misnomers, and misinformation that may be held as beliefs by the public or the media. To effectively deal with these issues, the road authority may reconsider some of their protocols used to exchange information with the public.

Throughout my days as a forensic transportation engineer, my assessments, calculations, opinion, and commentary have been under continuous review and evaluation by engineers who see the industry through an entirely different lens. Almost without exception, their views reinforce the status quo of the industry. Furthermore, their position is formulated according to current knowledge—often their own current knowledge.

Yet, I have consistently come across situations and conditions where system users have been harmed because of the manner in which they are treated by transportation authorities. Those harms often come about because of indifference at some level, but they can also be embedded in the protocols and standards of the industry. To serve those who have been harmed, one task has been to question why things are the way they are, to ask who benefits, and to point out what I believe to be weighted results. This process has led me to ponder certain aspects of the industry and voice my position on that material.

As this book is intended to recognize variation within the user population, it is self-evident to me that many may take exception to the information presented herein or the way it is presented. I consider those opinions to be important and hope to treat them with respect, for validation can occur only when knowledge is in the open. This has formed a secondary premise of the book, in which industry protocols and standards brought into an open public forum can be evaluated and gain acceptance in that public forum. If that does not happen, specific issues may find their way to acceptance through litigation.

It may well be found publicly or judicially that encompassing 85 percent of the user population within commonly applied standards provides acceptable safety for the public in transportation matters regardless of the share of the population that may be exempted for other reasons, such as medical toxicity. If that number is found to provide acceptable safety, then I will be content.

EXAMPLE OF THE EVOLUTION OF A THRESHOLD-BASED REGULATION

This first appendix sets out the development trend leading to the provision of a provincial regulation in Ontario for roadway maintenance. The second appendix discusses the reasonableness of the terms of the Minimum Maintenance Standards (MMS) as they existed in 2002 through 2010. While there have been significant changes since that time, much of the fundamental concepts of the standards remain or have been expanded on in the more recent revisions to the MMS.

A1.1 OGRA Standards 1995

In 1995, the Ontario Good Roads Association (OGRA) produced a guide for roadway service standards.[1] As an organization largely composed of municipal road authorities, OGRA produced the publication to help its members plan and maintain a consistent level of service for municipal roadways in consideration of growing budgetary pressures. As Ontario applies joint and several liability in motor vehicle crashes, the effort was well-founded to allow municipalities to improve system operations by reducing the contribution of the road system to collisions, while at the same time constructing a reasonable defense against claims.

The OGRA standards set out twenty-two service standards that identified a minimal requirement for road maintenance. The development of the standards represented excellent initiative in the creation of a common maintenance standard. The creation of the standards was a move toward enabling motorists to experience consistent roadway conditions when moving within and between jurisdictions.

The OGRA standards created a classification system for roadways according to traffic volume, location and setting (urban, semiurban, or rural), and travel speed. In addition, the standards identified two maintenance levels, including a minimal level and a desirable level. It was noted in the manual that the desirable standards meet not only the safety and legal obligations but also economic and social standards.[2] However, no explanation was provided as to how it was determined that the desirable standard satisfied some threshold of social acceptance.

Through this means in 1995, OGRA raised the issue that minimum standards were required to satisfy some standard held by the public, not simply those set by road authorities alone. Such musings were appropriate for several reasons. Some municipal road authorities of the time may have had well-established maintenance practices that went well beyond the minimums cited by the new standards.

The OGRA standards were intended to be performance-oriented. The winter maintenance provisions of the OGRA manual issued six standards related to the provision of winter maintenance. The standards were in some measure a composite of event-based and outcome-based approaches to winter maintenance. There were overriding considerations in the standards to reflect the need for operations during an event for producing a specific outcome during the event.

These included the following:

- **Winter inspections:** This standard indicated that the roadway authority was obligated to know the condition of its roads during the winter season, during both ambient and storm conditions. All roadways were required to undergo winter inspections on a routine basis by an inspector reporting to a supervisor and keeping appropriate records of the conditions observed. Inspections were to have regard for the maximum cycle time, which was defined as the maximum time between inspections. During storm events, desirable cycle times varied from four hours to one day, while minimum cycle times varied from eight hours to two days.

- **Ambient speed:** Where accumulated snow and/or ice on the traveled surface impedes vehicles' ability to travel, the minimum ambient travel speeds were to be restored within a specified lag time. Ambient speed was expressed as a percent of the reasonable "summer" travel speed.[3] This reflects the description of a hazard[4] where an adjustment to speed or path may be necessary.

- **Exposure:** This standard referred to the road surface exposure during ambient conditions throughout the winter. When snow and ice remained on the road after storm conditions, maintenance operations were to be directed in such a manner as to efficiently produce a specified surface exposure condition within a maximum lag time. Exposure conditions included bare, center bare, and snow-packed conditions. This standard reflects some desired operating condition and implicitly connects the notion of tying roadway friction conditions to maintenance activity, if perhaps somewhat obtusely.

- **Snowfall accumulation:** This was identified as the maximum depth to which newly fallen or general windblown snow is allowed to accumulate on the road surface. A caveat to this standard was that where it was not possible to maintain the depth of snow below required levels during a storm event, servicing would proceed on a priority basis. Snow removal operations were not required for roadways with fewer than four hundred vehicles per day or overnight between 15:00 hours (3:00 p.m.) and 06:00 hours (6:00 a.m.) the next morning.

- **Localized ice:** This standard recognized the effects of weather and traffic in creating road surface ice—compaction ice—on bridge decks, hills, curves, and intersections. It was indicated that where localized icing requires significant change in vehicle operation relative to the general conditions on the road, treatment was warranted. Snow removal operations were not required for roadways with fewer than four hundred vehicles per day or overnight between 15:00 hours (3:00 p.m.) and 06:00 hours (6:00 a.m.) the next morning.

- **Localized snow:** During ambient winter conditions, localized snow drifting may occur over the road surface. Where such drifts occur, the maximum condition (depth) measured across more than half of one travel lane in a localized area should be removed within the lag time. Overnight operations were not required for roadways having fewer than one thousand vehicles per day. With this standard, OGRA recognized the special circumstances related to windblown snow on the roadway and dealt with it in a manner that was different from newly fallen snow.

In assuming the role of a standards-issuing agency, OGRA had issued a set of standards that were considered reasonable by its representative road authorities. In establishing their standards, the agency provided explanatory notes related to why they were needed and what the standards were intended to achieve, including risk management. The standards were somewhat reflective of those used by the province of the time. However, it is understood there was reluctance to accept these standards by some road authorities. In any event, that all changed when roadway maintenance was brought under the umbrella of provincial regulation. Further to that, the nature of facilities in need of winter maintenance has been greatly expanded.

A1.2 Ministry of Transportation (Ontario)

In Ontario, the Ministry of Transportation (the Ministry) owned and operated connecting highways and freeways between municipalities. These roadways typically had speeds of 80 to 100 km/h (50 to 62 mph) in rural areas. As such, the Ministry is a well-funded senior road authority with research and development capabilities and a source to which less senior road authorities could turn for guidance and assistance in setting out maintenance programs.

The winter maintenance practice of the Ministry, much of which was set out as early as 1979 through 1995, was carried through to the Ministry's maintenance manual of 2003.[5] The manual is divided into two sections describing winter maintenance. The Maintenance Quality Standards (MQS) represent a minimum level of operational performance according to the nature of a defect, specified service levels, and response time. The Maintenance Best Practices (MBP) are guidelines that represent the Ministry's experience and expertise in the effective delivery of service. The guidelines of the MBP present additional activities undertaken for the maintenance of roadways and thus represent a reasonable standard of practice. However, the achievement may not be defined by a performance standard. The MBP also defines the materials necessary to achieve the MQS.

Since these standards were issued, the Ministry has moved to fully contracted winter maintenance services for its highways. The maintenance contracts impose on the contractors specific provisions for servicing its roadways. However, it is understood that as of 2023, the Ministry's own standards have not been revised. As it is not able to transfer responsibility for the operation of its roadways, it is understood these standards justly remain in place and, as such, underpin the requirements of the contractors.

A1.3 Ministry Classification

The section of the manual defining the MQS advises Ministry staff to conduct winter maintenance operations before, during, and after winter weather events. Section MQS-701 of the manual sets out the Ministry's level of service requirements for its highways. The requirements for winter maintenance are based on a roadway classification system using traffic volume.[6] There are only two classes of roadway with more than two thousand vehicles per day, which ensures there is a relatively consistent level of servicing for a broad group of roadways. In addition, there are only five classes of roadway with no further stratification, which makes the identification of the required service level a relatively simple matter.

The absence of speed in defining a roadway classification is appropriate. In the consideration of speed, vehicles involving a head-on collision on low-speed urban roadways with a 50 km/h (31 mph) legal speed limit can have a typical closing speed in excess of 100 km/h (62 mph). Where the speed limit is 80 km/h (50 mph), the closing speed can be well in excess of 160 km/h (100 mph). Both sets of closing speeds are sufficient to produce serious injuries or fatalities.

The propensity of any one driver to lose control of his vehicle on a slippery road is related to the actions of individual drivers within the driving population, not the volume of traffic on the roadway. Thus, it may be expected that any one driver on a low-traffic-volume road is just as likely to lose control as any one driver on a high-traffic-volume road, given they experience the same depth of snow or icy conditions. The Ministry therefore inherently recognized and accommodated this characteristic of vehicle operations by having a small number of roadway classifications with a wide range of traffic volume applicable to the two classifications with the most traffic.

In implicitly recognizing this characteristic of the driving population, the Ministry commences both its plowing and salting operations on all its roadways under identical conditions.[7] With this approach, drivers on a high-speed roadway with a low traffic volume are not penalized at the outset of winter operations by the road they are traveling at the time.

A1.4 Ministry Winter Patrols

During the frost months, roadway conditions are monitored by the Ministry using a system of road patrols that are available twenty-four hours per day, seven days per week. The purpose of patrolling is to maintain firsthand information related to road conditions, in real time and over a broad area. When major weather events move through, the patrols initiate winter maintenance, including both snowplowing and salting of highways when conditions warrant action. In the performance of this task, the patrols monitor roadways to ensure they are reasonably safe for use by the public.

The duties of road patrols during the winter weather months are set out in MQS-702. During storm events, patrols are undertaken as frequently as necessary to monitor and communicate roadway and weather conditions. Throughout an event, patrols continue to monitor road and weather conditions, direct and adjust snow and ice control operations, and ensure that the operations continue to be appropriate for the roadway and weather conditions.[8]

While the Ministry maintains many remote weather monitoring stations around the province, these devices do not provide an alternative to the patrol but rather provide assistance in the manner of additional documented information. In this regard, while Ontario highways may be electronically monitored, almost all decision-making is premised on firsthand knowledge obtained by inspectors.[9]

A1.5 Ministry Winter Operations

MQS-702 identifies the plowing priorities of the Ministry for mobilizing operations, the duties of winter patrols, plowing, and spreading chemicals and sand on the roadway. Within each activity, the standard identifies the activity level to be supplied and the priority of operations but does not determine performance criteria. In this way, the Ministry provides an event-based approach to winter maintenance. Events may take the form of winter storms but also include less dramatic events such as overnight frost.

The need for salting is defined by the friction provided by the road surface—a slippery condition—not by the definition of a physical contaminant on the road surface. The activity level is defined by the length of route or duration of time on a route. By this means, the Ministry becomes fully engaged in maintenance operations before or at the onset of an event and continues working until the cleanup is completed. However, the classification system allows the Ministry to prioritize service to some degree by enabling somewhat longer routes or circuit times on routes with a higher classification number (lower traffic volume).

The section defining the MBP of the manual presents the activities of Ministry staff for periods before, during, and after winter weather events. MBP-701 identifies the Ministry best practices with regard to the timing for plowing, salting, and sanding of roadways. The practice is to be proactive for winter maintenance rather than reactive. For example, the practice indicates when operations are to commence and how long to continue. With the onset of a storm, salting for all classifications begins when the depth of snow is greater than 0.5 cm (0.2 in.), although the need to service slippery conditions will supersede this criterion.[10] Plowing for all classifications is to begin before snow has reached a depth of 2 cm (0.8 in.), not after. Sand is to be applied for traction whenever slippery conditions are found and when salting is not likely to be effective.

As Ministry practice identifies measurable activity levels for winter operations, including circuit times for spreading routes and distances for plowing routes, the nature of the performance is independent of the weather conditions and remains tied to equipment in service and assigned to routes. Action is commenced as soon as the equipment and technology become effective in treating a condition. The approach is self-contained, as there is no dependency on the police or the public to be the eyes of the Ministry in finding hazardous conditions. The approach also prevents the Ministry from playing a waiting game to see when they may be notified of ice conditions or a triggering snow accumulation depth.

Through many years of experience and research, the Ministry had developed well-planned procedures for plowing and salting/sanding its highways. The application of combination units has been effective in the completion of these tasks. The blade at the front of the truck removes most of the snow from the road surface. However, for practical reasons, a film of snow is left on the road. If left unattended, the film of snow can develop into ice, allowing slippery conditions to develop. To prevent this, sand or salt may be applied by the truck from a chute or spinner behind the cab of snowplows or by separate salting vehicles.[11]

The Ministry standards also identify activities that are to be undertaken after the storm has passed through, once the travel lanes of the roadway have been adequately serviced. These operations include such matters as the clearing of roadway shoulders of snow, the removal of snow that may cause ramping at highway barriers, and the lowering of stored snow to restore required visibility conditions.

In summary, the Ministry standard attempts to maintain the operating condition of the roadway at a level defined by its operations, initiated in response to reduced friction and a need to satisfy circuit times. By the application of circuit times for plowing and salting, there is a limit to the extent that conditions are allowed to exist before servicing again takes place. In this way, when snow or slippery conditions exist, the Ministry operations are required to act promptly and continuously. Servicing is to remain ongoing to maintain roadways at a reasonable level of operation until a satisfactory end state, such as a wet pavement, is present.

In 2010, the Ministry expanded the circuit times for some highways from 1.3 hours to 1.6 hours, indicating that the circuit time commenced on the spreader leaving the yard until the time that it completed the route. The auditor general considered the change in circuit time to provide a reduction in service quality.[12] The reason why the change was made was not identified by the auditor general. Given these types of decisions, one is left to wonder if those making policy decisions adequately consider the public as paramount in providing a public service.

A1.6 The Unreported Development of the Standard

As referenced in the 1995 OGRA manual, substantial emphasis was placed on the relationship between roadway maintenance and litigation. It is an issue with the municipalities that continues to the present day. Perhaps because of that, Ontario municipalities sought to have their defense against claims embedded in legislation.

As of 2002, the new regulation, referred to as the Minimum Maintenance Standards (MMS), provided municipal road and bridge "outcome-based" standards and defined a minimum state of repair for roadways and bridges. The management of safety issues throughout the development of the process is not apparent in the document, and there is no publicly available background documentation related to its development. Further, no stakeholder participation in the preparation of the standards is apparent in the document. There is no evidence in the regulation that there was an independent assessment of the relationship of safety to winter maintenance.

A minimum standard inherently implies identification of the lowest level of service or level of acceptable safety to be provided by the road authority. For winter maintenance, this was interpreted in a manner whereby the MMS would only identify situations or conditions that would initiate a response. A response time was not actually defined but rather inferred. This was the maximum time allowed after notification or an event had ended to repair or remove the hazardous condition.[13] In setting these provisions, the standards were very generous in considering the delicacies of the municipal representatives, in the opinion of the author. This is particularly evident when they are compared to the standards of the province.

A1.7 A Need to Serve the Traveling Public

Drivers everywhere typically experience high friction levels, at least consistent with a wet pavement, for most of the year and even during the frost-prone months. As discussed previously, the reason for removing contaminants from the road surface is to allow drivers to perform the driving task in a manner consistent with their normal experience. Even during the winter months, the ambient condition of the pavement is typically dry (sometimes wet). Servicing returns the roadway to a condition consistent with driver expectancies, thereby enhancing opportunities for safe vehicle operation. The outcome-based standard may well have identified skid resistance—roadway friction—highlighting the need for a wet pavement as the defined outcome in accordance with speed (greater than 50 km/h [30 mph]) and type of roadway—freeway, arterial, collector. This could also have reasonably been tied to a time limit on servicing after the event has ended. However, no such provisions appear within the standard.

Consequently, the regulation suffered from providing a reasonable level of maintenance. The extent of changes made to the regulation over the years confirms this view but invites further reassessment. The fundamental premise of the MMS has not changed. In summary, the multiple revisions over the years place additional burdens on the municipalities, in some respects to improve service to the public, and moves the regulation in the direction of safety. However, other changes seem to be directed at improving the defense offered by the regulation. The author therefore encourages the province and the municipalities to undertake a full-blown safety assessment of the MMS considering a duty to the public as paramount. To provide additional insight to that process, Appendix 2 discusses several aspects of the provisions of the standard.

THE REGULATION THEN AND NOW

In review of provincial legislation and regulation, government agencies tailor laws to meet the needs of their citizens as well as their own. Due to the need to provide suitable travel conditions, there are common threads throughout, including a need to keep facilities in a state of repair. One definition indicates a "reasonable state of repair" means the condition of being structurally sound; free from significant damage, rot, or other deterioration; safe for intended use; and not presenting an unsightly condition.[1] "Safe for intended use" is unrestrained in this definition, and in that respect, is appropriate for public facilities. It may be contended that a more appropriate definition would refer to reasonable safety. However, as part of the definition, reasonable safety is insufficient since every individual using the facility within the bounds of reasonable behavior should not experience harm. Given the many situations and conditions that can develop within the right of way, a reasonable state of repair must be evaluated for each resulting harm, considering the common usage patterns and typical abilities of the users.

The definition of the highway includes all the lands between the property lines and thus includes all the services within the right of way. However, it may be argued there may be a shared responsibility with utility companies within the right of way that do not belong to the municipality.

With the above reference to the repair of the road, the character and location of the roadway or bridge must be considered. The character of the roadway or bridge includes the operating characteristics, such as speed and traffic volume, and other parameters arising from the design or traffic control. The location of the roadway or bridge may be interpreted to include such matters as an urban, suburban, or rural setting or the surrounding terrain such as hills, valleys, or nearby water.

In this case, the legislation was supplemented with a regulation specifying minimum standards for maintenance. As of November 2002, Regulation 239/02—Minimum Maintenance Standards, was enacted and remained in place until 2010. Since that time, additional modifications have recognized the public need while reinforcing the general provisions of the standard. In the following section, this examination sets out elements of the Regulation as it existed until modified in 2010. Commentary and opinion related to the effectiveness of the provisions of the standards is provided. Evaluation of revisions since that time is left for others to contemplate. In that task, some of the concepts and commentary contained in the following sections are applicable.

A2.1 Roadway Inspections

The need for routine patrolling was identified in 2002 and provided the following descriptive requirements and schedule for the activity:

3. (1) The minimum standard for the frequency of routine patrolling of highways is set out in the Table to this section. O. Reg. 239/02, s. 3 (1).

(2) Routine patrolling shall be carried out by driving on or by electronically monitoring the highway to check for conditions described in this Regulation. O. Reg. 239/02, s. 3 (2).

(3) Routine patrolling is not required between sunset and sunrise. O. Reg. 239/02, s. 3 (3).

TABLE: ROUTINE PATROLLING FREQUENCY

Class of Highway	Patrolling Frequency
1	3 times every 7 days
2	2 times every 7 days
3	once every 7 days
4	once every 14 days
5	once every 30 days

Table A2.1: O. Reg. 239/02, s. 3, Table.[2]

The standard for routine patrolling provided no instruction to those undertaking the patrolling. Further, no purpose for patrolling was identified, and no reference to a search for hazards to road users or to other problems with the road system was determined. The standard provided no general reference as to what may constitute a hazard. In terms of winter maintenance, there was no requirement to quantify either the depth of snow on the road or the road surface condition. The standards identified only the frequency that a patrol must travel the roadway. This approach to the provision of routine patrolling excluded any need to identify hazards not specified in the standard as areas of concern and codified liability. For example, snow that was piled up at the side of the road by the road authority and obstructing visibility would not be considered a condition for the patrol to initiate action.

The Ministry standard previously discussed indicates that patrols should "identify conditions that may adversely affect the conditions of the highway, the adjacent property, and the environment and to ensure adherence to the Maintenance Quality Standards and policies."[3] The open-endedness of the Ministry standard ensures that all manner of conditions along and beside the highway are identified and attended to in some manner. To perform that task, patrols require not only an understanding of the maintenance specifications but also an understanding of what constitutes a hazard.

Under the standard, the patrolling activity was to be undertaken by driving the road or via electronic monitoring to check for the conditions described by the Regulation. "Electronic monitoring" is likewise open-ended and subject to wide interpretation. While some road authorities have incident detection systems in place providing video surveillance of roadways, these systems are typically unable to identify specific hazards, such as debris or ice on the road, but may be able to identify the operating condition or snow accumulation on major highways. Remote weather information systems (RWIS) can identify conditions at a single location and can be used to initiate some winter operations. Still, these systems provide only limited and/or localized information.

As no definition is provided for electronic monitoring, it may include several other means. For example, many road authorities subscribe to weather services that fine-tune general forecasts for specific regions or cities. Similarly, for winter maintenance, it may be argued that this monitoring method could include simply listening to the radio or watching the weather station on TV.

In doing so, the road authority would not be required to leave the office or home to have been engaged in electronic monitoring. However, due to the broad areas of coverage provided, these means for monitoring are not sufficient to identify the extent of hazards. For example, the location of drifting snow or presence of black ice are difficult for electronic monitoring to detect, particularly in problem-prone locations. For the identification of these hazards, patrols are required. By far the most informative means to identify the operating condition of roadways is the patrol.

The Regulation provided significant latitude to the road authority regarding the use of road patrols. In the absence of any information related to the duties of the road patrol, there was no binding requirement for the patrol to identify, record, and take action on the conditions found.

By comparison, the Ministry has taken a flexible approach to patrolling. Some of the important elements of the Ministry program are stated below:

In addition to the stated frequencies, road patrols may be required to search for problems more often.[4]

Thus, under certain conditions such as during or following a severe weather event, the Ministry patrollers will be on the road to check for hazards.

All patrol observations and actions taken shall be documented in the Patrol Supervisor's Diary.[5]

Without the documentation, the road authority may contend to have "remained unaware" of certain conditions, which runs counter to the patrolling function in the first place. That function is to establish by documentation the safety readiness of the road system (and to provide a defense against claims). Documentation that records hazards found and acted upon is an important means to show the road authority was attending to its maintenance tasks.

"All conditions causing a Hazard shall be Addressed Immediately" (bold print shown in Ministry Manual).[6]

With this type of provision, one can appreciate that where there may be some doubt about the extent of the hazard, action is likely to be taken. Such provisions reveal the standard has considerable and explicit regard for road safety.

Finally, the effects of the patrolling requirement as stated in the table can be easily illustrated. For a Class 1 roadway, inspection is required three times every seven days. Therefore, for a roadway serving 12,000 vehicles per day at a speed of 80 km/h (50 mph), a road patrol can drive along the road once on Tuesday and again on Thursday and have the weekend off with the third patrol on Monday. The inspection exposure is therefore one inspection per every 28,000 vehicles with weekends off. A Class 2 roadway serving 12,000 less one vehicle per day at speeds of 80 km/h (50 mph) requires an inspection twice every seven days. Therefore, the inspection exposure is one inspection per 42,000 vehicles. Consequently, roadways having similar operational characteristics can have widely different inspection requirements.

The standard codified an ability to undertake no patrolling at specific times of day or on specific days of the week. For example, during the summer season, when traffic volumes are highest on weekends, no patrolling needed to be undertaken on the weekend. The daily time provisions allowed road authorities to do no patrolling after dark. However, when it is dark, visibility conditions can change significantly. There have been many collisions in which the problems road users encountered are not apparent until after dark. These typically relate to conditions where headlights remain invisible after dark (for example, due to a hill), where a vehicle is clearly visible during the day. Thus, the provision for patrolling could allow significant hazards to remain in place for a long time.

Consequently, the requirements for routine patrolling exclude all descriptors of the task and responsibilities of the patrollers, making the standard dysfunctional for winter maintenance. In addition, the standard codifies monitoring in a manner that cannot reveal the temporal extent of hazards found on the road system.

A2.2 The Exclusion of a Winter Patrol Standard

Prior to the development of the standard, the Ontario Good Roads Association (OGRA) had included in their general standards a reasonable and specific standard of practice for winter patrols. When the Ministry (which also issues design and traffic control manuals for Ontario) was developing its maintenance manual, about the same time that these regulations were being developed, it did not identify a separate winter patrol requirement but did include specific practices that were required for winter patrols. Clearly, the thinking of both these two standard-issuing agencies identified winter patrols as a necessary function of the standards. The standard was an important provision consistent with the provisions of the Municipal Act, which required road authorities to take "reasonable steps to prevent the default from arising."[7]

At the time of the Regulation's development, many road authorities did not undertake even routine winter patrols of their network. Obviously, these municipalities were reluctant to initiate a more rigorous winter maintenance standard and would not receive the protection of the standards if they failed to comply. However, routine patrolling remained within the standard, while winter patrolling provisions did not make it that far. Thus, with the removal of separate requirements for winter patrolling, the practice remained an open discussion.

Prior to the establishment of Regulation 239/02 (MMS), there was significant inconsistency between municipalities in the matter of winter patrols of roadways. Some municipalities and the Ministry patrolled roadways 24/7. Other municipalities did not patrol roadways overnight, and some did no patrolling at all.

While the standard appeared intent on establishing some consistency in the matter of road patrols, the attempt failed in the matter of winter patrols. The reasons why may be varied, but there was an apparent inability to establish a consensus between the stakeholders (the province and all municipalities) on the issue.[8] Rather than resolve the conflict or establish a trial standard, the issue was dropped. Likely the cost of maintaining inspections during the winter season was considered too high by some road authorities. Therefore, as of 2002, the Regulation established only routine patrols.

Due to the absence of the provisions for winter patrols, the requirements of Regulation 239/02 were not sufficient for winter maintenance operations. However, during the winter months, roadway friction can change significantly, and very quickly. Roadway surface conditions can change from dry and bare to dangerous, icy/slippery conditions, and even become impassable within minutes due to the accumulation of freezing rain, newly fallen snow, drifting snow, and ice. Therefore, during the frost-prone months, patrols must be more frequent and must consider road and weather conditions.

Despite the safety benefits provided by defining a requirement for winter patrol, some municipalities insisted their only obligation during the frost-prone months is identified by the general nature of the routine patrol.[9] This points to a discrepancy between the standard and a common-sense practice. It is a common practice for road authorities to engage winter patrols. However, the way this can be achieved is varied. Some road authorities maintain patrols on duty 24/7. To reduce costs, others provide for sixteen-hour coverage with provision for extending that time to twenty-four hours, as applicable. Other cost-effective means are available or may be developed. For example, the patrols of an upper-tier road authority could notify lower-tier road authorities of road conditions and even initiate operations as required. These types of actions are consistent with the Municipal Act in taking reasonable steps to prevent a default from arising.

Road patrols and other roadway personnel acquire an intimate knowledge of road conditions and should be able to predict roadway conditions according to environmental conditions, terrain, and experience. Based on the conditions found in one area, patrols can anticipate what conditions can be found elsewhere. To have developed these capabilities yet not use them because it is not required by the standard was not reasonable. Not all drivers can be expected to predict these conditions, especially where they may not be familiar with a road.

For a road authority to not have experienced personnel on patrol when conditions are deteriorating leaves drivers to cope on their own and plays the odds that collisions will not occur. Certainly, some savings in public expenditure will be accrued. The anticipated risk to the road authority is, on the one hand, that no collisions will occur, and on the other, that no claims will arise, filed claims will be withdrawn, the road authority will be determined to be unaware and their defense successful, or the damages will be small.

As previously discussed, the standards did not require patrolling between sunset and sunrise. Once again, this provision conflicts with the Municipal Act where reasonable steps are to be taken. Furthermore, even though the standards had no provision allowing municipalities to delay the commencement of operations, the absence of winter patrols codified an ability for the road authority to do just that. For example, where the removal of snow or ice from the roadway was to begin as soon as the municipality became aware, such operations might be delayed until patrols arrive for work or otherwise until after sunrise. Where such provisions are tied to time of day or the work schedules of employees, there is an inherent codified ability to delay the commencement of winter maintenance. Such measures are inherently contrary to road safety. For this reason, the absence of winter patrols from the standard remained unreasonable with respect to the frost-prone months.

As stated, patrolling is necessary to identify the safety readiness of the highway. The functional purpose of winter patrolling is to monitor the safety readiness of the roadway in real time, or close to it, and be ready when roadway conditions are expected to change. The Ministry indicated that patrolling should identity conditions that may adversely affect the condition of the highway, which is rather time dependent during the frost-prone months.[10]

To fulfill these tasks, the road authority must be vigilant and anticipate conditions that may develop in due course related to current environmental conditions, and further, to be ready to initiate winter operations at an appropriate time. These tasks can only be fulfilled where there is a reasonable winter patrolling program in place. The absence of winter patrolling from the standards removed the responsibility for road authorities to monitor the safety readiness of the roadway when it was expected that the hazardous extent of roadway conditions could change very quickly.

The 2013 version of the Regulation includes a requirement for patrolling if there is a substantial probability of snow on the roadway. One can only wonder how many motorists suffered and likely continue to suffer because of the patrolling provisions of the Regulation. It is left to others to evaluate the suitability of the current Regulation in this regard.

A2.3 Snow Accumulation

The snow accumulation provision of the 2002 Regulation was as follows:[11]

Snow accumulation

4.(1) The minimum standard for clearing snow accumulation is,

(a) while the snow continues to accumulate, to deploy resources to clear the snow as soon as practicable after becoming aware of the fact that the snow accumulation on a roadway is greater than the depth set out in the Table to this section; and

(b) after the snow accumulation has ended and after becoming aware that the snow accumulation is greater than the depth set out in the Table to this section, to clear the snow accumulation in accordance with subsections (2) and (3) or subsections (2) and (4), as the case may be, within the time set out in the Table. O. Reg. 239/02, s. 4 (1).

(2) The snow accumulation must be cleared to a depth less than or equal to the depth set out in the Table. O. Reg. 239/02, s. 4 (2).

(3) The snow accumulation must be cleared from the roadway to within a distance of 0.6 metres inside the outer edges of the roadway. O. Reg. 239/02, s. 4 (3).

(4)Despite subsection (3), for a Class 4 highway with two lanes or a Class 5 highway with two lanes, the snow accumulation on the roadway must be cleared to a width of at least 5 metres. O. Reg. 239/02, s. 4 (4).

(5) This section,

(a)does not apply to that portion of the roadway designated for parking; and

(b)only applies to a municipality during the season when the municipality performs winter highway maintenance. O. Reg. 239/02, s. 4 (5).

(6) In this section,

"snow accumulation" means the natural accumulation of new fallen snow or windblown snow that covers more than half a lane width of a roadway. O. Reg. 239/02, s. 4 (6).

TABLE: SNOW ACCUMULATION

Class of Highway	Depth	Time
1	2.5 cm	4 hours
2	5 cm	6 hours
3	8 cm	12 hours
4	8 cm	16 hours
5	10 cm	24 hours

Table A2.2: O. Reg. 239/02, s. 4, Table.[12]

A2.3.1 Terminology of the Snowfall Standard

The Regulation set the timing of when *snow reduction operations*[13] must commence according to the accumulated amount but also identified several caveats that could delay the commencement of operations as listed below:

- The snow must be on the roadway.
- Operations are to commence as soon as practical.
- Operations are to commence after becoming aware that some threshold amount of snow on the road has been satisfied.
- The snow continues to accumulate.

These criteria for the clearing of snow applied to both newly fallen snow and drifting snow. As the standard attempted to satisfy two different snow conditions with one criterion, it did not recognize the different effects of the contaminants and the specific requirements for treating each condition. In addition, the caveats gave rise to substantive confusion related to both when winter operations were considered to commence and the nature of the operation itself.

For example, a common interpretation of the standard was that the measured depth of snow refers to newly fallen snow uncompacted on the road.[14] However, it was argued in one trial that the compacted snow within the wheel tracks is the depth of snow at which winter operations were to commence. Two such widely divergent interpretations of the standard suggest that the language is vague, too open to argument, and not considerate of the road user.

In further consideration of the language of "after becoming aware," there was incentive for the road authority to simply not assess conditions to avoid initiating operations (and liability). This importantly allowed winter operations to be consolidated over a shorter time. Take, for example, overnight patrol conditions. A policy *not* to inspect roadways overnight allowed the road authority to wait to be notified by complaints or other means before operations were initiated. In other words, authorities could rely on others—police, public—to request winter maintenance before it was provided. This moved the standard away from road safety. Receipt of the complaints from the public or the police could occur well after the thresholds of accumulation had been satisfied and/or collisions had occurred. This type of language in the standard also enabled the road authority to ignore the prospect of initiating winter operations and to close for weekends and holidays. Such provisions also removed any *sense of urgency* for winter maintenance and enabled a culture of casualness and delay that was not supportive of road safety and remained unreasonable in the context of winter maintenance.

The term "as soon as practicable" was also open to interpretation. While the nature of winter operations is consistent with the need for other emergency services, this type of language distanced the operational aspects of the service from the need for a quick response. Any sense of urgency was removed from the standard. It was dramatically different from the Ministry's "immediate" call to action.

This language also codified the potential for significant delay, as any task a road authority undertakes could be argued as having greater priority than providing winter maintenance. There was no incentive with this language to ensure that reserve equipment or personnel were available. The language certainly ran counter to the sense of urgency adopted by the Ministry. The potential for delay allowed by this language was not reasonable in the context of winter maintenance.

Had the term "immediately" been incorporated into the standard, the priority for initiating operations would have been self-evident. Whether or not the road authority was able to get to the operations immediately is irrelevant provided that they had initiated activity. Getting to work, loading vehicles, and circle checks of vehicles are all part of an immediate response in satisfying the standard. This type of terminology in the standard would establish a strong tie between the need for an emergency service aimed at crash mitigation and the operations of that service.

Once the road authority is informed of a problem, some road authorities consider it their first order of business to verify the complaint even if it came from the police. In the case of a snowstorm, on-duty personnel may do this relatively quickly. However, in the case of windblown snow, long delays may be expected, especially if no personnel are on duty overnight. Upon being informed, travel to the location of the complaint may be considered necessary to determine if the threshold conditions have been satisfied. Thus, the inspection process can delay the start-up of operations even though the threshold conditions have been satisfied. If there are no personnel on duty, the commencement of service could be further delayed.

Given this potential for delay in commencing winter operations, it is reasonable to conclude that long servicing delays were possible for all classes of roadways. The standard readily accommodated these delays by providing:

- an ability to discontinue monitoring roadway conditions,
- allowance for long periods between when awareness is attained and the commencement of service, and
- extremely generous response times for when the treatment must be completed.

Due to the terminology that allowed operations to be delayed, the requirement that operations proceed "while the snow continues to accumulate" and "after the snow has ended" had little functional purpose. The other functional directives of the standard required that road authorities commence operations when the thresholds of accumulation have been satisfied yet permitted the stopping of service operations until the threshold conditions were again satisfied. These requirements remain independent of the snowstorm event. If the snow accumulation does not again exceed the thresholds, operations may cease, leaving substantial quantities of snow on the road according to the thresholds allowed. Such conditions move the standard in a direction *away* from safety. Allowing frozen moisture to remain on the roadway is unreasonable and challenges common sense.

A2.3.2 Residual Snow After Servicing

The standard allowed substantive quantities of snow to remain on the roadway after servicing. Based on this provision, this standard was apparently established in a manner to specifically permit using salt for snow melting on the roadway. The reasoning here is that any plowing operation would remove snow to a depth of approximately 1 cm (0.4 in.). It is beyond common sense that plow blades may be set in a manner that would allow 2.5 cm, 5.0 cm, or 8.0 cm (1 in., 2 in., or 3 in.) to remain on the road. On the other hand, salting may be considered as a means to simply lower the height of snow to some specified level, provided that sufficient salt is applied. This would allow snow to be removed from the roadway by the action of traffic rather than winter servicing operations.

Unsurprisingly, the nature of snowplowing operations does not have a capability to perform in the manner set out in the standard. The blade of a snowplow rests on sliding surfaces or shoes so that the blade is slightly raised from the road surface to accommodate surface imperfections. Typically, the blade is close enough to the road surface to sweep at least some of the residual snow from the surface by the movement of the truck. For this reason, plowing methods will remove almost all the snow from the road surface. Residual snow is typically (but not necessarily) removed by traffic and spreading operations. To consider that plowing operations for Class 2 roadways may leave 5 cm (2 in.) of snow on the road surface and 8 cm (3 in.) of snow on Class 3 roadways is unreasonable.

The provision for allowing residual snow on the roadway after servicing is completely irrational and would further allow roadways to remain in a hazardous state. Not only is this type of provision contrary to the purpose of winter maintenance, but it also defies common sense. It certainly moves the standard away from the direction of safety.

A2.3.3 Salt Applications for Snow Melting

Some road authorities of the time attempted to treat snowfall accumulation only with chemicals such as road salt. In one such case, where less than 7.5 cm (3 in.) of snow was expected, no plowing operations were initiated for the applicable classes of roadways.[15] The road authority contended compliance with the standard. With this type of policy, the road authority anticipated that the combined effects of daytime heating of the pavement and the movement of traffic would remove the snow from the road. The concept essentially outsourced some aspect of maintenance to the public with this expectation and seemed to rely on the traveling public to complete the task of snow removal. In essence, the concept places the public at indeterminate risk. If the depth of snow is 2 to 8 cm (1 to 3 in.), as permitted by the Regulation, the public could be at substantially more risk than if the snow was plowed off. These conditions could be expected four or more times each year.

It has been an advised practice since the late 1970s that salt should not be used to melt snow from the road surface, but rather, salt should be used to prepare the snow for plowing or for cleanup after plowing. As of 1977, the Ministry identified the amount of salt required to remove 1 cm (0.4 in.) of ice (i.e., 10 cm [4 in.] of snow) from a two-lane roadway one kilometer (0.6 mile) in length. At a temperature of -4°C (24.8°F), 16 tonnes (18 tons) of salt would be required over one hour.[16] Such large amounts of salt are not only too costly to apply but are also harmful to the environment.

A common spreading rate for road salt from a truck is 130 kg (287 lbs.) per two-lane kilometer (0.6 mi.). An application of this much salt is unlikely to melt a layer of snow that is approximately 2 mm (0.08 in.) in thickness at a temperature of -5°C (23°F). At temperatures of -12°C (10.4°F), approximately 2.5 times as much salt would be required to complete the transformation. Consequently, the application of salt to roadways at commonly used levels cannot be expected to clear the road of snow. Rather, the application of salt at commonly used rates is only intended to keep the snow from bonding with the pavement. The process creates a layer of snow and ice that floats on a brine layer. The floating material is broken up by traffic to create slush that can be plowed from the roadway.[17] One can appreciate, based on the limited application rates for salt, that snow is cleared from the roadway by plowing. Traffic will only remove snow and slush from the wheel path of vehicles.

Without removal of the slush by mechanical means, the brine solution will become increasingly diluted as more snow is converted to liquid brine. The mixture can eventually refreeze. Furthermore, without the removal of residual snow and slush, the width of pavement cleared of snow is that of the wheel path of vehicles and some undefined splash zone beside the wheel path. The width of the road that can be cleared for use by traffic cannot be assured. Consequently, plowing is required to remove snow from the road surface.

A2.3.4 Slush as a Form of Snow and Ice

Whether salt is applied to the road surface to create a brine solution or to "melt" snow from the road, a layer of brine solution overlain with a layer of snow will form with the additional accumulation of snow. As this occurs, the brine solution will become increasingly diluted, and eventually ice crystals will reform. As the solution becomes increasingly diluted, the amount of ice in the solution increases. As this composite mixture is compacted with the movement of traffic, the vehicles are effectively moving over a thin layer of ice. Where a layer of slush is sufficiently deep, a vehicle can commence hydroplaning, resulting in a loss of control, just as in the case of ponding water.

Further, a layer of slush can be converted to ice as temperatures drop overnight. One can readily see refrozen meltwater and slush on roadways in the early hours of the morning, when temperatures have dropped overnight. Qin and colleagues have shown that the duration that slush is allowed to remain on the road after salting and before plowing can lead to increased collision activity.[18] For this reason, it is important that the slush layer created by salt and snow be removed from the roadway by mechanical means before refreezing occurs.

However, the Regulation only required that the layer of snow (including slush) be lowered to threshold levels. Thus, the standard permits the slush layer to remain on the roadway. Further, there is no requirement within the standard that slush be removed from the road by plowing. These conditions leave the roadway in a hazardous condition after servicing. By not requiring the roadway to be returned to a reasonably safe operating condition, the standard also allowed the roadway to be left in a condition that permits no apparent servicing at all. Alternatively, the standard allows the road to be left in a condition that will transition into a potentially more hazardous state.

A2.3.5 Salt as a Toxic Substance

In 1995, road salt was placed on Environment Canada's Priority Substances List 2 for assessment as a toxic substance as defined under the Canadian Environmental Protection Act (CEPA).[19] Instead of declaring salt a toxic substance, a decision was made to work with national agencies such as the Transportation Association of Canada (TAC) and others to develop standards for the effective use of salt. One outcome of the effort was the TAC Salt Management Guide[20] and the Environment Canada Code of Practice.[21] Both of these documents were consistent with the Ministry advice for the use of salt as established in 1977.[22]

As of 2002, the Regulation permitted the removal of snow from the road either by attempts to melt it or to otherwise plow it from the road. The structure and language of the standard did not actually require the removal of snow (or ice) from the roadway, but rather only required that the depth of snow be reduced to some threshold limit. As indicated, some road authorities continued to attempt to melt substantial quantities of snow from the road without plowing at the time. This practice regarding the use of salt is not only contrary to the efforts and advice of Environment Canada and TAC but also other standards-issuing agencies.

A2.3.6 Deicing

The use of salt (or other freezing point depressants) may be used in two fundamentally different ways. Left unattended in the presence of traffic, snow will become compacted and bond with the roadway surface. Ice that has bonded with the road surface is more difficult to remove, as it requires additional treatments. At very low temperatures it may not be possible to remove this form of ice with typical chemical treatments. The winter operation that removes already-bonded snow and ice with the road surface is referred to as deicing.

However, deicing operations should not typically be necessary. Anti-icing (discussed in the following section) is a winter operations procedure that is used to *prevent* the formation of a bond between compacted snow (or ice) and the pavement surface, allowing a more effective removal of snow from the road surface. Since the mid-1990s, deicing is a practice that has been discouraged by most winter maintenance advisory agencies such as the US Federal Highway Administration (FHWA), AASHTO, TAC, and the Ontario Ministry of Transportation. As early as 1977, the Ministry discouraged the practice.[23] However, the terminology referring to deicing did not appear until some years later.

The practice of deicing is discouraged because the quantity of salt required to remove a bonded snow or an ice pack far exceeds the quantity of salt that is typically used in winter operations (130 kg/2-ln-km [287 lbs./2-ln-mi.]).[24] The amount of salt required is much greater because it must first mine its way through the layer of ice and snow before contact with the pavement is available. Once there is a bonded snowpack on the pavement, the ability of salt to perform its task can be rapidly reduced by the movement of traffic. The effectiveness of a salt application is also restricted by the quantity of snow and ice that must be broken up and the inability of any liquid to migrate across the road. As a result, the process of deicing takes longer and requires more salt to expose the pavement surface. In essence, anti-icing prevents the bond from forming through early application of salt. Anti-icing is more cost-effective and provides a safer road faster than deicing later.[25] For this reason, deicing programs as a principal means for removing ice and snow is much less cost-effective as a winter operation and a move away from the safety offered by anti-icing practices.

While a snow or ice pack remains on the road surface, the value of winter maintenance is diminished. Further, the changing nature of the snow or ice pack can bring about enhanced hazards. For example, as temperatures rise, snow becomes more slippery.[26] Therefore, where a road authority may delay operations or otherwise depend on a warming trend to assist in removing the snow or ice pack with salting, the road surface condition can become more hazardous. With a cooling trend, the reverse would be true, thus limiting the effectiveness of the salt.

Deicing as a bond-breaking operation stems from its timing: It is required after only approximately 2.5 cm (1 in.) of snow has accumulated and bonded to the road.[27] The approach of the standard in allowing snow to accumulate on the road surface to a minimum depth of not less than 2.5 cm (1 in.) therefore established a winter maintenance program that is primarily a deicing program. Consequently, the standard strategy for winter maintenance is effectively one of deicing only and is inconsistent with modern winter maintenance practices.

A2.3.7 Anti-Icing

The 1977 M-703 training manual of the Ministry (Ontario) advised winter maintenance operations to salt early in the storm to prevent snow from sticking to the pavement.[28] By the late 1990s, this practice had become encompassed in a broader range of practices referred to as anti-icing.[29] Anti-icing is the practice that prevents the bonding of snow and ice to the roadway. The practice allows the road to return to an acceptable condition earlier and at less cost, with less frequent servicing, and/or with less salt required if the snow has not bonded with the pavement.

Anti-icing now includes a range of activity such as direct liquid applications prior to the onset of a winter event or laying down salt shortly after the snowfall commences. Once a roadway is treated, a dried residue of the brine can remain on the roadway for several days in the absence of moisture. Ergo, it is an effective means to deal with anticipated frost. With anti-icing, salt is placed on the road before or at the beginning of the storm. In the case of dry or prewetted salt applications, a small amount of snowfall is necessary to provide sufficient moisture for the salt to stick and be effective. The practice of anti-icing is a strategy designed to minimize the use of salt. Of course, the use of salt will be required during a storm to mitigate slippery conditions as snow further accumulates and plowing removes brine from the road surface.

The Regulation in its 2002–2010 form delayed the onset of operations until some threshold amount of snow had fallen. By the time plowing was undertaken, snow on roadways with even moderate volumes of traffic may have already bonded to the pavement. Consequently, the standard remained completely contrary to the acknowledged practice of anti-icing.

A2.3.8 Newly Fallen Snow

One of the most dramatic differences between the approach of the OGRA standards and the Regulation as discussed previously concerned the manner in which snowfall and windblown snow was treated. The OGRA standards identified the maximum amount of snow permitted on the roadway. For example, the maximum amount of snow permitted on high-priority classes of roadway, such as Class 2, was 5 cm (2 in.). To ensure the standard was satisfied, plowing operations would need to begin early in the snowstorm or early under conditions of windblown snow to ensure that the threshold would not be exceeded by the time servicing of roadways were approaching the end of routes. Plowing operations would clean the road surface, effectively removing all snow. Consequently, the depth of snow for this important class of roadway would not exceed 5 cm (2 in.) at any time along the route.

The Ministry used a slightly different approach for snowfall accumulation, in which salting commences when there is greater than 0.5 cm

(0.2 in.) of accumulation, *for all classifications of roadways*. Similarly, plowing commences when there is 2 cm (0.8 in.) or more of snow, *for all classifications of roadways*. Therefore, the Ministry was required to start their winter operations with the onset of snow and continue through the event.

However, the terminology of the Regulation was significantly different from the procedures recommended by OGRA and the Ministry. In the case of Class 2 roadways (e.g., AADT = 7,000 vpd, speed = 90 km/h [56 mph]), operations needed not commence until the threshold amount had been exceeded. Thus, no plowing or salting operations needed to be initiated at any time if the expected accumulation was less than 5 cm (2 in.) and snow in that amount never materialized. Where the threshold was exceeded, the start-up delay (due to notification and "as soon as practicable") could be several hours while the servicing delay could add many more hours.

During the start-up delay, snow continues to accumulate. Based on a moderate average hourly snowfall of 2.5 cm (1 in.) per hour and a delay of six hours, the amount of snow on a Class 2 roadway prior to servicing could easily be 20 cm (8 in.).[30] Allowing that much snow to accumulate on a roadway with high travel speeds and high traffic volumes is beyond the bounds of common sense and certainly is not supportive of road safety. In allowing dangerous conditions to prevail, the congestion and/or collision experience permitted by the Regulation can eventually terminate traffic movement. For this reason, the Regulation cannot be relied upon and is irrelevant to many road authorities.

Indeed, with that amount of accumulation for rural high-speed roadways, it is highly unlikely that a conscientious road authority would delay its operations until it was known that the threshold of snow accumulation would be exceeded. In any event, the standard allowed unreasonable amounts of snow to collect on the roadway before operations were required to attend to the problem. In review of these types of provisions, the obvious conclusion is that the standard was set excessively low to capture a wide range of nonperformance in winter maintenance. Further, the standard was of little real value for winter maintenance but constituted a walled defense against claims.

In considering the thresholds of accumulation necessary to commence operations as well as the caveats, the standard was heavily weighted toward allowing road authorities to commence operations in their own good time. Not only did the thresholds of snow accumulation universally not support prompt service of important roadways, neither did the servicing times permitted by the standard.

A primary benefit to the road authorities of the snowfall accumulation standards was allowing them to wait until the storm event had moved off before they needed to commence operations. This offered considerable opportunity for the road authorities to consolidate serving and thus reduce the number of servicing hours. If thresholds of accumulation were not satisfied, theoretically no operation needed to be initiated. With this approach, the likelihood of having to perform plowing operations more than once was substantially reduced to produce significant cost savings.

Additionally, during storms of low intensity but long duration, there was no incentive for the road authority to commence operations. Drivers were left on their own to cope with storm conditions. However, as the duration of the event increased, the collision experience and a police request for servicing were likely to drive decisions to commence plowing rather than the regulatory standard. This was the circumstance referenced previously—a sense of urgency. In that case where the driver spent the afternoon washing his truck, the trial evaluated the reasonableness of this type of standard ruling against the municipality. Road users should not have to depend on these actions for winter maintenance to commence.

As written, the standard would allow up to 10 cm (4 in.) of snow to remain on Class 5 roadways and an infinite amount of snow on Class 6 roadways without servicing them. For those road authorities with only Class 3 to Class 5 roadways, there is a potential for substantial delay, allowing grossly unreasonable depths of snow on roadways. These provisions for snow clearance also defy common sense and are not supportive of road safety or a sense of urgency.

A2.3.9 Windblown Snow

As previously indicated, the standard applied to windblown snow as well as to newly fallen snow. In recognition of the differing nature of these weather phenomena, the standard included additional limitations respecting windblown snow. In this case, it was required that at least half the lane be covered with snow to the respective depth before operations were initiated. While the two types of snow conditions on the road were treated in the same manner, their effects on vehicle operations can be very different due to different physical properties.

In Ontario, drifting snow as opposed to falling snow is responsible for about 30 percent of road maintenance budgets in agricultural areas.[31] Road authorities must be just as vigilant in monitoring the effects of drifting snow as newly fallen snow. Due to the characteristics of drifting snow, the potential hazards may be the same or greater than hazards presented by newly fallen snow on the roadway. Snowdrift formation occurs where the flow of an air mass bearing snow is disrupted. At locations where wind speeds drop, snow particles stop moving or otherwise fall out of the airflow. Typically, wind speeds drop in locations where the moving air mass expands to fill a void. This can occur over very large areas or relatively small areas. Typical locations where wind speeds drop include ground depressions or low spots such as ditches, fencing, hills or ridges (including roads), wood-lots, buildings, trees, and utility poles, to name a few.

As the snow particles in a drift are small, of various sizes, and rounded in shape, snow deposited in drifts is more dense than newly fallen snow. For example, the density of newly fallen snow averages about 100 kg/ cu. m (6.24 lbs./cu. ft.), while the density of newly deposited drifted snow may be as high as 300 kg/cu. m (18.7 lbs./cu. ft.), approximately three times that of newly fallen snow.[32] In addition, wind-deposited snow par-ticles can freeze together upon contact. The bonds grow and strengthen through sintering, which involves heating without melting. For this rea-son, wind-deposited snow can become resistant to subsequent erosion within only a few hours of deposition. As snowdrifts tend to be variable in depth across the road, their effect on a vehicle that strikes even a small drift can destabilize its motion or cause a surprised driver to inappropriately react, increasing the potential for collision.

While the standard required half the roadway to be covered by a depth of snow exceeding the threshold amount before plowing operations need commence, the depth of snow near the outside edge can be substantially greater. Thus, the effects of striking a snowdrift defined by the standard can result in a substantively different impact on vehicle operations than passing through newly fallen snow of similar depth. An appropriate modification to the standard in the direction of road safety may be to apply the threshold standard to the edge of the road, not one half.

As of 2002–2010, the standard did not specify a length over which the drifting snow must be present to the threshold depth to initiate plowing operations. The effect of this was to require plowing for a single drift even where the longitudinal length of the drift along the roadway was relatively short. From a safety perspective, this is likely to be one aspect of the standard that was favorable to drivers. However, the standard left open to interpretation the extent to which the longitudinal magnitude of the drift presented a hazard.

Due to the density of snow in the drift, an excursion from the common wheel path of vehicles (if there is one) can destabilize a vehicle's motion, enhancing the opportunity for collision due to differential drag on either side of the vehicle. At any speed, a loss of vehicle control can occur over very short distances including just a couple of meters (yards). As vehicles track through snowdrifts of any depth, the compacted snow becomes polished and the road surface can become slippery. However, the standard did not recognize this condition as a hazard and did not encourage servicing for the slippery condition.

As a final note regarding the standard, Section 3 of Snow Accumulation indicates that the road surface is to be cleared to a distance within 0.6 m

(2 ft.) inside of the outer edges of the roadway, which did not include the shoulder. Consequently, for a typical width of travel lane up to 3.65 m (12 ft.), a clearing width of snowplows would need to be as wide as 3.05 m (10 ft.). Most plows can clear a width of 3.05 m (10 ft.) or less. Plows would be required to make a second trip along the route to clear a path where bicycle lanes were present.[33] The resulting width of roadway as a result of plowing in two directions would be 6.10 m (20 ft.), which is considered a narrow roadway. For wider lanes, additional trips would be required.

A2.3.10 Slippery Conditions Associated with Snow Accumulation

A reduction of roadway friction is brought about whenever there is a layer of snow on the road surface. Snow on a road surface will accumulate rapidly with heavy snowfalls, and the need for servicing becomes quickly apparent. However, it can take very little frozen moisture for slippery conditions to develop. An overnight frost in the frost-prone season can produce slippery conditions. The ice lens in this situation is thin and transparent, giving drivers no visual cue of the hazard. The ice lens is perishable and may be present for only a short time or may linger for quite some time. Servicing operations are required for these slippery conditions as appropriate.

One condition that can catch road authorities off guard is that of flurries and very light ongoing snowfalls. Too often in this situation, light or wispy snowfalls of several hours do not present cues of a hazardous condition, as there can be no significant change in the appearance of the road surface as the ice forms over time. Some road authorities contend that under such conditions the movement of traffic will blow the snow off the road (or out of the wheel tracks) to maintain good quality friction. To drivers, it continues to look like a dry or damp pavement, but that is not the case. Ice is forming and thickening throughout this event.

Where there is no winter maintenance with these conditions, as traffic moves along the roadway, it entraps small amounts of snow between the vehicle tires and road surface. Over time and the passage of vehicles, a buildup of compacted snow creates an ice lens. To drivers, the roadway or wheel tracks may appear to offer some friction. Even when that is the case in the early stages of formation, roadway friction is dropping with the passage of time. With these conditions, an unsuspecting driver can be very surprised when attempting some maneuver that fails, resulting in collision.

As snow is compacted by passing traffic, the frictional properties of the surface are reduced and the roadway becomes slippery. Additional snowfall will add to the depth of compacted snow. This can create various depths of snow on the road, ranging from low-depth, high-density conditions within the wheel paths to greater depth, low-density conditions outside of the wheel path. Snow that is entrapped within the wheel paths is pressed and polished by the movement of more traffic. Consequently, the compacted snow on the road surface exhibits similar properties to that of ice. It is a condition that the Regulation did not recognize as a hazard. In reality, the depth of accumulation is of little relevance, and very little snow can create slippery conditions.

As roadways become slippery with falling snow, the standard related to snowfall accumulation has little relevance to the need for winter maintenance, and the likelihood of collisions is primarily related to the surface friction conditions present. However, according to the standard, there was no provision for slippery conditions. Common sense should tell a road authority that slippery conditions are hazardous and should be remedied.

The standard required road authorities to attend to snow on the roadway but not remove it from the road surface. Yet, there was no provision for slippery conditions or a need to respond to hazardous road surface conditions that remain after servicing. However, the preceding discussion indicates that this condition should be untenable because it will be transformed into ice by traffic, and that ice will bond with the road surface. In this way, the standard moved away from safety.

A2.4 Icy Roadways

The provisions of the 2002 MMS, Regulation 29/02 for servicing icy roadways was as follows:

5.(1) The minimum standard for treating icy roadways is,

(a) to deploy resources to treat an icy roadway as soon as practicable after becoming aware that the roadway is icy; and

(b) to treat the icy roadway within the time set out in the Table to this section after becoming aware that the roadway is icy. O. Reg. 239/02, s. 5 (1).

(2) This section only applies to a municipality during the season when the municipality performs winter highway maintenance. O. Reg. 239/02, s. 5 (2).

TABLE: ICY ROADWAYS

Class of Highway	Time
1	3 hours
2	4 hours
3	8 hours
4	12 hours
5	16 hours

Table A2.3: O. Reg. 239/02, s. 5, Table.[34]

The Regulation in this matter dealt with a contaminant on the road surface as distinct from a surface condition. Consequently, there can be confusion concerning whether the hazardous condition involving a slippery road surface was to be treated or not. Common sense suggests there should be no doubt. Research has shown that compacted snow assumes friction characteristics similar to that of ice. For this reason, research of the friction associated with road surface moisture encompasses both compacted snow and ice. For example, Hunter found the typical friction of untracked snow, snow and ice, and ice to be 0.35, 0.32, and 0.24, respectively.[35] Martin and Schaefer found coefficients of friction for snow and ice to have a range of 0.11 to 0.23 depending on temperature.[36] The latter can be referred to as polished snow.

The language of the standard in dealing with snow and ice deflected attention from the real issue. More specifically, the real need to undertake action is not related to the presence of ice (or snow) but rather to the frictional properties of the road surface, typically expressed as a slippery or icy/slippery condition. In the collision investigations of police involving winter collisions, motor vehicle accident reports cite the presence of snow or ice as a checkbox. However, it is typical for hand notes and duty notes to independently identify the surface condition using the widely accepted term of "slippery."

As of 2002–2010, the standard indicated that the condition was to be treated within a time set out in a table. Due to the nature of the classification system, the table created discontinuities between servicing times for similar roadways. For example, the delay in servicing a roadway serving 11,000 vehicles per day could be 1.5 times as long as another roadway serving 11,000 vehicles per day less one vehicle, both having posted speeds of 80 km/h (50 mph). This reasoning cannot be rationalized, as there is no difference in the operations of these two roadways. As a crude measure of roadway safety, collision experience is often reported as a function of traffic volume. It is reasonable to expect therefore that the collision experience of these two facilities would be almost identical. However, the collision experience may become weighted toward the facility of lower traffic volume simply due to the servicing requirements of each facility. With these volumes of traffic moving at these speeds through a hazard of low roadway friction, there is clearly a need to have such locations treated with haste.

One can appreciate that the lag times for treatment must reflect the nature of winter operations. In the case of slippery conditions arising from predicted snowfalls or snow showers, it is reasonable that servicing operators are on duty and the maximum lag time for treatment would be the time taken to complete the route. Ministry circuit times for salting operations on high-speed and arterial roads were set at 1.3 to 1.5 hours. In the case of having received a complaint from the police, a nighttime patrol may order out the equipment to commence road servicing. Allowing thirty minutes of transit time for the operator to arrive at the yard from home, and ten to fifteen minutes for loading a vehicle, the operator should be on his route within forty-five minutes. If only a road patrol is sent to inspect the route, checking for the presence of ice, this could take up to 2.75 hours. This time could be substantively shorter if the problem location is near the beginning of the route, but the whole of the route would be attended to in the longer period.

If a complaint is received from the public, it may be necessary for a road patrol to attend to the location of the complaint prior to calling out a vehicle operator. This type of delay can be mitigated when patrols routinely use equipment capable of dealing with localized problems.

The ice provisions of the standard also contain caveats similar in nature to those pertaining to snowfall accumulation. These have been discussed previously and are not repeated here.

A2.5 Other Winter Exclusions

A2.5.1 Uniquely Hazardous Locations

Much of the following has been discussed in Chapter 15 dealing with situational hazards with winter maintenance but is repeated here for completeness of the section. Weather events and their effects on road conditions are highly predictable. Similarly, locations likely to present problems for drivers can be predictable. Road authorities are in a unique position to be able to identify hazardous locations within the road network that are prone to certain types of weather events. These locations are commonly referred to as trouble spots or hot spots or by similar identifiers. They include locations that are prone to frost formation or icing, such as low-lying roadways and roadways over or beside streams, hills with roadway curves, structures, bridges, or locations conducive to drifting snow.

By checking these marker locations, the authority has a simple convenient predictor of the road conditions found elsewhere. In a similar vein, the patrols of road authorities could reasonably inspect certain hazard-prone locations as a priority to determine when and where local conditions may be hazardous. However, the Regulation did not recognize these types of locations. In this regard, the standard moved away from the provision of safety.

A2.5.2 Visibility

It has long been known that the visibility provided to drivers at intersecting roadways is related to collision experience. Adequate visibility at intersections can reduce the frequency and/or severity of collisions. To this end, engineering practice has adopted the concept of using visibility triangles at Stop-controlled intersections to allow drivers the opportunity to avoid collisions. Over time, the visibility triangles can experience reduced effectiveness because of overgrown brush, the presence of visibility obstructions such as installed barriers and signs, and/or a lack of maintenance. However, the Regulation made no reference to the maintenance of these important safety devices. The omission of language about maintaining the visibility conditions runs contrary to the design of roadways and is also contrary to maintaining adequately safe roads for public use.

As snow is removed from the roadway, it is placed in windrows along the side of the road or stored at the side of the road at intersections. As the height of the windrow increases, it can begin to affect the visibility conditions at intersections, whether a visibility triangle is present or not. Once the height of a windrow exceeds 1.05 m (3.4 ft.), the designated height of a driver's eye used for design, the windrow can affect the design features of the highway as well as the visibility of intersections and driveways. To accommodate the visibility needs of drivers, snowbanks at intersections (and driveways) should be lowered.

Language to ensure this important driver consideration is maintained would have made the standard more consistent with the Ministry practice,[37] while allowing the design features of the roadway to function properly. Where a visibility triangle exists, lowered snowbanks should encompass the whole of the triangle. Where no visibility triangle exists, conditions may be set according to the non-frost-month visibility available at the intersection. However, the standard contains no provision for maintaining visibility triangles in winter. In this regard, the standard moved away from the provision of safety.

A2.5.3 Ramping

When snow is removed from the road, it is stored in windrows along the side of the roads. Where the windrow has solidified, it is able to act as a ramp, causing errant vehicles to vault over barriers intended to keep vehicles on the roadway. In this circumstance, the function of the barrier system is disabled by the presence of the frozen windrow. To prevent the failure of barrier systems in this manner, a standard is required. However, the Regulation had no provision for this important winter phenomenon. In this regard, the standard moved away from the provision of safety.

A2.5.4 Bicycles and Other Vehicles

The 2002 Regulation did not include provisions for the winter maintenance of bicycle facilities. Since that time, changes have been made for the standards to include these vehicles to some extent. However, with the promotion of more active forms of transportation, there is much greater likelihood that these modes will be active all year. To manage the safety of these facilities and to allow them to function as designed, standards need to consider these facilities in the same manner as they do other parts of the roadway.

A2.6 Developing an Appropriate Municipal Standard

The development of an appropriate standard has not been undertaken in this examination of one standard, the Regulation. However, the examination contains several guiding principles that can be used for that purpose and move the Regulation in the direction of safety.

In review of the Regulation as of 2010, it is readily evident that there was a preoccupation with maintenance cost and issues of liability. Certainly, there is no doubt that an appropriate standard can recognize the ability of municipalities to fund the service. In this regard, the concept that the roadways with the highest frequency and severity of collisions should be attended to first has some relevance. It should also be recognized that the likelihood of collision is related to individual experience, which is to say that not all drivers encountering a slippery road condition have the same probability of losing control. Furthermore, motorists traveling at speeds of 50 km/h (30 mph) or more are more likely to experience serious injury in a crash.

Finally, it is important to service roadways in a manner that will keep traffic moving at all times. Again, a standard that explicitly recognizes this attribute of roadway operation can move the standard in the direction of safety for the traveling public.

In dealing with these realities, measures can be found to improve the economy of winter maintenance operations. For example, as municipalities routinely identify freeway, arterial, collector, and local roadways, the priority for winter maintenance may be tied to these functions, as was done in the past. Beyond that, roadways with operating speeds of 50 km/h (30 mph) or more are appropriately served with a similar response time.

In considering the language and performance measures of the standard, it is required that there be a match between what the maintenance activity does and the way in which maintenance is performed. For example, it is nonsense that a snowplow could perform in such a way as to leave 2.5 cm (1 in.) or more snow on the road surface or that plowing is not needed if there is less than the threshold amount. Furthermore, as a recognized contaminant of waterways, road salt should not be used to "melt" snow from the road surface.[38] Since plowing is the *means* of removing snow from the road surface, the nature of the plowing task should be recognized in the standard.

The Ministry's winter maintenance standards and practices provide several guiding elements. For example, servicing of all roadways commences when roadway conditions begin to deteriorate. The servicing of roadways continues until cleanup operations are complete. The process both takes steps to prevent defaults from occurring and maintains activity until roadways are returned to an appropriate operating condition. Equipment is effectively utilized by allowing longer servicing times on routes with a higher numerical classification. There is no delay in operations on start-up, and the activity is undertaken based on need rather than some predetermined schedule of delay.

The snowfall thresholds of the Ministry (0.5 cm [0.2 in.] to initiate salting) are set to minimize the road user's exposure to excessive depths of snow on the roadway. In this respect, the thresholds are user-oriented rather than service-oriented, as they are with the preceding Regulation. The former (Ministry) approach is compatible with safety objectives.

In addition, the Ministry approach to winter maintenance has no provision for ice as a physical contaminant but rather uses the operation initiative of a slippery road surface. Operations to deal with the slippery condition are initiated as required. Therefore, there is no confusion about whether compacted snow may be ice, slush, or snow, or whether frost formation is a type of ice. Servicing is required to attend to slippery conditions in any form. Due to the nature of winter storms, the Ministry is required to maintain the road surface friction to the best of its ability as the winter weather event continues. All these measures have a direction toward safety relative to the municipal standard. Finally, the Ministry standards and practices deal with a wide manner of winter hazards that are not only a product of the environmental conditions but also a product of winter maintenance itself. As these hazards are well-known, dealing with them in a standard for municipal road authorities would assist those organizations defending themselves in litigation.

On the issue of inspections, the municipal standard contained no information in this regard. However, the Ministry manual provides patrols with an instructive framework for the completion of that task. They are informed of the duties they are required to perform and the order of performance in directing winter operations. The Ministry requires patrols to maintain reasonable records of activity, decisions, and environmental conditions. This data assists in establishing an effective means of defense against claims. A minimum maintenance standard identifying the need to maintain consistent and accessible records of operations by both patrols and equipment operators is necessary to accomplish this task.

The Ministry's approach has cost-saving features built in. Operationally, the Ministry standards provide what is deemed to be a reasonable standard of safety and attempt to maintain that standard throughout the winter. In attempting to establish a nominal level of safety for winter maintenance, a standard may use the operating characteristics of vehicles (including bicycles), as did the Ministry, OGRA (Section A1.1), and presumedly, many others. Creation of a nominal level of safety provided by a standard could identify an operational level for winter maintenance. Such a standard would contribute to driver expectancies across jurisdictions. The alternative to developing a standard, in which the municipality has a free hand to provide winter maintenance based on the lowest expenditures that only a few municipalities are willing to pay, is not contributory to a nominal standard of safety for road users. While it may be the position of road authorities that standards based on these principles are impossible to maintain from a cost perspective, they have an option for adopting a reasonable standard or assuming the risks associated with litigation.

The Ministry model of winter maintenance is simply used for comparative purposes to illustrate some of the desirable elements of a winter standard. There are many resources available at national or state/provincial levels that could also provide an excellent reference for developing an appropriate municipal standard.

In the experience of the author, the Regulation as set out in 2002–2010 did little to establish either common-sense practice or an appropriate nominal standard of safety. The standard exposed road users to excessive risk of collision. This problem had been recognized by responsible road authorities who maintained their own standards of practice in a manner offering a significant improvement when compared to the Regulation. Several municipalities exercise an approach that is similar to the Ministry's for arterial and collector roadways but use a modified approach to local and/or low-speed roadways. This approach recognizes the need to have operations oriented toward safety performance on high-speed and/or busy facilities and effectively exploits the tolerance of the public to have less intense servicing of local roadways or where operating speeds are less than 50 km/h (30 mph).

A2.7   Closing Comment on the Regulation

Perhaps the most important guidance set forth by the Municipal Act is that road authorities must take reasonable steps to prevent the default from arising. Since the Regulation as formulated was reactive in nature with a codified proclivity for enabling delay, the basic formulation of the standard was completely contrary to the requirements of the Act. Furthermore, in considering that winter maintenance was necessary according to the snow accumulation or icing, the standard was almost wholly directed by its terminology and performance criteria toward setting out provisions that allowed the delay of operations or alternatively opened the door to reasons why winter maintenance could not be performed, or may not have been performed in a timely fashion.

Consequently, in this form, the Regulation remained disconnected from the need to achieve key objectives, which is to return the road system to reasonably safe conditions for road users. In a similar vein, the standard promoted, or at least enabled, a culture of delay and failed to instill a meaningful sense of urgency in getting to the task of winter maintenance and completion of service within a reasonable time.

While functionally similar to emergency operations, there was a disconnect between the need for servicing and the propensity for collisions to occur until the winter operations were completed. The overall effect was to produce a standard that was overwhelmingly oriented toward reducing the cost of operations, or otherwise limiting the opportunity for claims relative to returning the roadway to reasonably safe operating conditions. One can only wonder about the number of system users who came to harm as a result of the concepts embedded in the Regulation.

For the reasons set out in this assessment, the standards as set out in 2002 to 2010 were functionally inappropriate in meeting the needs of road users and required substantial revision to provide adequate road safety in a common-sense approach to winter maintenance. An assessment of the current regulation in a similar manner will reveal the extent to which these issues have been overcome.

NOTES

CHAPTER 2

1. Red Hill Valley Parkway Inquiry, http://rhvpi.ca/.

CHAPTER 4

1. Jerry J. Eubanks and Paul F. Hill, *Pedestrian Accident Reconstruction and Litigation*, 2nd ed. (Lawyers and Judges, 1998), 76.

2. Ann Coffin and John Morrall, "Walking Speeds of Elderly Pedestrians at Crosswalks," *Transportation Research Record* 1478 (1995): 63.

3. Harold Lunenfeld and Gerson J. Alexander, *A User's Guide to Positive Guidance*, 3rd ed. (Federal Highway Administration, 1990).

4. Alison Smiley and Geni Bahar, *An Introduction to Road Safety Science*, course material presented by Human Factors North Inc. and iTrans Consulting Inc., Ramada Plaza Hotel, Toronto, October 23–25, 2001.

5. Smiley and Bahar, *An Introduction to Road Safety Science*; more recent information has indicated that both numbers cited here may be somewhat low. The point is that there are limitations on how much of the information in the visual field may be processed.

6. R. R. Mourant and T. H. Rockwell, "Mapping Eye Movement Patterns to the Visual Scene in Driving: An Exploratory Study," *Human Factors* 12, no. 1 (1970): 85, Table 1, doi: 10.1177/001872087001200112.

7. Eubanks and Hill, *Pedestrian Accident Reconstruction and Litigation*, 300.

8. Paraphrased from: Wolfgang Homburger, ed., *Transportation and Traffic Engineering Handbook*, 2nd ed. (Prentice Hall, 1982).

9.   James L. Pline, ed., *Traffic Engineering Handbook*, 2nd ed. (Prentice Hall, 1992), 5.

10. T. J. Post et al., *A User's Guide to Positive Guidance*, 2nd ed. (Federal Highway Administration, 1981), 1–7.

11. Gerson J. Alexander and Harold Lunenfeld, *Driver Expectancy in Highway Design and Traffic Operations* (Federal Highway Administration, 1986), 3.

12. Alexander and Lunenfeld, *Driver Expectancy*, 27.

13. *Geometric Design Guide for Canadian Roads* (Transportation Association of Canada, 1999).

CHAPTER 5

1.   Paul L. Olson, *Driver Perception Response Time* (Society of Automotive Engineers, 1989), SAE Publication 890731.

2.   Heikki Summala, "Driver/Vehicle Steering Response Latencies," *Human Factors: The Journal of the Human Factors and Ergonomics Society* 23, no. 6 (1981): 683, doi: 10.1177/001872088102300605.

3.   Louis J. Pignataro, *Traffic Engineering: Theory and Practice* (Prentice Hall, 1973), in reference to the American Association of State Highway Officials, "A Policy on Geometric Design of Rural Highways," 1965.

4.   Dilkhaz Zakhoy, *A Policy on Geometric Design of Highways and Streets* (American Association of State Highway and Transportation Officials, 2011), 2–41.

5.   Zakhoy, *A Policy on Geometric Design*, 2–41.

6.   Robert H. Wortman and Judson S. Matthias, "Evaluation of Driver Behavior at Signalized Intersections," *Transportation Research Record* 904 (1983); George T. Taoka, "An Analytical Model for Driver Response," *Transportation Research Record* 1213 (1981): 1.

7.   Dilkhaz Zakhoy, *A Policy on Geometric Design of Highways and Streets* (American Association of State Highway and Transportation Officials, 2011), 3–7.

8.   Hugh W. McGee, Wagner-McGee Associates, Inc., "Decision Sight Distance for Highway Design and Traffic Control Requirements," *Transportation Research Record* 736 (1979).

9.   Geoffrey Ho, Julian Rozental, and Svetozar Majstorovic, *Decision Sight Distance for Freeway Exit Ramps—A Road Safety Perspective*, prepared for the 2016 Conference of the Transportation Association of Canada.

10. Ezra Hauer, *Safety Review of Highway 407: Confronting Two Myths* (Transportation Research Board, 1999).

11. Dilkhaz Zakhoy, *A Policy on Geometric Design of Highways and Streets* (American Association of State Highway and Transportation Officials, 2011), 3-3; the manual recommends that different response times apply to different situations, such as complex intersections.

12. Rudolf Mortimer, "Human Factors in Highway-Railway Grade Crossing Accidents," *Accident Reconstruction Journal* (1993).

13. Paul Olson and Eugene Farber, *Forensic Aspects of Driver Perception and Response*, 2nd ed. (Lawyers and Judges, 2003), 111–117.

14. Nathan Gartner, C. Messer, and A. Rathi, *Revised Monograph on Traffic Flow Theory* (Federal Highway Administration, 1999), 3–14.

15. Louis Tijerina, Frank S. Barickman, and Elizabeth Mazzae, *Driver Eye Glance Behavior During Car Following* (US Department of Transportation, National Highway Traffic Safety Administration, 2004), 10.

16. Ontario Ministry of Transportation, *Geometric Design Standards for Ontario Highways* (Surveys and Design Office, 1994).

17. Paul L. Olson and Eugene Farber, *Forensic Aspects of Driver Perception and Response*, 2nd ed. (Lawyers and Judges, 2003).

18. G. H. Robinson, D. J. Erickson, G. L. Thurston, and R. L. Clark, "Visual Search by Automobile Drivers," *Human Factors* 14, no. 4 (1972): 315–323 (Stop and search techniques, merge search techniques), doi: 10.1177/001872087201400404.

19. Pignataro, *Traffic Engineering: Theory and Practice*, 14.

20. *Driver Attitude to Speeding and Speed Management: A Quantitative and Qualitative Study—Final Report* (EKOS Research Associates, 2005).

21. *Survey of Speed Zoning Practices: An Informational Report* (Institute of Transportation Engineers, 2001); "Setting Speed Limits," Institute of Transportation Engineers.org, https://www.ite.org/technical-resources/topics/speed-management-for-safety/setting-speed-limits/.

22. Other methods for setting speed limits also can exclude a share of the drivers who assume that they are performing reasonably. The share of drivers excluded can be expected to increase with unreasonably low speed limits.

23. *Geometric Design Guide for Canadian Roads* (Transportation Association of Canada, 1999).

24. *A Policy on Geometric Design of Highways and Streets* (American Association of State Highway and Transportation Officials, 2001).

25. Ontario Ministry of Transportation, *Geometric Design Standards for Ontario Highways* (Surveys and Design Office, 1994).

26. Ontario Ministry, *Geometric Design Standards*, Glossary, p.2.

27. Ontario Ministry, Geometric Design Standards, A5-5.

28. Takashi Wakasugi, *A Study on Warning Timing for Lane Change Decision Aid Systems Based on Driver's Lane Change Maneuver* (Japan Automobile Research Institute, 2005); Dario D. Salvucci and Andrew Liu, "The Time Course of a Lane Change: Driver Control and Eye-Movement Behavior," *Transportation Research Part F: Traffic Psychology and Behaviour* 5, no. 2 (2002): 123–132, doi: 10.1016/S1369-8478(02)00011-6; Shannon Hetrick, "Examination of Driver Lane Change Behavior and the Potential Effectiveness of Warning Onset Rules for Lane Change or 'Side' Crash Avoidance Systems," master's thesis (Virginia Polytech, 1997).

29. Alison Smiley, ed., *Human Factors in Traffic Safety*, 3rd ed. (Lawyers and Judges, 2015), 114.

30. Research of Wortman and Matthias (1983) reported in Smiley, *Human Factors in Traffic Safety*, 92.

31. Wortman and Matthias in Smiley, *Human Factors in Traffic Safety*, 92.

CHAPTER 6

1. James L. Pline, ed., *Traffic Engineering Handbook*, 4th ed. (Prentice Hall, 1992), 4; James L. Pline, ed., *Traffic Engineering Handbook*, 5th ed. (Institute of Transportation Engineers, 1999), 7.

2. *Ontario Traffic Manual, Positive Guidance Toolkit*, Book 1C (Ministry of Transportation, 2001), Appendix C, 11.

3. *Ontario Traffic Manual, Temporary Conditions*, Book 7 (Ministry of Transportation, 2001), Figure 1, 22.

CHAPTER 7

1. "Locomotive Acts," Wikipedia, accessed January 26, 2023, https://en.wikipedia.org/wiki/Locomotive_Acts.

2. Case work in which a pedestrian on a busy downtown sidewalk tripped as a result of a defective water shutoff valve; personal experience with a friend who fell and sustained a serious broken elbow injury requiring surgery, weeks of recovery, and physiotherapy while having lasting effects, 2019.

3. *Highway Capacity Manual*, Special Report 209 (Transportation Research Board, 1985), Chapter 13.

CHAPTER 8

1. This matter was settled out of court.

2. *Guideline, Professional Practice* (Association of Professional Engineers of Ontario, 1988).

3. Carson Morrison and Philip Hughes, *Professional Engineering Practice, Ethical Aspects*, 2nd ed. (McGraw-Hill, 1988).

4. Parentheses added by author.

5. "Road Design: 13. One-Way/Two-Way Street Conversions," FHWA Highway Safety Programs, https://safety.fhwa.dot.gov/saferjourney1/library/countermeasures/13.htm; "One-way/Two-way Street Conversions," Pedsafe, http://www.pedbikesafe.org/pedsafe/countermeasures_detail.cfm?CM_NUM=23.

6. *Guideline: Transportation and Traffic Engineering* (Association of Professional Engineers of Ontario, 1994).

7. *Guideline: Transportation and Traffic Engineering.*

8. "Code of Ethics," Professional Engineers Ontario, https://www.peo.on.ca/licence-holders /code-ethics; see also "Regulation 538/84," Association of Professional Engineers of Ontario, 1984, https://openlibrary.org/books/OL17511444M/Regulation_538_84; George Comrie, "Lessons for PEO from Jack Welch," *Engineering Dimensions* (2006).

9. The Association of Professional Engineers of Ontario produces guidelines for: services in land development and redevelopment; services in transportation and traffic engineering; services with respect to roads, bridges, and associated facilities; services for municipalities; services in forensic engineering investigations; and much more.

10. This does not include the braking distance.

11. Myung-Soon Chang, Carroll J. Messer, and Alberto J. Santiago, "Timing Traffic Signal Change Intervals Based on Driver Behavior," *Transportation Research Record* 1027 (1985): 20.

CHAPTER 9

1. Wolfgang S. Homburger et al., eds., *Transportation and Traffic Engineering Handbook*, 2nd ed. (Prentice Hall, 1982), 556.

2. "Black ice" is referenced here because it is a term that some use to refer to a slippery condition that is not observable or is poorly visible. This is simply a form of ice that may be transparent or translucent. It can include polished ice, freezing rain, and frost.

3. Ezra Hauer, *Safety Review of Highway 407: Confronting Two Myths* (Transportation Research Board, 1999).

4. Other standards have differing criteria for driver eye heights and object heights.

5. Dilkhaz Zakhoy, *A Policy on Geometric Design of Highways and Streets* (American Association of State Highway and Transportation Officials, 2011), 3–15.

6. *Manual of Uniform Traffic Control Devices for Canada* (Transportation Association of Canada, 1982).

7. *Ontario Traffic Manual, Warning Signs*, Book 6 (Ministry of Transportation, 2001), 54.

8. Ontario Traffic Manual, *Positive Guidance Toolkit*, Book 1C (Ministry of Transportation, 2001), Appendix C, 11.

9. "Manual on Uniform Traffic Control Devices," sections 2C.20–2C.21, US Department of Transportation, https://mutcd.fhwa.dot.gov/kno-millennium_12.18.00.htm.

10. *Ontario Traffic Manual*, Book 1C, 14 (Hazards).

11. Ontario Traffic Manual, Book 1C, 14–15 (Highway conditions).

12. Ontario Traffic Manual, Book 1C, 14–15 (Drivers avoiding hazards).

13. Ezra Hauer, *Safety in Geometric Design Standards*, published with revisions as two papers in the Proceedings of the 2nd International Symposium of Highway Geometric Design, 1999.

14. Other jurisdictions often label the standards the *Manual of Uniform Traffic Control Devices*.

15. Carson Morrison and Philip Hughes, *Professional Engineering Practice, Ethical Aspects*, 2nd ed. (McGraw-Hill, 1988); Provincial codes indicate engineers state in various ways that the engineer has a first or highest priority to public welfare, and in several provinces, safety is an integral part of that welfare.

16. "Professional Engineers Act, Revised Statutes of Ontario, 1990, Regulation 941," Professional Engineers Ontario, Section 72 (2b), https://www.peo.on.ca/about-peo/what-peo/acts-regulations-and-laws/professional-misconduct-section-72-regulation-o-reg.

17. "Professional Engineers Act, Revised Statutes of Ontario, RSO 1990, C. P.28," section 2(3), https://www.ontario.ca/laws/statute/90p28.

CHAPTER 10

1. Robert Dewar and Paul Olson, *Human Factors in Traffic Safety*, 1st ed. (Lawyers and Judges, 2001), 19.

2. Wolfgang S. Homburger et al., eds., *Transportation and Traffic Engineering Handbook*, 2nd ed. (Prentice Hall, 1982), 558.

3. Tapan Datta, *Risk Management System, A Procedural Guide*, a report prepared with the cooperation of the Michigan Office of Highway Planning and the US Department of Transportation, 1991.

4. *Ontario Traffic Manual, Positive Guidance Toolkit*, Book 1C (Ministry of Transportation, 2001), Appendix C, Chapter 3.2, 25.

5. James L. Pline, ed., *Traffic Engineering Handbook*, 4th ed. (Prentice Hall, 1992), 24.

6. Martin L. Reiss, "Young Pedestrian Behaviour," *Transportation Engineering* (1977): 40–44; H. D. Robertson and E. C. Carter, "The Safety, Operational Impacts, and Cost of Impacts of Pedestrians at Signalized Intersections," *Transportation Research Record* 959 (1989); Wolfgang S. Homburger and James H. Kell, *Fundamentals of Traffic Engineering*, 12th ed. (Institute of Transportation Studies, University of California at Berkeley, 1988): 22–1; *Design and Safety of Pedestrian Facilities: A Recommended Practice of the Institute of Transportation Engineers* (Institute of Transportation Engineers, 1994), 45.

7. G. C. Avery, *The Capacity of Young Children to Cope with the Traffic System: A Review* (Traffic Accident Research Unit, Department of Motor Transport, 1974).

8. Stina Sandels, *Children in Traffic* (Paul Elek, 1968).

9. Marie Connelly, Helen Conaglen, Barry Parsonson, and Robert Isler, "Child Pedestrians' Crossing Gap Thresholds," *Accident Analysis & Prevention* 30, no. 4 (1998): 443–453, doi: 10.1016/S0001-4575(97)00109-7.

10. "Analysis of Relevant Psychological Functions and Process and their Development," section IV.3 in *Traffic Safety of Children* (Organisation for Economic Co-operation and Development, 1983).

11. Martin L. Reiss, "Knowledge and Perceptions of Young Pedestrians," paper presented at the 56th Annual Meeting of the Transportation Research Board, January 1977.

12. "Analysis of Relevant Psychological Functions," section IV.3 in *Traffic Safety of Children*.

13. Marvin Malek, Bernard Guyer, and Ilana Lescohier, "The Epidemiology and Prevention of Child Pedestrian Injury," *Accident Analysis & Prevention* 22, no. 4 (1990): 301–313, doi: 10.1016/0001-4575(90)90046-N.

14. Reiss, "Young Pedestrian Behaviour," 40–44.

15. H. T. Zwahlen, "Distance Judgement Capabilities of Children and Adults in a Pedestrian Situation," paper presented at the 3rd International Congress of Automotive Safety, San Francisco, California, July 1974.

16. Connelly et al., "Child Pedestrians' Crossing Gap Thresholds."

17. Errol R. Hoffmann, Anthony Payne, and Stephen Prescott, "Children's Estimates of Vehicle Approach Times," *Human Factors: The Journal of the Human Factors and Ergonomics Society* 22, no. 2 (1980), doi: 10.1177/001872088002200212.

18. Santo Salvatore, "The Ability of Elementary and Secondary School Children to Sense Oncoming Car Velocity," *Highway Research Record* 436 (1973): 19–28.

19. Sandels, *Children in Traffic*.

CHAPTER 11

1. *Highway Safety Design and Operations Guide* (American Association of State and Highway Transportation Officials, 1997).

CHAPTER 12

1. Ontario Good Roads Association, "Letter to Municipal Road Managers," September 13, 2002.

2. "Revised Statutes of Ontario, Municipal Act, 2001, c. 25," s. 44 (1), Province of Ontario, https://www.ontario.ca/laws/statute/01m25.

3. "Municipal Act, 2001, S.O. 2001, c. 25," O. Reg. 239/02: Minimum Maintenance Standard for Municipal Highways, Province of Ontario, https://www.ontario.ca/laws/statute/01m25.

4. "Ontario Regulation 239/02: Minimum Maintenance Standards for Municipal Highways," Province of Ontario, https://www.ontario.ca/laws/regulation/020239/v1. Note: The text of v1, the online version of 2003, is identical to the text of the version that came into force on November 1, 2002.

5. *A Guide for the Development of Policy for Roadway Service Standards in Ontario* (Ontario Good Roads Association, 1995).

6. *A Guide for the Development of Policy*, 5.

7. "Priorities—MMS and Roadway Liability," Ontario Good Roads Association, https://goodroads.ca/priority_article/mms-and-roadway-liability/.

8. "Ontario Regulation 239/02," Province of Ontario.

9. This stratification has not changed as of 2024.

10. "Ontario Regulation 239/02," Province of Ontario.

11. "Ontario Regulation 239/02," Province of Ontario.

12. "Ontario Regulation 239/02," Province of Ontario.

13. *Manual of Low-Cost Roadway Safety Improvements for Rural Highways* (Transport Canada, 1981).

14. *Highway Safety Design and Operations Guide*, American Association of State Highway and Transportation Officials, 1997.

CHAPTER 13

1. *Salt Management Guide* (Transportation Association of Canada, 1999).

2. *Ontario Annual Road Safety Report*, Table 3.5 for years 2006 through 2010 (Ministry of Transportation, 2006–2010).

3. "Historical Climate Data," Government of Canada, https://climate.weather.gc.ca/; "Canadian Climate Normals," 1981–2010, Government of Canada, https://climate.weather.gc.ca/climate_normals.

4. *A Policy on Geometric Design of Highways and Streets* (American Association of State Highway and Transportation Officials, 2001).

5. *A Policy on Geometric Design of Highways and Streets*, Exhibit 2-27, p. 52.

6. Carl-Gustaf Wallman, Peter Wretling, and Gudrun Öberg, *Effects of Winter Road Maintenance: State of the Art*, VTI report 423A (Swedish National Road and Transport Research Institute, 1997), Summary.

7. Jean Andrey, Brian Mills, and Jessica Adams, "Weather Information and Road Safety," The Institute for Catastrophic Loss Reduction, ICLR Paper Series No. 15, 2001.

8. Jonas Norrman, Marie Eriksson, and Sven Lindqvist, "Relationships Between Road Slipperiness, Traffic Accident Risk and Winter Road Maintenance," *Climate Research* 15 (2000): 185–193, doi: 10.3354/CR015185.

9. Xiao Qin, David A. Noyce, Chanyoung Lee, and John R. Kinar, "Snowstorm Event-Based Crash Analysis," *Transportation Research Record: Journal of the Transportation Research Board* 1948 (2006), 135–141.

10. Manjunathan Kumar and Shaowei Wang, *Impacts of Weather on Rural Highway Operations*, prepared for the US Department of Transportation, 2006.

11. Robert E. Dewar and Paul L. Olson, *Human Factors in Traffic Safety*, 2nd ed. (Lawyers and Judges, 2007), 390.

12. Personal observation of the author.

13. *2020 Traffic Safety Culture Index* (AAA Foundation for Traffic Safety, 2020), 28.

14. "Winter Tires: A Review of Research on Effectiveness and Use," Traffic Injury Research Foundation, https://tirf.ca/projects/winter-tires-review-research-effectiveness-use/.

15. The Transportation Association of Canada (TAC) accepted research completed in Norway by the Directorate of Public Roads evaluating the effects of winter maintenance as stated in a major publication, *Salt Management Guide* (Transportation Association of Canada, 1999), 1–12.

CHAPTER 14

1. Jean Andrey, Brian Mills, and Jessica Adams, "Weather Information and Road Safety," The Institute for Catastrophic Loss Reduction, ICLR Paper Series No. 15, 2001.

2. Xiao Qin, David A. Noyce, Chanyoung Lee, and John R. Kinar, "Snowstorm Event-based Crash Analysis," *Transportation Research Record: Journal of the Transportation Research Board* 1948 (2006), 135–141.

3. "Municipal Act, 2001, S.O. 2001, c. 25," O. Reg. 239/02: Minimum Maintenance Standard for Municipal Highways, Province of Ontario, https://www.ontario.ca/laws/statute/01m25.

4. *Ontario Traffic Manual, Positive Guidance Toolkit*, Book 1C (Ministry of Transportation, 2001), Appendix C, 14; It is worthwhile to check the meaning of a highway or roadway in any jurisdiction. In Ontario, all roadways are described as highways in various acts and regulations.

CHAPTER 15

1. "Weather and Meteorology Glossary," Government of Canada, https://www.canada.ca/en /environment-climate-change/services/weather-general-tools-resources/glossary.html.

2. Cumulus-type clouds are most often detached clouds, generally dense and with sharp outlines, developing vertically in the form of rising mounds, domes, or towers, having their bases located in the low-level étage (ground level to 2,000 m [1.24 mi.]). The sunlit parts of these clouds are mostly brilliant white. Their base is relatively dark and nearly horizontal. Since these clouds may grow from regions above freezing to levels well below freezing, they may be composed solely of water droplets, supercooled water droplets, ice crystals, snowflakes, ice pellets, or a combination of all. These clouds form in an unstable environment, which allows air parcels to continue to rise once started either through forced lifting or heating, and are sometimes referred to as "clouds of ascending air currents."

3.   *Salt Management Guide* (Transportation Association of Canada, 1999), 3–89.

4.   A fill section of roadway is a location where earth or other available material has been used to raise the road surface above the surrounding terrain.

5.   Ronald D. Tabler, *Design Guidelines for the Control of Blowing and Drifting Snow*, prepared for the Strategic Highway Research Program (SHRP), 1994, 56.

6.   Estimated from topographic mapping of Atlas of Canada: "The Atlas of Canada—Toporama," Government of Canada, https://atlas.gc.ca/toporama/en/index.html.

7.   Measuring of the grade used a Vericom 4000, vehicle-mounted computer.

8.   "About Canadian Weather Radar: How Radar Works," Environment Canada, radar interpretation, summary extracts, https://www.canada.ca/en/environment-climate-change /services/weather-general-tools-resources/radar-overview/about.html.

9.   In the past, Ontario allowed free access to the real-time RWIS data provided by the Ministry of Transportation stations. Access was lost when the Ministry and Ontario Municipalities contracted the reporting service to their current service provider.

10. "Road Weather Management Program, Frequently Asked Questions," US Department of Transportation, Federal Highway Administration, http://www.ops.fhwa.dot.gov/weather /faq.htm.

11. "Anti-icing and RWIS Technology in Canada," *C-SHRP Technical Brief* 20 (2000). While seven provinces as well as Calgary and other municipalities were using or testing anti-icing as of 2000, Alberta was not. Similar results were found for RWIS technology development.

CHAPTER 16

1.   "Backovers Resources," kidsandcars.org, https://www.kidsandcars.org/how-kids-get-hurt /backovers/.

2.   Ezra Hauer, *Safety Review of Highway 407: Confronting Two Myths* (Transportation Research Board, 1999), TRID, https://trid.trb.org/view/514279.

3.   University of New Brunswick, *Road Safety Audit Guidelines*, Eric Hildebrand and Frank Wilson, eds., UNB Transportation Group, 1999, removed from online access July 2023.

4.   "FHWA Road Safety Audit Guidelines," US Department of Transportation, https://highways.dot.gov/safety/data-analysis-tools/rsa/fhwa-road-safety-audit-guidelines.

5.   "The Canadian Road Safety Audit Guide: A Book in the Canadian Road Safety Engineering Handbook (CRaSH) (2001)," Transportation Association of Canada, https://www.tac-atc.ca /en/knowledge-centre/technical-resources-search/publications/ptm-crsag-e/.

6.   Warren Hughes, Kim Eccles, Douglas Harwood, Ingrid Potts, and Ezra Hauer, *Development of a Highway Safety Manual*, National Cooperative Highway Research Program (Transportation Research Board, 2004).

7. "Highway Safety Manual," American Association of State Highway and Transportation Officials, https://www.highwaysafetymanual.org/Pages/About.aspx.

8. "CMF/CRF Details, CMF ID: 2346, Install TWLTL (Two-Way Left Turn Lane) on Two Lane Road," Crash Modifications Factors Clearinghouse, https://cmfclearinghouse.fhwa.dot.gov/detail.php?facid=2346.

9. C. Fragomeni, "Taking a Circuitous Route to Safety," *The Hamilton Spectator* (2005).

APPENDIX 1

1. *A Guide for the Development of Policy for Roadway Service Standards in Ontario* (Ontario Good Roads Association, 1995).

2. *A Guide for the Development of Policy*, 5.

3. This may be considered to be a wet pavement condition.

4. *Ontario Traffic Manual, Positive Guidance Toolkit*, Book 1C (Ministry of Transportation, 2001), Appendix C, 14.

5. In moving to fully contracted maintenance services, the Ministry has adjusted the elements of the 2003 standards accordingly. While the conditions imposed on contractors mirror these standards, there remains an issue as to whether those standards delegate responsibility for the road condition to contractors, or whether the Ministry's own standards remain applicable in civil litigation. The author had used the Ministry's own standards as a measure of the standard of care in litigation.

6. *Maintenance Manual* (Ontario Ministry of Transportation, 2003), MQS-701 "Winter Maintenance – Level of Service."

7. *Maintenance Manual*, MQS-701, "Winter Maintenance – Level of Service."

8. *Maintenance* Manual, MQS-702, "Winter Maintenance – Operations."

9. The Ministry has also set in place automatic spray systems for some bridge decks to deal with icing problems.

10. In the absence of pre-event anti-icing operations, some moisture in the form of snow was required on the roadway to allow a solid salt application to become activated while also allowing the salt to adhere to the surface to some degree. Thus, a minimal amount of snow was required for the salting operation to be effective.

11. Modern technologies are capable of performing similarly using rear-mounted equipment.

12. Bonnie Lysyk, *Winter Highway Maintenance* (Office of the Auditor General of Ontario, 2015), 1, "Our work at regional offices in contract areas throughout Ontario found that it is now taking much longer to return highways to a safer state after a snowfall than prior to the introduction of performance-based contracts, and the amount of salt, sand, and anti-icing liquid used declined substantially."

13. In reference to snow accumulation: "Municipal Act, 2001, S.O. 2001, c. 25," O. Reg. 239/02: Minimum Maintenance Standard for Municipal Highways, Province of Ontario, November 2002, Subsection 4. (1)(b) and other Subsections of the regulation tables indicating a time limit, https://www.ontario.ca/laws/regulation/020239/v1. Note: The text of v1, the online version of 2003, is identical to the text of the version that came into force on November 1, 2002.)

APPENDIX 2

1. "Reasonable State of Repair," LawInsider.com, https://www.lawinsider.com/dictionary/reasonable-state-of-repair. Note: This is a general legal description for the state of repair; however, it broadly covers the elements applicable to the safe use by the public.

2. "Municipal Act, 2001, S.O. 2001, c. 25," O. Reg. 239/02: Minimum Maintenance Standard for Municipal Highways, Province of Ontario, referenced as table appears in the Regulation, https://www.ontario.ca/laws/statute/01m25.

3. *Maintenance Manual* (Ontario Ministry of Transportation, 2003), MQS-395 "Road Patrol."

4. Maintenance *Manual*, MQS-395, "Road Patrol."

5. Maintenance Manual, MQS-395, "Road Patrol."

6. Maintenance Manual, MQS-395, "Road Patrol."

7. "Municipal Act, 2001, S.O. 2001, c. 25."

8. Ontario Good Roads, Slide Presentation of Ontario's New Minimum Maintenance Standards, February 5, 2003, p. 23.

9. Case work of the author.

10. *Maintenance Manual*, MQS-395, "Road Patrol."

11. "Municipal Act, 2001, S.O. 2001, c. 25," O. Reg. 239/02: Minimum Maintenance Standard for Municipal Highways, Province of Ontario, https://www.ontario.ca/laws/statute/01m25.

12. "Municipal Act, 2001, S.O. 2001, c. 25," referenced as table appears in the Regulation.

13. The standard did not require that snow be removed from roadways.

14. Experience of the author.

15. Experience of the author.

16. *Use of Salt for Snow and Ice Control*, M-803 Training Guide, Metric Edition (Ministry of Transportation and Communications—Ontario, 1977).

17. *Salt Management Guide* (Transportation Association of Canada, 1999), 3–33.

18. Xiao Qin, David A. Noyce, Chanyoung Lee, and John R. Kinar, "Snowstorm Event-Based Crash Analysis," *Transportation Research Record: Journal of the Transportation Research Board* 1948 (2006), 135–141.

19. "Second Priority Substances List (PSL2)," Government of Canada, https://www.canada.ca /en/environment-climate-change/services/evaluating-existing-substances/second-priority -substances-list-psl2.html.

20. *Salt Management Guide* (Transportation Association of Canada, 1999).

21. "Code of Practice for the Environmental Management of Road Salts," Government of Canada, https://www.canada.ca/en/environment-climate-change/services/pollutants/road-salts /code-practice-environmental-management.html.

22. *Use of Salt for Snow and Ice Control*, M703 Training Guide (Ministry of Transportation and Communications, 1977).

23. *Use of Salt for Snow and Ice Control.*

24. Use of Salt for Snow and Ice *Control*, 12.

25. *Salt Management Guide* (Transportation Association of Canada, 1999), 3–73.

26. Francis Navin, Michael Macnabb, and Connie Nicolletti, "Vehicle Traction Experiments on Snow and Ice," *Journal of Passenger Cars* 105, no. 6 (1996): 702–713, https://www.jstor.org /stable/44720791.

27. Stephen A. Ketcham, L. David Minsk, Robert R. Blackburn, Edward J. Fleege, *Manual of Practice for an Effective Anti-icing Program: A Guide for Highway Maintenance Personnel* (US Federal Highway Administration, 1995), section 2.3.

28. *Use of Salt for Snow and Ice Control.*

29. Ketcham et al., *Manual of Practice for an Effective Anti-icing Program.*

30. This level of snowfall on the road would include 2.5 cm (1 in.) of snow required to achieve the threshold to activate plowing, and assumed two hours of start-up delay until complaint is received, and a nominal two-hour delay for travel on a designated snow plow route.

31. *Salt Management Guide* (Transportation Association of Canada, 1999), 3–89.

32. Ronald D. Tabler, *Design Guidelines for the Control of Blowing and Drifting Snow*, prepared for the Strategic Highway Research Program (SHRP), 1994, 56.

33. The expense of having to make a second trip along roadways with bicycle lanes was removed by revision to the language of the Regulation. This was accomplished by indicating that the Regulation was applicable to motorized vehicles only. Thus, cyclists were required to ride in mixed traffic even though bicycle lanes may be present on the roadway. It is also noted that bicycle lanes would provide a storage location for snow removed from mixed traffic lanes.

34. "Municipal Act, 2001, S.O. 2001, c. 25," referenced as table appears in the Regulation.

35. Dimensionless quantity (force to move object divided by force of gravity (g-force); friction is a dimensionless quantity, which is the result of the friction force divided by the normal force. It may be thought of as a share of the force of gravity (g) where g = 1; John R. Hunter, *Reconstructing Collisions Involving Ice and Slippery Surfaces*, SAE Technical Paper 930896, 1993.

36. Dennis P. Martin and Gerard F. Schaefer, "Tire-Road Friction in Winter Conditions for Accident Reconstruction," *Journal of Passenger Cars* 105, no 6 (1996): 732–750.

37. *Maintenance Manual* (Ontario Ministry of Transportation, 2003), MQS-702 "Winter Maintenance – Operations."

38. Under the Canadian Environmental Protection Act, 1999, the Government of Canada published a *Code of Practice for the Environmental Management of Road Salts* on April 3, 2004. The Code is designed to help municipalities and other road authorities better manage their use of road salts in a way that reduces harm to the environment while maintaining road safety. The Code was updated in 2022. https://www.canada.ca/en/environment-climate-change/services /pollutants/road-salts/code-practice-environmental-management-overview-data.html.

GLOSSARY

1. "Highway Traffic Act, R.S.O. 1990, c. H.8," Province of Ontario, https://www.ontario.ca /laws/statute/90h08.

2. *Maintenance Manual* (Ontario Ministry of Transportation, 2023), Introduction, 2.

3. Maintenance Manual (Ontario Ministry of Transportation, 2023), Introduction, 1.

GLOSSARY

AADT: Annual Average Daily Traffic. This is an estimated value obtained through traffic counts that sample traffic volumes at various times of the year which are then adjusted in accordance with estimates of seasonal knowledge.

AASHTO: American Association of State Highway and Transportation Officials.

Active transportation: Human-powered transportation including walking and cycling.

Anti-icing: Preemptive methods to keep newly fallen snow, frost, or freezing rain from bonding with the road surface. This servicing is required before or as a winter weather event commences.

Black ice: Typically, a thin layer of ice on the road surface that is difficult to detect by casual observation. It can be transparent or translucent.

Blast button: Winter maintenance sand and salt spreading control having a special button or trigger that significantly increases the amount of material spread, typically over a short section of roadway as the button is held.

Complete streets: This concept of urban design recognizes that roadways are multipurpose facilities that need to allow for various types of activities and interactions besides just the movement of traffic. The street is therefore repurposed to accommodate greater range of human interaction.

Condition hazard: See Hazards.

Conflict points: Locations where road or system users merge, diverge, or cross.

Crash or collision: Typically, exchangeable terms with "crashes" used in the US and "collisions" used for reference in Canada.

Creep: The motion of windblown snow particles rolling across a stationary surface.

Deadheading: Maintenance vehicles that are traveling to or from a location or route without servicing roadways.

Decision sight distance: The distance at which a driver must detect information or a hazard that may be vague in its presentation or difficult to perceive due to visual clutter or poor reference cues. The distance includes that required for detection, identification, decision response, volition, and to safely complete a response such as a stopping lane change.

Defects and defaults: Defects refer to facility conditions (or conditions on the property of the transportation authority) that may adversely affect the facility's use or present a potential source of harm. Defaults occur when conditions fall below the thresholds of nominal standards.

Deicing: The servicing of roadways to remove ice that has bonded with the road surface. Typically, this requires greater amounts of salt than is used when ice has not bonded with the surface.

Design speed: A speed that is selected for the purpose of design and correlation of the geometric features of a road and is a measure of the quality of design offered by the road. It is the highest continuous speed at which individual vehicles can travel with safety on a road when weather conditions are favorable.

Eight-hour warrant (US) or Justification (CA) for traffic control signals: As of 2012 in Ontario, this method for determining the need for signals used traffic counts in each hour of eight hours. The traffic counts identified vehicle through and turning movements as well as counts of pedestrians and other systems users. The hours did not need to be consecutive. Attainment of the minimum thresholds of the vehicle movements to a level of 100 percent in each of the hours would trip the need for signals. The need for signals could also be considered in combination with other intersection operations if 80 percent of the thresholds was attained. As traffic volumes exceeding the thresholds are not acknowledged in the method, shorter-term periods of vehicle movements with high-demand periods are not explicitly relevant and would not trip the need for traffic control signals.

Engineered products: Products that have been developed as the result of applied science and engineering principles. Not all manufactured products are engineered. Engineered ground transportation facilities involve time, motion, and force calculations. They include both the means of conveyance and the facilities used in the conveyance. They can include all elements used directly—roadways, sidewalks, multiuse paths—by system users as well as supporting facilities—roadside barriers, handrails, streetlights, push buttons for traffic signals, etc.

Event-based maintenance: See Maintenance.

Fetch: The distance of terrain that wind can blow across to pick up or otherwise move snow about.

Fill section of roadway: A location where earth or granular material has been used to raise the road surface above the surrounding terrain. The material may have come from a cut section of roadway where the ground elevation is lowered to the desired road elevation.

Forensic engineering: An investigation of why failures occur. Transportation-related failures can occur in the infrastructures available for use by the public—roadways, sidewalks, pathways, cycling facilities. It includes failures that occur in the design, operation, and maintenance of infrastructure. There can also be failures in the corporate management and oversight provisions of facilities.

Four-hour warrant (US) or Justification (CA) for traffic control signals: These requirements or standards set the thresholds needed for traffic control signals based on a four-hour period of traffic passing through an intersection. The four-hour period can occur at any time when traffic volumes are at their highest daily levels and need not be consecutive hours. The information is obtained through traffic counts at the location.

Friction or roadway friction: Friction is the resistance offered to a sliding standing object. It is a dimensionless quantity that is the result of the force required to move a stationary object divided by the normal (downward) force. It may be thought of as a share of the force of gravity (g), where $g = 1$.

G-force: The normal (downward) force applied to an object. For example, the downward force of an object at rest on a surface is 1 g.

Hazards, condition: Infrastructure features that may cause harm to system users if users are not properly informed of their presence and instructed on how to perform. For example, drivers may experience an expectancy violation and crash where control inputs (throttle, brake) and guidance (steering) are required but appropriate signs are absent.

Hazards, situation: Hazards confronted by drivers that tend to be transitory or temporal in nature. They can arise from the onset of frost or rain. These are typically associated with two or more events and/or conditions coming together. It is the combination of contributing elements that make them particularly hazardous. The completion of a turn at a signalized intersection with a bike lane present and significant pedestrian activity is one example.

Highway: This facility includes a common and public highway, street, avenue, parkway, driveway, and so on, which is intended for or used by the public for the passage of vehicles and includes the area between the lateral property lines thereof.[1]

Highway defaults: Infrastructure elements that have deteriorated beyond the threshold of conditions that adequately serve their design function and are now in need of repair.

Hot spots or trouble spots: In winter maintenance, these are typically locations within the road system that deteriorate more quickly than other locations. They may include river crossings and hills or open stretches of terrain that are subject to drifting snow. When monitored, they can be indicators of when servicing action needs to be initiated.

Hydrostatic drag: The resisting force applied to a moving vehicle on attempting to pass through a static body of water or accumulated snow.

Maintenance, event-based: This proactive approach recognizes the importance of getting ready for any environmental event, maintaining the best possible conditions throughout the event, and an expeditious return of the system attributes to their ambient conditions after the event has passed. It may include regular vegetation trimming before visibility obstructions occur or the action of spreading a brine solution on bridge decks when overnight frost is possible. The safety of the traveling public is maintained to the lowest extent possible throughout winter weather events.

Maintenance, outcome-based: This method sets preconditions and outcomes that are qualitative statements that describe a state of being or condition specification rather than the activities and procedures used to achieve the results. The preconditions allow a period of deterioration before action is undertaken, thus assuming *all* system users will be able to cope with the conditions. When servicing is complete, a final specification is used to determine the conditions that may be left unattended, again assuming *all* system users will be able to cope with the final state. For example, a pothole does not require servicing before reaching a certain size, while after servicing, the pothole only needs to be smaller than a certain size.

MBP or Maintenance Best Practices: These practices are guidelines that represent the Ontario Ministry of Transportation's experience and expertise in the effective delivery of the maintenance program.[2]

MQS or Maintenance Quality Standards: This Ontario standard describes the remedial work, response times, and service levels required to address the infrastructure defects and the safety of the motoring public.[3]

Nowcast: A broadcast via social media that is made in real time.

OGRA: Ontario Good Roads Association, an association of municipal representatives from roads departments of municipalities in Ontario, Canada.

Outcome-based maintenance: See Maintenance.

Platoon, vehicle: A moving queue of vehicles.

Ramping: The action of a snow windrow having a slope that has hardened by the action of weather and time on contact by a vehicle.

Road and roadway: In this publication, these terms generally refer to the traveled surface used for vehicular traffic. The definition of a road or roadway is likely described in legislation in many jurisdictions where there is a distinction between the two terms. A roadway may be defined by the limits of the area used by vehicles including shoulders and parking lanes, whereas a road is only that portion of the roadway used for traveling vehicles. However, the meaning may not be as precise when described by system users. Also, in this publication, the roadside refers to the area adjacent to the road including the shoulders where applicable. Also see Highway.

Road safety vs. Safe roads: Safe roads are not capable of causing harm to system users. Road safety is the extent of risk assigned to system users. Road authorities can undertake actions to move risk *in the direction of safety*, resulting in reduced likelihood of harm, or *moving away from safety*, resulting in greater likelihood of harm.

RWIS: Remote weather information systems, reporting road and weather conditions for key locations with a road network. These are remote weather stations.

Safety, acceptable or reasonable: The extent of safety that has been provided and accepted through explicit evaluation. The evaluation may include explicit assessment by industry professionals in accordance with standards of practice. However, a more meaningful application of the term occurs when the evaluation has been further vetted through public means such as transportation tribunals or judicial decisions.

Safety, nominal: The extent of safety provided by the minimum limit of documented standards.

Safety, substantive: The safety determined through collision evaluations for specific locations, compared with collisions at other similar locations and found to be operating within an expected or normally accepted degree of tolerance.

Saltation: The motion of windblown snow particles bouncing or moving along close to the surface layer of ground snow.

Sintering: A process that involves heating without melting, by which wind-deposited snow becomes resistant to subsequent erosion within only a few hours of deposition. Wind- (or plow-) deposited snow particles bond together upon contact. The bonds may strengthen over time and may create a solid structure.

Spinners: A pinwheel-like device on either or both sides or the back of spreading trucks undertaking winter maintenance service. Salt or sand is dropped onto the spinner at a prescribed rate according to the temperature, speed of vehicle, and roadway conditions being serviced.

Spreading: The winter maintenance action of placing sand on the roadway for traction or placing chemicals such as salt solids or brine for the removal of frozen moisture.

Streetscaping: Areas not assigned to traffic that can include dining areas, benches, parking for mobility devices, shelters for waiting, and more.

System users: Individuals using a transportation element—sidewalk, roadway, path, stairs, bike lane—who may be drivers, pedestrians, cyclists, or using any other mode of travel.

Traffic signal warrants (US) and justification (CA): A set of up to eleven threshold requirements (standards) used to determine the need for traffic control signals. These were previously referred to as warrants in both the US and Canada. The terminology in Ontario changed in 2001, when a new manual was issued recognizing only five thresholds for signal installation rather than eleven, as used in the US. The warrants are determined by field studies of intersection operations. The Ontario warrants included: minimum vehicle volume, delay to cross traffic, combined minimum volume and delay to cross traffic, minimum pedestrian volume, and collision experience. The 1988 *MUTCD* included warrants for school crossings, progressive movements through successive signals, systems considerations to organize traffic, and three for traffic peaking conditions at intersections.

Transportation or travel authority: State/provincial and municipal corporations or agencies providing travel facilities for public use. They can include public works departments, conservation authorities, parks departments, parkway commissions, state parks, private corporations such as shopping centers, and more.

Turbulent diffusion: When windblown particles are carried along in the airflow without ground contact.

Vulnerable road or system users: System users that are more likely to be injured as a result of a crash because they have little in the way of protections. Moving vehicles, people, or objects can make direct contact with vulnerable system users.

Wet pavement condition: A pavement condition which has little or no residual water or frozen moisture on it. Wet pavements are typically representative of the design condition.

INDEX

Felton, William, 90
fetch, 275–76, 381
FHWA. *See* US Federal Highway
    Administration
fill sections, 273, 374n4, 382
forensic transportation engineering, 11–25. *See*
    also failures, examples of; road and travel
    authorities; system users; transportation
    planning, engineering, and safety
    behind-the-scenes means of fixing defi-
        cient facilities, 31
    broad evaluation, 187–88
    defined, 6, 382
    definitive conclusions where there is sub-
        stantive uncertainty, 127–29
    design decisions to omit sidewalks, 108–11
    design parameter contribution to collisions,
        60–61
    disconnected disciplines, 23
    documentation of design decisions, 107
    driver contribution to collisions, 11–13,
        131
    focus of, 3, 5–6, 44
    infrastructure contribution to collisions, 12,
        60, 132, 205
    knowledge gaps from staff turnover, 22–23
    lane changes and weaving areas, 74
    legal profession and litigation, 20–25, 181
    licensed versus unlicensed professionals, 24
    maintenance issues, 190–91
    mismatch between "wished for" and actual
        behaviors, 6, 44, 81
    positive guidance, 77
    resource shortfalls, 20, 181
    response time algorithms, 56
    standards in force at time of construction,
        137
    threshold standards, 198
    travel authority failings, 14–16, 18
    updating of manuals, 161
    vague and inconsistent guidelines, 23–24
    variety and availability of industry stan-
        dards and information, 21–22
    winter maintenance, 271
four-hour justifications/warrants, 158–61,
    163, 382
friction
    bumps, 150–51
    defined, 382
    dimensionless quantity, 232, 377n35

    low levels of friction on curvilinear high-
        way section, 15
    winter driving and maintenance, 194,
        232–33, 237, 268, 273, 322–23, 325,
        352–53, 355

G

Geometric Design Guide for Canadian Roads
    (TAC), 50–51
g-force, 83, 377n35, 382
Green Book (*A Policy on Geometric Design of
    Highways and Streets*) (AASHTO), 57,
    59, 61
Guyer, Bernard, 176

H

hazards, 165–77. *See also* failures, examples
    of; maintenance issues; winter driving;
    winter maintenance; *names of specific
    hazards and conditions*
    acceptable/reasonable safety, 17–18,
        185–88
    children as, 174–77
    condition hazards, 256–59, 382
    defined, 166, 382
    identifying, 166–69
    inspections, 181–84
    looming problem, 63
    network screening approach, 167–69
    perception/reaction process, 57, 72–73
    proactively examining noncollision sites
        for, 168
    situation hazards, 258–59, 383
    traffic control provisions warning of, 23,
        35, 77, 79
    urgency in dealing with, 168–74
headlights
    height of, 144
    lack of, 92
    looming problem, 62
    obstructed, 76, 332
    oncoming, 46
    winter hazards, 259
Highway 407, 141, 296–98, 304
Highway Capacity Manual (TRB), 95
highway defaults. *See also* hazards
    defined, 380, 383
    reasonable steps to prevent, 201, 254–55,
        262, 333–34, 362

ABOUT THE AUTHOR

Author photograph by Christopher Gilchrist

Robert Gilchrist, PEng, has been a licensed professional engineer in Ontario since 1978. He received degrees in civil engineering from the University of Waterloo (1976, BASc) and McMaster University (1988, MEng). Both degree programs focused on transportation and traffic engineering. He is a lifetime member of the Institute of Transportation Engineers (1976) and acquired the designation of Professional Traffic Operations Engineer (1999, PTOE, now retired), both of Washington, DC.

His career has taken him through positions in transportation planning, transportation engineering, and traffic engineering, where he has been a partner and/or owner of firms providing services to the public. He has been actively engaged in forensic transportation engineering since 1992, when he and two partners established AT Traffic Safety Corporation; he later purchased the company from the partners in 2010. The corporation mainly provided forensic engineering services to the legal community. Through his work and training, he became qualified to provide human factors opinions on transportation matters in Ontario's Superior Court.

www.ingramcontent.com/pod-product-compliance
Lightning Source LLC
Chambersburg PA
CBHW020916140626
46545CB00015B/73